The Ultimate

Air Fryer Cookbook

for Beginners

2000 Days of Crispy, Flavorful, & Guilt-Free Recipes to Revolutionize Your Cooking and Satisfy Every Craving—Perfect for Newbies and Seasoned Chefs

Lionel Miller

Table of Contents

INTRODUCTION

Imagine a kitchen appliance that could simplify your life, cut down your cooking time, and help you prepare healthier meals with ease. The air fryer is just that — a versatile tool that has quickly become a staple in kitchens around the world. Whether you're a novice cook or a seasoned chef, this cookbook will open your eyes to a new way of cooking that is faster, healthier, and incredibly satisfying.

The air fryer's ability to replicate the crispy texture of fried foods with a fraction of the oil has made it an indispensable appliance for anyone looking to enjoy delicious meals without the added calories. But that's not all the air fryer can do. In this cookbook, you'll discover that the air fryer is much more than a frying device; it's a multi-purpose cooker capable of baking, grilling, roasting, and even dehydrating. Get ready to embark on a culinary journey that will transform the way you think about cooking.

Why This Air Fryer Cookbook Is Different

This cookbook is not just another collection of recipes. It is a guide to mastering the art of air frying, helping you unlock all the benefits this appliance has to offer. Here, you will find an array of recipes designed to maximize flavor while minimizing effort. From breakfast to dinner, appetizers to desserts, we've carefully crafted dishes that cater to every meal of the day, ensuring that you can use your air fryer to its fullest potential.

Unlike traditional cooking methods, which often require multiple pots, pans, and cooking techniques, the air fryer simplifies the process by doing it all in one compact appliance. The recipes in this book are designed with simplicity in mind — minimal ingredients, straightforward instructions, and quick preparation times. This means less time spent in the kitchen and more time enjoying delicious, home-cooked meals.

Healthy Meals Without Compromise

One of the greatest challenges in today's fast-paced world is maintaining a healthy diet without sacrificing flavor. The air fryer is a perfect solution to this problem. By using hot air to cook food to a crispy perfection, it allows you to enjoy all the textures and flavors of deep-fried dishes without the added fats and calories. This cookbook focuses on healthy, balanced recipes that use fresh, wholesome ingredients. Whether you're following a specific diet plan or simply looking to eat better, you'll find a variety of options that cater to your nutritional needs.

We've also made sure to include a range of recipes that accommodate different dietary preferences, including vegetarian, gluten-free, low-carb, and low-fat options. You can feel confident that every dish you prepare from this cookbook will support your health goals while delighting your taste buds.

A Tool for Every Occasion

The beauty of the air fryer lies in its versatility. It's not just for making French fries or chicken wings (although it excels at those too!). This cookbook will show you how to use your air fryer for everything from weekday breakfasts to weekend brunches, from quick weeknight dinners to festive holiday feasts. You'll find:

- Breakfasts: Start your day with air-fried classics like fluffy pancakes, crispy bacon, or even a quick frittata.

- Lunches and Dinners: Enjoy everything from crispy fish tacos to perfectly roasted chicken breasts, with a variety of sides that complement each main dish.

- Snacks and Appetizers: Entertain guests with homemade mozzarella sticks, crispy onion rings, or stuffed mushrooms, all with a fraction of the oil.

- Desserts: Indulge your sweet tooth with treats like air-fried apple crisps, chocolate chip cookies, or banana bread, all made in the air fryer.

Each recipe is designed to be as easy and efficient as possible, using ingredients you likely already have in your kitchen. This means no long shopping lists, no complicated techniques — just simple, delicious meals that anyone can make.

Tips for Getting the Most Out of Your Air Fryer

To help you become an air fryer pro, we've included a chapter filled with tips and tricks. You'll learn how to properly preheat your air fryer, how to avoid overcrowding the basket, and how to adapt traditional oven recipes for air frying. We'll also cover the best ways to clean and maintain your air fryer, ensuring it lasts for years to come.

Understanding the nuances of air frying will help you avoid common pitfalls like uneven cooking or soggy textures. You'll find advice on choosing the right accessories, such as baking pans or skewers, that can expand your air fryer's capabilities even further.

Cooking with Confidence

This cookbook is about more than just recipes; it's about building confidence in the kitchen. We believe that cooking should be a joyful, creative experience — not a chore. With the right tools, ingredients, and techniques, anyone can create delicious meals that bring comfort, joy, and satisfaction. The air fryer is the perfect tool to help you achieve this. It's forgiving, easy to use, and incredibly adaptable, making it ideal for cooks of all skill levels.

Even if you've never used an air fryer before, this book will guide you step-by-step through each recipe, providing you with the knowledge and skills you need to become an air fryer aficionado. And if you're already a fan of air frying, you'll find plenty of new and exciting recipes to expand your culinary horizons.

Your Culinary Adventure Awaits

There's a whole world of possibilities waiting for you with the air fryer, and this cookbook is your gateway to explore them all. Whether you're looking to make healthier versions of your favorite fried foods or want to try new dishes that push the boundaries of what the air fryer can do, this book has you covered.

So, take a deep breath, plug in your air fryer, and get ready to cook. Your culinary adventure begins now, and with this cookbook by your side, you'll soon discover that the air fryer is more than just a kitchen gadget — it's your new best friend. Welcome to a world of delicious, healthy, and hassle-free cooking!

Let's Get Frying!

Chapter 1

Breakfasts

Easy Sausage Pizza

Prep time: 10 minutes | Cook time: 6 minutes | Serves 4

- 2 tablespoons ketchup
- 1 pita bread
- ⅓ cup sausage
- ½ pound (227 g)
- Mozzarella cheese
- 1 teaspoon garlic powder
- 1 tablespoon olive oil

1. Preheat the air fryer to 340°F (171°C). 2. Spread the ketchup over the pita bread. 3. Top with the sausage and cheese. Sprinkle with the garlic powder and olive oil. 4. Put the pizza in the air fryer basket and bake for 6 minutes. 5. Serve warm.

Two-Cheese Grits

Prep time: 10 minutes | Cook time: 10 to 12 minutes | Serves 4

- ⅔ cup instant grits
- 1 teaspoon salt
- 1 teaspoon freshly ground black pepper
- ¾ cup milk, whole or 2%
- 1 large egg, beaten
- 3 ounces (85 g) cream
- cheese, at room temperature
- 1 tablespoon butter, melted
- 1 cup shredded mild Cheddar cheese
- 1 to 2 tablespoons oil

1. In a large bowl, combine the grits, salt, and pepper. Stir in the milk, egg, cream cheese, and butter until blended. Stir in the Cheddar cheese. 2. Preheat the air fryer to 400°F (204°C). Spritz a baking pan with oil. 3. Pour the grits mixture into the prepared pan and place it in the air fryer basket. 4. Cook for 5 minutes. Stir the mixture and cook for 5 minutes more for soupy grits or 7 minutes more for firmer grits.

Berry Muffins

Prep time: 15 minutes | Cook time: 12 to 17 minutes | Makes 8 muffins

- 1⅓ cups plus 1 tablespoon all-purpose flour, divided
- ¼ cup granulated sugar
- 2 tablespoons light brown sugar
- 2 teaspoons baking powder
- 2 eggs
- ⅔ cup whole milk
- ⅓ cup safflower oil
- 1 cup mixed fresh berries

1. In a medium bowl, stir together 1⅓ cups of flour, the granulated sugar, brown sugar, and baking powder until mixed well. 2. In a small bowl, whisk the eggs, milk, and oil until combined. Stir the egg mixture into the dry ingredients just until combined. 3. In another small bowl, toss the mixed berries with the remaining 1 tablespoon of flour until coated. Gently stir the berries into the batter. 4. Double up 16 foil muffin cups to make 8 cups. 5. Insert the crisper plate into the basket and the basket into the unit.

Preheat the unit by selecting BAKE, setting the temperature to 315°F (157°C), and setting the time to 3 minutes. Select START/STOP to begin. 6. Once the unit is preheated, place 4 cups into the basket and fill each three-quarters full with the batter. 7. Select BAKE, set the temperature to 315°F (157°C), and set the time for 17 minutes. Select START/STOP to begin. 8. After about 12 minutes, check the muffins. If they spring back when lightly touched with your finger, they are done. If not, resume cooking. 9. When the cooking is done, transfer the muffins to a wire rack to cool. 10. Repeat steps 6, 7, and 8 with the remaining muffin cups and batter. 11. Let the muffins cool for 10 minutes before serving.

Cheddar-Ham-Corn Muffins

Prep time: 10 minutes | Cook time: 6 to 8 minutes per batch | Makes 8 muffins

- ¾ cup yellow cornmeal
- ¼ cup flour
- 1½ teaspoons baking powder
- ¼ teaspoon salt
- 1 egg, beaten
- 2 tablespoons canola oil
- ½ cup milk
- ½ cup shredded sharp Cheddar cheese
- ½ cup diced ham
- 8 foil muffin cups, liners removed and sprayed with cooking spray

1. Preheat the air fryer to 390°F (199°C). 2. In a medium bowl, stir together the cornmeal, flour, baking powder, and salt. 3. Add egg, oil, and milk to dry ingredients and mix well. 4. Stir in shredded cheese and diced ham. 5. Divide batter among the muffin cups. 6. Place 4 filled muffin cups in air fryer basket and bake for 5 minutes. 7. Reduce temperature to 330°F (166°C) and bake for 1 to 2 minutes or until toothpick inserted in center of muffin comes out clean. 8. Repeat steps 6 and 7 to cook remaining muffins.

Savory Sweet Potato Hash

Prep time: 15 minutes | Cook time: 18 minutes | Serves 6

- 2 medium sweet potatoes, peeled and cut into 1-inch cubes
- ½ green bell pepper, diced
- ½ red onion, diced
- 4 ounces (113 g) baby
- bella mushrooms, diced
- 2 tablespoons olive oil
- 1 garlic clove, minced
- ½ teaspoon salt
- ½ teaspoon black pepper
- ½ tablespoon chopped fresh rosemary

1. Preheat the air fryer to 380°F (193°C). 2. In a large bowl, toss all ingredients together until the vegetables are well coated and seasonings distributed. 3. Pour the vegetables into the air fryer basket, making sure they are in a single even layer. (If using a smaller air fryer, you may need to do this in two batches.) 4. Roast for 9 minutes, then toss or flip the vegetables. Roast for 9 minutes more. 5. Transfer to a serving bowl or individual plates and enjoy.

Butternut Squash and Ricotta Frittata

Prep time: 10 minutes | Cook time: 33 minutes | Serves 2 to 3

- 1 cup cubed (½-inch) butternut squash (5½ ounces / 156 g)
- 2 tablespoons olive oil
- Kosher salt and freshly ground black pepper, to
- taste
- 4 fresh sage leaves, thinly sliced
- 6 large eggs, lightly beaten
- ½ cup ricotta cheese
- Cayenne pepper

1. In a bowl, toss the squash with the olive oil and season with salt and black pepper until evenly coated. Sprinkle the sage on the bottom of a cake pan and place the squash on top. Place the pan in the air fryer and bake at 400°F (204°C) for 10 minutes. Stir to incorporate the sage, then cook until the squash is tender and lightly caramelized at the edges, about 3 minutes more. 2. Pour the eggs over the squash, dollop the ricotta all over, and sprinkle with cayenne. Bake at 300°F (149°C) until the eggs are set and the frittata is golden brown on top, about 20 minutes. Remove the pan from the air fryer and cut the frittata into wedges to serve.

Ham and Cheese Crescents

Prep time: 5 minutes | Cook time: 7 minutes | Makes 8 rolls

- Oil, for spraying
- 1 (8 ounces / 227 g) can refrigerated crescent rolls
- 4 slices deli ham
- 8 slices American cheese
- 2 tablespoons unsalted butter, melted

1. Line the air fryer basket with parchment and spray lightly with oil. 2. Separate the dough into 8 pieces. 3. Tear the ham slices in half and place 1 piece on each piece of dough. Top each with 1 slice of cheese. 4. Roll up each piece of dough, starting on the wider side. 5. Place the rolls in the prepared basket. Brush with the melted butter. 6. Air fry at 320°F (160°C) for 6 to 7 minutes, or until puffed and golden brown and the cheese is melted.

Potatoes Lyonnaise

Prep time: 10 minutes | Cook time: 31 minutes | Serves 4

- 1 Vidalia onion, sliced
- 1 teaspoon butter, melted
- 1 teaspoon brown sugar
- 2 large russet potatoes (about 1 pound / 454 g in
- total), sliced ½-inch thick
- 1 tablespoon vegetable oil
- Salt and freshly ground black pepper, to taste

1. Preheat the air fryer to 370°F (188°C). 2. Toss the sliced onions, melted butter and brown sugar together in the air fryer basket. Air fry for 8 minutes, shaking the basket occasionally to help the onions cook evenly. 3. While the onions are cooking, bring a saucepan of salted water to a boil on the stovetop. Par-cook the potatoes in boiling water for 3 minutes. Drain the potatoes and pat them dry with a clean kitchen towel. 4. Add the potatoes to the onions in the air fryer basket and drizzle with vegetable oil. Toss to coat the potatoes with the oil and season with salt and freshly ground black pepper. 5. Increase the air fryer temperature to 400°F (204°C) and air fry for 20 minutes, tossing the vegetables a few times during the cooking time to help the potatoes brown evenly. 6. Season with salt and freshly ground black pepper and serve warm.

Strawberry Toast

Prep time: 10 minutes | Cook time: 8 minutes | Makes 4 toasts

- 4 slices bread, ½-inch thick
- Butter-flavored cooking
- spray
- 1 cup sliced strawberries
- 1 teaspoon sugar

1. Spray one side of each bread slice with butter-flavored cooking spray. Lay slices sprayed side down. 2. Divide the strawberries among the bread slices. 3. Sprinkle evenly with the sugar and place in the air fryer basket in a single layer. 4. Air fry at 390°F (199°C) for 8 minutes. The bottom should look brown and crisp and the top should look glazed.

Whole Wheat Blueberry Muffins

Prep time: 10 minutes | Cook time: 15 minutes | Serves 6

- Olive oil cooking spray
- ½ cup unsweetened applesauce
- ¼ cup raw honey
- ½ cup nonfat plain Greek yogurt
- 1 teaspoon vanilla extract
- 1 large egg
- 1½ cups plus 1
- tablespoon whole wheat flour, divided
- ½ teaspoon baking soda
- ½ teaspoon baking powder
- ½ teaspoon salt
- ½ cup blueberries, fresh or frozen

1. Preheat the air fryer to 360°F(182°C). Lightly coat the inside of six silicone muffin cups or a six-cup muffin tin with olive oil cooking spray. 2. In a large bowl, combine the applesauce, honey, yogurt, vanilla, and egg and mix until smooth. 3. Sift in 1½ cups of the flour, the baking soda, baking powder, and salt into the wet mixture, then stir until just combined. 4. In a small bowl, toss the blueberries with the remaining 1 tablespoon flour, then fold the mixture into the muffin batter. 5. Divide the mixture evenly among the prepared muffin cups and place into the basket of the air fryer. Bake for 12 to 15 minutes, or until golden brown on top and a toothpick inserted into the middle of one of the muffins comes out clean. 6. Allow to cool for 5 minutes before serving.

Mini Shrimp Frittata

Prep time: 15 minutes | Cook time: 20 minutes | Serves 4

- 1 teaspoon olive oil, plus more for spraying
- ½ small red bell pepper, finely diced
- 1 teaspoon minced garlic
- 1 (4-ounce / 113-g) can of
- tiny shrimp, drained
- Salt and freshly ground black pepper, to taste
- 4 eggs, beaten
- 4 teaspoons ricotta cheese

1. Spray four ramekins with olive oil. 2. In a medium skillet over medium-low heat, heat 1 teaspoon of olive oil. Add the bell pepper and garlic and sauté until the pepper is soft, about 5 minutes 3. Add the shrimp, season with salt and pepper, and cook until warm, 1 to 2 minutes. Remove from the heat. 4. Add the eggs and stir to combine. 5. Pour one quarter of the mixture into each ramekin. 6. Place 2 ramekins in the air fryer basket and bake at 350ºF (177ºC) for 6 minutes. 7. Remove the air fryer basket from the air fryer and stir the mixture in each ramekin. Top each frittata with 1 teaspoon of ricotta cheese. Return the air fryer basket to the air fryer and cook until eggs are set and the top is lightly browned, 4 to 5 minutes. 8. Repeat with the remaining two ramekins.

Fried Chicken Wings with Waffles

Prep time: 10 minutes | Cook time: 30 minutes | Serves 4

- 8 whole chicken wings
- 1 teaspoon garlic powder
- Chicken seasoning, for preparing the chicken
- Freshly ground black pepper, to taste
- ½ cup all-purpose flour
- Cooking oil spray
- 8 frozen waffles
- Pure maple syrup, for serving (optional)

1. In a medium bowl, combine the chicken and garlic powder and season with chicken seasoning and pepper. Toss to coat. 2. Transfer the chicken to a resealable plastic bag and add the flour. Seal the bag and shake it to coat the chicken thoroughly. 3. Insert the crisper plate into the basket and the basket into the unit. Preheat the unit by selecting AIR FRY, setting the temperature to 400ºF (204ºC), and setting the time to 3 minutes. Select START/STOP to begin. 4. Once the unit is preheated, spray the crisper plate with cooking oil. Using tongs, transfer the chicken from the bag to the basket. It is okay to stack the chicken wings on top of each other. Spray them with cooking oil. 5. Select AIR FRY, set the temperature to 400ºF (204ºC), and set the time to 20 minutes. Select START/STOP to begin. 6. After 5 minutes, remove the basket and shake the wings. Reinsert the basket to resume cooking. Remove and shake the basket every 5 minutes until the chicken is fully cooked. 7. When the cooking is complete, remove the cooked chicken from the basket; cover to keep warm. 8. Rinse the basket and crisper plate with warm water. Insert them back into the unit. 9.

Select AIR FRY, set the temperature to 360ºF (182ºC), and set the time to 3 minutes. Select START/STOP to begin. 10. Once the unit is preheated, spray the crisper plate with cooking spray. Working in batches, place the frozen waffles into the basket. Do not stack them. Spray the waffles with cooking oil. 11. Select AIR FRY, set the temperature to 360ºF (182ºC), and set the time to 6 minutes. Select START/STOP to begin. 12. When the cooking is complete, repeat steps 10 and 11 with the remaining waffles. 13. Serve the waffles with the chicken and a touch of maple syrup, if desired.

Baked Egg and Mushroom Cups

Prep time: 5 minutes | Cook time: 15 minutes | Serves 6

- Olive oil cooking spray
- 6 large eggs
- 1 garlic clove, minced
- ½ teaspoon salt
- ½ teaspoon black pepper
- Pinch red pepper flakes
- 8 ounces (227 g) baby bella mushrooms, sliced
- 1 cup fresh baby spinach
- 2 scallions, white parts and green parts, diced

1. Preheat the air fryer to 320°F (160ºC). Lightly coat the inside of six silicone muffin cups or a six-cup muffin tin with olive oil cooking spray. 2. In a large bowl, beat the eggs, garlic, salt, pepper, and red pepper flakes for 1 to 2 minutes, or until well combined. 3. Fold in the mushrooms, spinach, and scallions. 4. Divide the mixture evenly among the muffin cups. 5. Place into the air fryer and bake for 12 to 15 minutes, or until the eggs are set. 6. Remove and allow to cool for 5 minutes before serving.

Easy Buttermilk Biscuits

Prep time: 5 minutes | Cook time: 18 minutes | Makes 16 biscuits

- 2½ cups all-purpose flour
- 1 tablespoon baking powder
- 1 teaspoon kosher salt
- 1 teaspoon sugar
- ½ teaspoon baking soda
- 8 tablespoons (1 stick) unsalted butter, at room temperature
- 1 cup buttermilk, chilled

1. Stir together the flour, baking powder, salt, sugar, and baking powder in a large bowl. 2. Add the butter and stir to mix well. Pour in the buttermilk and stir with a rubber spatula just until incorporated. 3. Place the dough onto a lightly floured surface and roll the dough out to a disk, ½ inch thick. Cut out the biscuits with a 2-inch round cutter and re-roll any scraps until you have 16 biscuits. 4. Preheat the air fryer to 325ºF (163ºC). 5. Working in batches, arrange the biscuits in the air fryer basket in a single layer. Bake for about 18 minutes until the biscuits are golden brown. 6. Remove from the basket to a plate and repeat with the remaining biscuits. 7. Serve hot.

Turkey Breakfast Sausage Patties

Prep time: 5 minutes | Cook time: 10 minutes | Serves 4

- 1 tablespoon chopped fresh thyme
- 1 tablespoon chopped fresh sage
- 1¼ teaspoons kosher salt
- 1 teaspoon chopped fennel seeds
- ¾ teaspoon smoked paprika
- ½ teaspoon onion powder
- ½ teaspoon garlic powder
- ⅛ teaspoon crushed red pepper flakes
- ⅛ teaspoon freshly ground black pepper
- 1 pound (454 g) 93% lean ground turkey
- ½ cup finely minced sweet apple (peeled)

1. Thoroughly combine the thyme, sage, salt, fennel seeds, paprika, onion powder, garlic powder, red pepper flakes, and black pepper in a medium bowl. 2. Add the ground turkey and apple and stir until well incorporated. Divide the mixture into 8 equal portions and shape into patties with your hands, each about ¼ inch thick and 3 inches in diameter. 3. Preheat the air fryer to 400°F (204°C). 4. Place the patties in the air fryer basket in a single layer. You may need to work in batches to avoid overcrowding. 5. Air fry for 5 minutes. Flip the patties and air fry for 5 minutes, or until the patties are nicely browned and cooked through. 6. Remove from the basket to a plate and repeat with the remaining patties. 7. Serve warm.

Hearty Blueberry Oatmeal

Prep time: 10 minutes | Cook time: 25 minutes | Serves 6

- 1½ cups quick oats
- 1¼ teaspoons ground cinnamon, divided
- ½ teaspoon baking powder
- Pinch salt
- 1 cup unsweetened vanilla almond milk
- ¼ cup honey
- 1 teaspoon vanilla extract
- 1 egg, beaten
- 2 cups blueberries
- Olive oil
- 1½ teaspoons sugar, divided
- 6 tablespoons low-fat whipped topping (optional)

1. In a large bowl, mix together the oats, 1 teaspoon of cinnamon, baking powder, and salt. 2. In a medium bowl, whisk together the almond milk, honey, vanilla and egg. 3. Pour the liquid ingredients into the oats mixture and stir to combine. Fold in the blueberries. 4. Lightly spray a baking pan with oil. 5. Add half the blueberry mixture to the pan. 6. Sprinkle ⅛ teaspoon of cinnamon and ½ teaspoon sugar over the top. 7. Cover the pan with aluminum foil and place gently in the air fryer basket. 8. Air fry at 360°F (182°C) for 20 minutes. Remove the foil and air fry for an additional 5 minutes. Transfer the mixture to a shallow bowl. 9. Repeat with the remaining blueberry mixture, ½ teaspoon of sugar, and ⅛ teaspoon of cinnamon. 10. To serve, spoon into bowls

and top with whipped topping.

Baked Peach Oatmeal

Prep time: 5 minutes | Cook time: 30 minutes | Serves 6

- Olive oil cooking spray
- 2 cups certified gluten-free rolled oats
- 2 cups unsweetened almond milk
- ¼ cup raw honey, plus more for drizzling (optional)
- ½ cup nonfat plain Greek
- yogurt
- 1 teaspoon vanilla extract
- ½ teaspoon ground cinnamon
- ¼ teaspoon salt
- 1½ cups diced peaches, divided, plus more for serving (optional)

1. Preheat the air fryer to 380°F(193°C). Lightly coat the inside of a 6-inch cake pan with olive oil cooking spray. 2. In a large bowl, mix together the oats, almond milk, honey, yogurt, vanilla, cinnamon, and salt until well combined. 3. Fold in ¾ cup of the peaches and then pour the mixture into the prepared cake pan. 4. Sprinkle the remaining peaches across the top of the oatmeal mixture. Bake in the air fryer for 30 minutes. 5. Allow to set and cool for 5 minutes before serving with additional fresh fruit and honey for drizzling, if desired.

Greek Bagels

Prep time: 10 minutes | Cook time: 10 minutes | Makes 2 bagels

- ½ cup self-rising flour, plus more for dusting
- ½ cup plain Greek yogurt
- 1 egg
- 1 tablespoon water
- 4 teaspoons everything bagel spice mix
- Cooking oil spray
- 1 tablespoon butter, melted

1. In a large bowl, using a wooden spoon, stir together the flour and yogurt until a tacky dough forms. Transfer the dough to a lightly floured work surface and roll the dough into a ball. 2. Cut the dough into 2 pieces and roll each piece into a log. Form each log into a bagel shape, pinching the ends together. 3. In a small bowl, whisk the egg and water. Brush the egg wash on the bagels. 4. Sprinkle 2 teaspoons of the spice mix on each bagel and gently press it into the dough. 5. Insert the crisper plate into the basket and the basket into the unit. Preheat the unit by selecting BAKE, setting the temperature to 330°F (166°C), and setting the time to 3 minutes. Select START/STOP to begin. 6. Once the unit is preheated, spray the crisper plate with cooking spray. Drizzle the bagels with the butter and place them into the basket. 7. Select BAKE, set the temperature to 330°F (166°C), and set the time to 10 minutes. Select START/STOP to begin. 8. When the cooking is complete, the bagels should be lightly golden on the outside. Serve warm.

Easy Buttermilk Biscuits

Prep time: 5 minutes | Cook time: 18 minutes | Makes 16 biscuits

- 2½ cups all-purpose flour
- 1 tablespoon baking powder
- 1 teaspoon kosher salt
- 1 teaspoon sugar
- ½ teaspoon baking soda
- 8 tablespoons (1 stick) unsalted butter, at room temperature
- 1 cup buttermilk, chilled

1. Stir together the flour, baking powder, salt, sugar, and baking powder in a large bowl. 2. Add the butter and stir to mix well. Pour in the buttermilk and stir with a rubber spatula just until incorporated. 3. Place the dough onto a lightly floured surface and roll the dough out to a disk, ½ inch thick. Cut out the biscuits with a 2-inch round cutter and re-roll any scraps until you have 16 biscuits. 4. Preheat the air fryer to 325°F (163°C). 5. Working in batches, arrange the biscuits in the air fryer basket in a single layer. Bake for about 18 minutes until the biscuits are golden brown. 6. Remove from the basket to a plate and repeat with the remaining biscuits. 7. Serve hot.

Onion Omelet

Prep time: 10 minutes | Cook time: 12 minutes | Serves 2

- 3 eggs
- Salt and ground black pepper, to taste
- ½ teaspoons soy sauce
- 1 large onion, chopped
- 2 tablespoons grated Cheddar cheese
- Cooking spray

1. Preheat the air fryer to 355°F (179°C). 2. In a bowl, whisk together the eggs, salt, pepper, and soy sauce. 3. Spritz a small pan with cooking spray. Spread the chopped onion across the bottom of the pan, then transfer the pan to the air fryer. 4. Bake in the preheated air fryer for 6 minutes or until the onion is translucent. 5. Add the egg mixture on top of the onions to coat well. Add the cheese on top, then continue baking for another 6 minutes. 6. Allow to cool before serving.

Spinach and Mushroom Mini Quiche

Prep time: 10 minutes | Cook time: 15 minutes | Serves 4

- 1 teaspoon olive oil, plus more for spraying
- 1 cup coarsely chopped mushrooms
- 1 cup fresh baby spinach, shredded
- 4 eggs, beaten
- ½ cup shredded Cheddar cheese
- ½ cup shredded Mozzarella cheese
- ¼ teaspoon salt
- ¼ teaspoon black pepper

1. Spray 4 silicone baking cups with olive oil and set aside. 2. In a medium sauté pan over medium heat, warm 1 teaspoon of olive oil. Add the mushrooms and sauté until soft, 3 to 4 minutes. 3. Add the spinach and cook until wilted, 1 to 2 minutes. Set aside. 4. In a medium bowl, whisk together the eggs, Cheddar cheese, Mozzarella cheese, salt, and pepper. 5. Gently fold the mushrooms and spinach into the egg mixture. 6. Pour ¼ of the mixture into each silicone baking cup. 7. Place the baking cups into the air fryer basket and air fry at 350°F (177°C) for 5 minutes. Stir the mixture in each ramekin slightly and air fry until the egg has set, an additional 3 to 5 minutes.

Veggie Frittata

Prep time: 7 minutes | Cook time: 21 to 23 minutes | Serves 2

- Avocado oil spray
- ¼ cup diced red onion
- ¼ cup diced red bell pepper
- ¼ cup finely chopped broccoli
- 4 large eggs
- 3 ounces (85 g) shredded sharp Cheddar cheese, divided
- ½ teaspoon dried thyme
- Sea salt and freshly ground black pepper, to taste

1. Spray a pan well with oil. Put the onion, pepper, and broccoli in the pan, place the pan in the air fryer, and set to 350°F (177°C). Bake for 5 minutes. 2. While the vegetables cook, beat the eggs in a medium bowl. Stir in half of the cheese, and season with the thyme, salt, and pepper. 3. Add the eggs to the pan and top with the remaining cheese. Set the air fryer to 350°F (177°C). Bake for 16 to 18 minutes, until cooked through.

Kale and Potato Nuggets

Prep time: 10 minutes | Cook time: 18 minutes | Serves 4

- 1 teaspoon extra virgin olive oil
- 1 clove garlic, minced
- 4 cups kale, rinsed and chopped
- 2 cups potatoes, boiled
- and mashed
- ⅛ cup milk
- Salt and ground black pepper, to taste
- Cooking spray

1. Preheat the air fryer to 390°F (199°C). 2. In a skillet over medium heat, sauté the garlic in the olive oil, until it turns golden brown. Sauté with the kale for an additional 3 minutes and remove from the heat. 3. Mix the mashed potatoes, kale and garlic in a bowl. Pour in the milk and sprinkle with salt and pepper. 4. Shape the mixture into nuggets and spritz with cooking spray. 5. Put in the air fryer basket and air fry for 15 minutes, flip the nuggets halfway through cooking to make sure the nuggets fry evenly. 6. Serve immediately.

Spinach and Swiss Frittata with Mushrooms

Prep time: 10 minutes | Cook time: 20 minutes | Serves 4

- Olive oil cooking spray
- 8 large eggs
- ½ teaspoon salt
- ½ teaspoon black pepper
- 1 garlic clove, minced
- 2 cups fresh baby spinach
- 4 ounces (113 g) baby
- bella mushrooms, sliced
- 1 shallot, diced
- ½ cup shredded Swiss cheese, divided
- Hot sauce, for serving (optional)

1. Preheat the air fryer to 360°F(182°C). Lightly coat the inside of a 6-inch round cake pan with olive oil cooking spray. 2. In a large bowl, beat the eggs, salt, pepper, and garlic for 1 to 2 minutes, or until well combined. 3. Fold in the spinach, mushrooms, shallot, and ¼ cup of the Swiss cheese. 4. Pour the egg mixture into the prepared cake pan, and sprinkle the remaining ¼ cup of Swiss over the top. 5. Place into the air fryer and bake for 18 to 20 minutes, or until the eggs are set in the center. 6. Remove from the air fryer and allow to cool for 5 minutes. Drizzle with hot sauce (if using) before serving.

Pumpkin Donut Holes

Prep time: 15 minutes | Cook time: 14 minutes | Makes 12 donut holes

- 1 cup whole-wheat pastry flour, plus more as needed
- 3 tablespoons packed brown sugar
- ½ teaspoon ground cinnamon
- 1 teaspoon low-sodium baking powder
- ⅓ cup canned no-salt-
- added pumpkin purée (not pumpkin pie filling)
- 3 tablespoons 2% milk, plus more as needed
- 2 tablespoons unsalted butter, melted
- 1 egg white
- Powdered sugar (optional)

1. In a medium bowl, mix the pastry flour, brown sugar, cinnamon, and baking powder. 2. In a small bowl, beat the pumpkin, milk, butter, and egg white until combined. Add the pumpkin mixture to the dry ingredients and mix until combined. You may need to add more flour or milk to form a soft dough. 3. Divide the dough into 12 pieces. With floured hands, form each piece into a ball. 4. Cut a piece of parchment paper or aluminum foil to fit inside the air fryer basket but about 1 inch smaller in diameter. Poke holes in the paper or foil and place it in the basket. 5. Put 6 donut holes into the basket, leaving some space around each. Air fry at 360°F (182°C) for 5 to 7 minutes, or until the donut holes reach an internal temperature of 200°F (93°C) and are firm and light golden brown. 6. Let cool for 5 minutes. Remove from the basket and roll in powdered sugar, if

desired. Repeat with the remaining donut holes and serve.

Gluten-Free Granola Cereal

Prep time: 7 minutes | Cook time: 30 minutes | Makes 3½ cups

- Oil, for spraying
- 1½ cups gluten-free rolled oats
- ½ cup chopped walnuts
- ½ cup chopped almonds
- ½ cup pumpkin seeds
- ¼ cup maple syrup or honey
- 1 tablespoon toasted sesame oil or vegetable oil
- 1 teaspoon ground cinnamon
- ½ teaspoon salt
- ½ cup dried cranberries

1. Preheat the air fryer to 250°F (121°C). Line the air fryer basket with parchment and spray lightly with oil. (Do not skip the step of lining the basket; the parchment will keep the granola from falling through the holes.) 2. In a large bowl, mix together the oats, walnuts, almonds, pumpkin seeds, maple syrup, sesame oil, cinnamon, and salt. 3. Spread the mixture in an even layer in the prepared basket. 4. Cook for 30 minutes, stirring every 10 minutes. 5. Transfer the granola to a bowl, add the dried cranberries, and toss to combine. 6. Let cool to room temperature before storing in an airtight container.

Maple Granola

Prep time: 5 minutes | Cook time: 40 minutes | Makes 2 cups

- 1 cup rolled oats
- 3 tablespoons pure maple syrup
- 1 tablespoon sugar
- 1 tablespoon neutral-flavored oil, such as refined coconut,
- sunflower, or safflower
- ¼ teaspoon sea salt
- ¼ teaspoon ground cinnamon
- ¼ teaspoon vanilla extract

1. Insert the crisper plate into the basket and the basket into the unit. Preheat the unit by selecting BAKE, setting the temperature to 250°F (121°C), and setting the time to 3 minutes. Select START/STOP to begin. 2. In a medium bowl, stir together the oats, maple syrup, sugar, oil, salt, cinnamon, and vanilla until thoroughly combined. Transfer the granola to a 6-by-2-inch round baking pan. 3. Once the unit is preheated, place the pan into the basket. 4. Select BAKE, set the temperature to 250°F (121°C) and set the time to 40 minutes. Select START/STOP to begin. 5. After 10 minutes, stir the granola well. Resume cooking, stirring the granola every 10 minutes, for a total of 40 minutes, or until the granola is lightly browned and mostly dry. 6. When the cooking is complete, place the granola on a plate to cool. It will become crisp as it cools. Store the completely cooled granola in an airtight container in a cool, dry place for 1 to 2 weeks.

Breakfast Meatballs

Prep time: 10 minutes | Cook time: 15 minutes | Makes 18 meatballs

- 1 pound (454 g) ground pork breakfast sausage
- ½ teaspoon salt
- ¼ teaspoon ground black pepper
- ½ cup shredded sharp Cheddar cheese
- 1 ounce (28 g) cream cheese, softened
- 1 large egg, whisked

1. Combine all ingredients in a large bowl. Form mixture into eighteen 1-inch meatballs. 2. Place meatballs into ungreased air fryer basket. Adjust the temperature to 400°F (204°C) and air fry for 15 minutes, shaking basket three times during cooking. Meatballs will be browned on the outside and have an internal temperature of at least 145°F (63°C) when completely cooked. Serve warm.

Super Easy Bacon Cups

Prep time: 5 minutes | Cook time: 20 minutes | Serves 2

- 3 slices bacon, cooked, sliced in half
- 2 slices ham
- 1 slice tomato
- 2 eggs
- 2 teaspoons grated Parmesan cheese
- Salt and ground black pepper, to taste

1. Preheat the air fryer to 375°F (191°C). Line 2 greased muffin tins with 3 half-strips of bacon 2. Put one slice of ham and half slice of tomato in each muffin tin on top of the bacon 3. Crack one egg on top of the tomato in each muffin tin and sprinkle each with half a teaspoon of grated Parmesan cheese. Sprinkle with salt and ground black pepper, if desired. 4. Bake in the preheated air fryer for 20 minutes. Remove from the air fryer and let cool. 5. Serve warm.

Red Pepper and Feta Frittata

Prep time: 10 minutes | Cook time: 20 minutes | Serves 4

- Olive oil cooking spray
- 8 large eggs
- 1 medium red bell pepper, diced
- ½ teaspoon salt
- ½ teaspoon black pepper
- 1 garlic clove, minced
- ½ cup feta, divided

1. Preheat the air fryer to 360°F(182°C). Lightly coat the inside of a 6-inch round cake pan with olive oil cooking spray. 2. In a large bowl, beat the eggs for 1 to 2 minutes, or until well combined. 3. Add the bell pepper, salt, black pepper, and garlic to the eggs, and mix together until the bell pepper is distributed throughout. 4. Fold in ¼ cup of the feta cheese. 5. Pour the egg mixture into the prepared cake pan, and sprinkle the remaining ¼ cup of feta over the top. 6. Place into the air fryer and bake for 18 to 20 minutes, or

until the eggs are set in the center. 7. Remove from the air fryer and allow to cool for 5 minutes before serving.

Italian Egg Cups

Prep time: 5 minutes | Cook time: 10 minutes | Serves 4

- Olive oil
- 1 cup marinara sauce
- 4 eggs
- 4 tablespoons shredded Mozzarella cheese
- 4 teaspoons grated
- Parmesan cheese
- Salt and freshly ground black pepper, to taste
- Chopped fresh basil, for garnish

1. Lightly spray 4 individual ramekins with olive oil. 2. Pour ¼ cup of marinara sauce into each ramekin. 3. Crack one egg into each ramekin on top of the marinara sauce. 4. Sprinkle 1 tablespoon of Mozzarella and 1 tablespoon of Parmesan on top of each egg. Season with salt and pepper. 5. Cover each ramekin with aluminum foil. Place two of the ramekins in the air fryer basket. 6. Air fry at 350°F (177°C) for 5 minutes and remove the aluminum foil. Air fry until the top is lightly browned and the egg white is cooked, another 2 to 4 minutes. If you prefer the yolk to be firmer, cook for 3 to 5 more minutes. 7. Repeat with the remaining two ramekins. Garnish with basil and serve.

Breakfast Calzone

Prep time: 15 minutes | Cook time: 15 minutes | Serves 4

- 1½ cups shredded Mozzarella cheese
- ½ cup blanched finely ground almond flour
- 1 ounce (28 g) full-fat cream cheese
- 1 large whole egg
- 4 large eggs, scrambled
- ½ pound (227 g) cooked breakfast sausage, crumbled
- 8 tablespoons shredded mild Cheddar cheese

1. In a large microwave-safe bowl, add Mozzarella, almond flour, and cream cheese. Microwave for 1 minute. Stir until the mixture is smooth and forms a ball. Add the egg and stir until dough forms. 2. Place dough between two sheets of parchment and roll out to ¼-inch thickness. Cut the dough into four rectangles. 3. Mix scrambled eggs and cooked sausage together in a large bowl. Divide the mixture evenly among each piece of dough, placing it on the lower half of the rectangle. Sprinkle each with 2 tablespoons Cheddar. 4. Fold over the rectangle to cover the egg and meat mixture. Pinch, roll, or use a wet fork to close the edges completely. 5. Cut a piece of parchment to fit your air fryer basket and place the calzones onto the parchment. Place parchment into the air fryer basket. 6. Adjust the temperature to 380°F (193°C) and air fry for 15 minutes. 7. Flip the calzones halfway through the cooking time. When done, calzones should be golden in color. Serve immediately.

Turkey Sausage Breakfast Pizza

Prep time: 15 minutes | Cook time: 24 minutes | Serves 2

- 4 large eggs, divided
- 1 tablespoon water
- ½ teaspoon garlic powder
- ½ teaspoon onion powder
- ½ teaspoon dried oregano
- 2 tablespoons coconut flour
- 3 tablespoons grated Parmesan cheese
- ½ cup shredded provolone cheese
- 1 link cooked turkey sausage, chopped (about 2 ounces / 57 g)
- 2 sun-dried tomatoes, finely chopped
- 2 scallions, thinly sliced

1. Preheat the air fryer to 400°F (204°C). Line a cake pan with parchment paper and lightly coat the paper with olive oil. 2. In a large bowl, whisk 2 of the eggs with the water, garlic powder, onion powder, and dried oregano. Add the coconut flour, breaking up any lumps with your hands as you add it to the bowl. Stir the coconut flour into the egg mixture, mixing until smooth. Stir in the Parmesan cheese. Allow the mixture to rest for a few minutes until thick and dough-like. 3. Transfer the mixture to the prepared pan. Use a spatula to spread it evenly and slightly up the sides of the pan. Air fry until the crust is set but still light in color, about 10 minutes. Top with the cheeses, sausage, and sun-dried tomatoes. 4. Break the remaining 2 eggs into a small bowl, then slide them onto the pizza. Return the pizza to the air fryer. Air fry 10 to 14 minutes until the egg whites are set and the yolks are the desired doneness. Top with the scallions and allow to rest for 5 minutes before serving.

Broccoli-Mushroom Frittata

Prep time: 10 minutes | Cook time: 20 minutes | Serves 2

- 1 tablespoon olive oil
- 1½ cups broccoli florets, finely chopped
- ½ cup sliced brown mushrooms
- ¼ cup finely chopped
- onion
- ½ teaspoon salt
- ¼ teaspoon freshly ground black pepper
- 6 eggs
- ¼ cup Parmesan cheese

1. In a nonstick cake pan, combine the olive oil, broccoli, mushrooms, onion, salt, and pepper. Stir until the vegetables are thoroughly coated with oil. Place the cake pan in the air fryer basket and set the air fryer to 400°F (204°C). Air fry for 5 minutes until the vegetables soften. 2. Meanwhile, in a medium bowl, whisk the eggs and Parmesan until thoroughly combined. Pour the egg mixture into the pan and shake gently to distribute the vegetables. Air fry for another 15 minutes until the eggs are set. 3. Remove from the air fryer and let sit for 5 minutes to cool slightly. Use a silicone spatula to gently lift the frittata onto a plate before serving.

Sausage and Cheese Balls

Prep time: 10 minutes | Cook time: 12 minutes | Makes 16 balls

- 1 pound (454 g) pork breakfast sausage
- ½ cup shredded Cheddar cheese
- 1 ounce (28 g) full-fat cream cheese, softened
- 1 large egg

1. Mix all ingredients in a large bowl. Form into sixteen (1-inch) balls. Place the balls into the air fryer basket. 2. Adjust the temperature to 400°F (204°C) and air fry for 12 minutes. 3. Shake the basket two or three times during cooking. Sausage balls will be browned on the outside and have an internal temperature of at least 145°F (63°C) when completely cooked. 4. Serve warm.

Vanilla Granola

Prep time: 5 minutes | Cook time: 40 minutes | Serves 4

- 1 cup rolled oats
- 3 tablespoons maple syrup
- 1 tablespoon sunflower oil
- 1 tablespoon coconut sugar
- ¼ teaspoon vanilla
- ¼ teaspoon cinnamon
- ¼ teaspoon sea salt

1. Preheat the air fryer to 248°F (120°C). 2. Mix together the oats, maple syrup, sunflower oil, coconut sugar, vanilla, cinnamon, and sea salt in a medium bowl and stir to combine. Transfer the mixture to a baking pan. 3. Place the pan in the air fryer basket and bake for 40 minutes, or until the granola is mostly dry and lightly browned. Stir the granola four times during cooking. 4. Let the granola stand for 5 to 10 minutes before serving.

Bourbon Vanilla French Toast

Prep time: 15 minutes | Cook time: 6 minutes | Serves 4

- 2 large eggs
- 2 tablespoons water
- ⅔ cup whole or 2% milk
- 1 tablespoon butter, melted
- 2 tablespoons bourbon
- 1 teaspoon vanilla extract
- 8 (1-inch-thick) French bread slices
- Cooking spray

1. Preheat the air fryer to 320°F (160°C). Line the air fryer basket with parchment paper and spray it with cooking spray. 2. Beat the eggs with the water in a shallow bowl until combined. Add the milk, melted butter, bourbon, and vanilla and stir to mix well. 3. Dredge 4 slices of bread in the batter, turning to coat both sides evenly. Transfer the bread slices onto the parchment paper. 4. Bake for 6 minutes until nicely browned. Flip the slices halfway through the cooking time. 5. Remove from the basket to a plate and repeat with the remaining 4 slices of bread. 6. Serve warm.

Parmesan Sausage Egg Muffins

Prep time: 5 minutes | Cook time: 20 minutes | Serves 4

- 6 ounces (170 g) Italian sausage, sliced
- 6 eggs
- ⅛ cup heavy cream
- Salt and ground black pepper, to taste
- 3 ounces (85 g) Parmesan cheese, grated

1. Preheat the air fryer to 350ºF (177ºC). Grease a muffin pan. 2. Put the sliced sausage in the muffin pan. 3. Beat the eggs with the cream in a bowl and season with salt and pepper. 4. Pour half of the mixture over the sausages in the pan. 5. Sprinkle with cheese and the remaining egg mixture. 6. Bake in the preheated air fryer for 20 minutes or until set. 7. Serve immediately.

Breakfast Sammies

Prep time: 15 minutes | Cook time: 20 minutes | Serves 5

- Biscuits:
- 6 large egg whites
- 2 cups blanched almond flour, plus more if needed
- 1½ teaspoons baking powder
- ½ teaspoon fine sea salt
- ¼ cup (½ stick) very cold unsalted butter (or lard for dairy-free), cut into
- ¼-inch pieces
- Eggs:
- 5 large eggs
- ½ teaspoon fine sea salt
- ¼ teaspoon ground black pepper
- 5 (1 ounce / 28 g) slices Cheddar cheese (omit for dairy-free)
- 10 thin slices ham

1. Spray the air fryer basket with avocado oil. Preheat the air fryer to 350ºF (177ºC). Grease two pie pans or two baking pans that will fit inside your air fryer. 2. Make the biscuits: In a medium-sized bowl, whip the egg whites with a hand mixer until very stiff. Set aside. 3. In a separate medium-sized bowl, stir together the almond flour, baking powder, and salt until well combined. Cut in the butter. Gently fold the flour mixture into the egg whites with a rubber spatula. If the dough is too wet to form into mounds, add a few tablespoons of almond flour until the dough holds together well. 4. Using a large spoon, divide the dough into 5 equal portions and drop them about 1 inch apart on one of the greased pie pans. (If you're using a smaller air fryer, work in batches if necessary.) Place the pan in the air fryer and bake for 11 to 14 minutes, until the biscuits are golden brown. Remove from the air fryer and set aside to cool. 5. Make the eggs: Set the air fryer to 375ºF (191ºC). Crack the eggs into the remaining greased pie pan and sprinkle with the salt and pepper. Place the eggs in the air fryer to bake for 5 minutes, or until they are cooked to your liking. 6. Open the air fryer

and top each egg yolk with a slice of cheese (if using). Bake for another minute, or until the cheese is melted. 7. Once the biscuits are cool, slice them in half lengthwise. Place 1 cooked egg topped with cheese and 2 slices of ham in each biscuit. 8. Store leftover biscuits, eggs, and ham in separate airtight containers in the fridge for up to 3 days. Reheat the biscuits and eggs on a baking sheet in a preheated 350ºF (177ºC) air fryer for 5 minutes, or until warmed through.

Spaghetti Squash Fritters

Prep time: 15 minutes | Cook time: 8 minutes | Serves 4

- 2 cups cooked spaghetti squash
- 2 tablespoons unsalted butter, softened
- 1 large egg
- ¼ cup blanched finely
- ground almond flour
- 2 stalks green onion, sliced
- ½ teaspoon garlic powder
- 1 teaspoon dried parsley

1. Remove excess moisture from the squash using a cheesecloth or kitchen towel. 2. Mix all ingredients in a large bowl. Form into four patties. 3. Cut a piece of parchment to fit your air fryer basket. Place each patty on the parchment and place into the air fryer basket. 4. Adjust the temperature to 400ºF (204ºC) and set the timer for 8 minutes. 5. Flip the patties halfway through the cooking time. Serve warm.

Smoky Sausage Patties

Prep time: 30 minutes | Cook time: 9 minutes | Serves 8

- 1 pound (454 g) ground pork
- 1 tablespoon coconut aminos
- 2 teaspoons liquid smoke
- 1 teaspoon dried sage
- 1 teaspoon sea salt
- ½ teaspoon fennel seeds
- ½ teaspoon dried thyme
- ½ teaspoon freshly ground black pepper
- ¼ teaspoon cayenne pepper

1. In a large bowl, combine the pork, coconut aminos, liquid smoke, sage, salt, fennel seeds, thyme, black pepper, and cayenne pepper. Work the meat with your hands until the seasonings are fully incorporated. 2. Shape the mixture into 8 equal-size patties. Using your thumb, make a dent in the center of each patty. Place the patties on a plate and cover with plastic wrap. Refrigerate the patties for at least 30 minutes. 3. Working in batches if necessary, place the patties in a single layer in the air fryer, being careful not to overcrowd them. 4. Set the air fryer to 400ºF (204ºC) and air fry for 5 minutes. Flip and cook for about 4 minutes more.

Chapter 2

Family Favorites

Mixed Berry Crumble

Prep time: 10 minutes | Cook time: 11 to 16 minutes | Serves 4

- ½ cup chopped fresh strawberries
- ½ cup fresh blueberries
- ⅓ cup frozen raspberries
- 1 tablespoon freshly squeezed lemon juice
- 1 tablespoon honey
- ⅔ cup whole-wheat pastry flour
- 3 tablespoons packed brown sugar
- 2 tablespoons unsalted butter, melted

1. In a baking pan, combine the strawberries, blueberries, and raspberries. Drizzle with the lemon juice and honey. 2. In a small bowl, mix the pastry flour and brown sugar. 3. Stir in the butter and mix until crumbly. Sprinkle this mixture over the fruit. 4. Bake at 380ºF (193ºC) for 11 to 16 minutes, or until the fruit is tender and bubbly and the topping is golden brown. Serve warm.

Meringue Cookies

Prep time: 15 minutes | Cook time: 1 hour 30 minutes | Makes 20 cookies

- Oil, for spraying
- 4 large egg whites
- 1 cup sugar
- Pinch cream of tartar

1. Preheat the air fryer to 140ºF (60ºC). Line the air fryer basket with parchment and spray lightly with oil. 2. In a small heatproof bowl, whisk together the egg whites and sugar. Fill a small saucepan halfway with water, place it over medium heat, and bring to a light simmer. Place the bowl with the egg whites on the saucepan, making sure the bottom of the bowl does not touch the water. Whisk the mixture until the sugar is dissolved. 3. Transfer the mixture to a large bowl and add the cream of tartar. Using an electric mixer, beat the mixture on high until it is glossy and stiff peaks form. Transfer the mixture to a piping bag or a zip-top plastic bag with a corner cut off. 4. Pipe rounds into the prepared basket. You may need to work in batches, depending on the size of your air fryer. 5. Cook for 1 hour 30 minutes. 6. Turn off the air fryer and let the meringues cool completely inside. The residual heat will continue to dry them out.

Berry Cheesecake

Prep time: 5 minutes | Cook time: 10 minutes | Serves 4

- Oil, for spraying
- 8 ounces (227 g) cream cheese
- 6 tablespoons sugar
- 1 tablespoon sour cream
- 1 large egg
- ½ teaspoon vanilla extract
- ¼ teaspoon lemon juice
- ½ cup fresh mixed berries

1. Preheat the air fryer to 350ºF (177ºC). Line the air fryer basket with parchment and spray lightly with oil. 2. In a blender, combine the cream cheese, sugar, sour cream, egg, vanilla, and lemon juice and blend until smooth. Pour the mixture into a 4-inch springform pan. 3. Place the pan in the prepared basket. 4. Cook for 8 to 10 minutes, or until only the very center jiggles slightly when the pan is moved. 5. Refrigerate the cheesecake in the pan for at least 2 hours. 6. Release the sides from the springform pan, top the cheesecake with the mixed berries, and serve.

Fish and Vegetable Tacos

Prep time: 15 minutes | Cook time: 9 to 12 minutes | Serves 4

- 1 pound (454 g) white fish fillets, such as sole or cod
- 2 teaspoons olive oil
- 3 tablespoons freshly squeezed lemon juice, divided
- 1½ cups chopped red cabbage
- 1 large carrot, grated
- ½ cup low-sodium salsa
- ⅓ cup low-fat Greek yogurt
- 4 soft low-sodium whole-wheat tortillas

1. Brush the fish with the olive oil and sprinkle with 1 tablespoon of lemon juice. Air fry in the air fryer basket at 390ºF (199ºC) for 9 to 12 minutes, or until the fish just flakes when tested with a fork. 2. Meanwhile, in a medium bowl, stir together the remaining 2 tablespoons of lemon juice, the red cabbage, carrot, salsa, and yogurt. 3. When the fish is cooked, remove it from the air fryer basket and break it up into large pieces. 4. Offer the fish, tortillas, and the cabbage mixture, and let each person assemble a taco.

Buffalo Cauliflower

Prep time: 15 minutes | Cook time: 5 minutes | Serves 6

- 1 large head cauliflower, separated into small florets
- 1 tablespoon olive oil
- ½ teaspoon garlic powder
- ⅓ cup low-sodium hot wing sauce
- ⅔ cup nonfat Greek yogurt
- ½ teaspoons Tabasco sauce
- 1 celery stalk, chopped
- 1 tablespoon crumbled blue cheese

1. In a large bowl, toss the cauliflower florets with the olive oil. Sprinkle with the garlic powder and toss again to coat. Put half of the cauliflower in the air fryer basket. Air fry at 380ºF (193ºC) for 5 to 7 minutes, until the cauliflower is browned, shaking the basket once during cooking. 2. Transfer to a serving bowl and toss with half of the wing sauce. Repeat with the remaining cauliflower and wing sauce. 3. In a small bowl, stir together the yogurt, Tabasco sauce, celery, and blue cheese. Serve with the cauliflower for dipping.

Scallops with Green Vegetables

Prep time: 15 minutes | Cook time: 8 to 11 minutes | Serves 4

- 1 cup green beans
- 1 cup frozen peas
- 1 cup frozen chopped broccoli
- 2 teaspoons olive oil
- ½ teaspoon dried basil
- ½ teaspoon dried oregano
- 12 ounces (340 g) sea scallops

1. In a large bowl, toss the green beans, peas, and broccoli with the olive oil. Place in the air fryer basket. Air fry at 400°F (204°C) for 4 to 6 minutes, or until the vegetables are crisp-tender. 2. Remove the vegetables from the air fryer basket and sprinkle with the herbs. Set aside. 3. In the air fryer basket, put the scallops and air fry for 4 to 5 minutes, or until the scallops are firm and reach an internal temperature of just 145°F (63°C) on a meat thermometer. 4. Toss scallops with the vegetables and serve immediately.

Elephant Ears

Prep time: 5 minutes | Cook time: 5 minutes | Serves 8

- Oil, for spraying
- 1 (8 ounces / 227 g) can buttermilk biscuits
- 3 tablespoons sugar
- 1 tablespoon ground
- cinnamon
- 3 tablespoons unsalted butter, melted
- 8 scoops vanilla ice cream (optional)

1. Line the air fryer basket with parchment and spray lightly with oil. 2. Separate the dough. Using a rolling pin, roll out the biscuits into 6- to 8-inch circles. 3. Place the dough circles in the prepared basket and spray liberally with oil. You may need to work in batches, depending on the size of your air fryer. 4. Air fry at 350°F (177°C) for 5 minutes, or until lightly browned. 5. In a small bowl, mix together the sugar and cinnamon. 6. Brush the elephant ears with the melted butter and sprinkle with the cinnamon-sugar mixture. 7. Top each serving with a scoop of ice cream (if using).

Pork Stuffing Meatballs

Prep time: 10 minutes | Cook time: 12 minutes | Makes 35 meatballs

- Oil, for spraying
- 1½ pounds (680 g) ground pork
- 1 cup bread crumbs
- ½ cup milk
- ¼ cup minced onion
- 1 large egg
- 1 tablespoon dried
- rosemary
- 1 tablespoon dried thyme
- 1 teaspoon salt
- 1 teaspoon freshly ground black pepper
- 1 teaspoon finely chopped fresh parsley

1. Line the air fryer basket with parchment and spray lightly with oil. 2. In a large bowl, mix together the ground pork, bread crumbs, milk, onion, egg, rosemary, thyme, salt, black pepper, and parsley. 3. Roll about 2 tablespoons of the mixture into a ball. Repeat with the rest of the mixture. You should have 30 to 35 meatballs. 4. Place the meatballs in the prepared basket in a single layer, leaving space between each one. You may need to work in batches, depending on the size of your air fryer. 5. Air fry at 390°F (199°C) for 10 to 12 minutes, flipping after 5 minutes, or until golden brown and the internal temperature reaches 160°F (71°C).

Coconut Chicken Tenders

Prep time: 10 minutes | Cook time: 12 minutes | Serves 4

- Oil, for spraying
- 2 large eggs
- ¼ cup milk
- 1 tablespoon hot sauce
- 1½ cups sweetened flaked coconut
- ¾ cup panko bread
- crumbs
- 1 teaspoon salt
- ½ teaspoon freshly ground black pepper
- 1 pound (454 g) chicken tenders

1. Line the air fryer basket with parchment and spray lightly with oil. 2. In a small bowl, whisk together the eggs, milk, and hot sauce. 3. In a shallow dish, mix together the coconut, bread crumbs, salt, and black pepper. 4. Coat the chicken in the egg mix, then dredge in the coconut mixture until evenly coated. 5. Place the chicken in the prepared basket and spray liberally with oil. 6. Air fry at 400°F (204°C) for 6 minutes, flip, spray with more oil, and cook for another 6 minutes, or until the internal temperature reaches 165°F (74°C).

Buffalo Cauliflower

Prep time: 15 minutes | Cook time: 5 minutes | Serves 6

- 1 large head cauliflower, separated into small florets
- 1 tablespoon olive oil
- ½ teaspoon garlic powder
- ⅓ cup low-sodium hot wing sauce
- ⅔ cup nonfat Greek yogurt
- ½ teaspoons Tabasco sauce
- 1 celery stalk, chopped
- 1 tablespoon crumbled blue cheese

1. In a large bowl, toss the cauliflower florets with the olive oil. Sprinkle with the garlic powder and toss again to coat. Put half of the cauliflower in the air fryer basket. Air fry at 380°F (193°C) for 5 to 7 minutes, until the cauliflower is browned, shaking the basket once during cooking. 2. Transfer to a serving bowl and toss with half of the wing sauce. Repeat with the remaining cauliflower and wing sauce. 3. In a small bowl, stir together the yogurt, Tabasco sauce, celery, and blue cheese. Serve with the cauliflower for dipping.

Beef Jerky

Prep time: 30 minutes | Cook time: 2 hours | Serves 8

- Oil, for spraying
- 1 pound (454 g) round steak, cut into thin, short slices
- ¼ cup soy sauce
- 3 tablespoons packed
- light brown sugar
- 1 tablespoon minced garlic
- 1 teaspoon ground ginger
- 1 tablespoon water

1. Line the air fryer basket with parchment and spray lightly with oil. 2. Place the steak, soy sauce, brown sugar, garlic, ginger, and water in a zip-top plastic bag, seal, and shake well until evenly coated. Refrigerate for 30 minutes. 3. Place the steak in the prepared basket in a single layer. You may need to work in batches, depending on the size of your air fryer. 4. Air fry at 180ºF (82ºC) for at least 2 hours. Add more time if you like your jerky a bit tougher.

Churro Bites

Prep time: 5 minutes | Cook time: 6 minutes | Makes 36 bites

- Oil, for spraying
- 1 (17¼ ounces / 489 g) package frozen puffed pastry, thawed
- 1 cup granulated sugar
- 1 tablespoon ground cinnamon
- ½ cup confectioners' sugar
- 1 tablespoon milk

1. Preheat the air fryer to 400ºF (204ºC). Line the air fryer basket with parchment and spray lightly with oil. 2. Unfold the puff pastry onto a clean work surface. Using a sharp knife, cut the dough into 36 bite-size pieces. 3. Place the dough pieces in one layer in the prepared basket, taking care not to let the pieces touch or overlap. 4. Cook for 3 minutes, flip, and cook for another 3 minutes, or until puffed and golden. 5. In a small bowl, mix together the granulated sugar and cinnamon. 6. In another small bowl, whisk together the confectioners' sugar and milk. 7. Dredge the bites in the cinnamon-sugar mixture until evenly coated. 8. Serve with the icing on the side for dipping.

Steak Tips and Potatoes

Prep time: 10 minutes | Cook time: 20 minutes | Serves 4

- Oil, for spraying
- 8 ounces (227 g) baby gold potatoes, cut in half
- ½ teaspoon salt
- 1 pound (454 g) steak, cut into ½-inch pieces
- 1 teaspoon
- Worcestershire sauce
- 1 teaspoon granulated garlic
- ½ teaspoon salt
- ½ teaspoon freshly ground black pepper

1. Line the air fryer basket with parchment and spray lightly

with oil. 2. In a microwave-safe bowl, combine the potatoes and salt, then pour in about ½ inch of water. Microwave for 7 minutes, or until the potatoes are nearly tender. Drain. 3. In a large bowl, gently mix together the steak, potatoes, Worcestershire sauce, garlic, salt, and black pepper. Spread the mixture in an even layer in the prepared basket. 4. Air fry at 400ºF (204ºC) for 12 to 17 minutes, stirring after 5 to 6 minutes. The cooking time will depend on the thickness of the meat and preferred doneness.

Cheesy Roasted Sweet Potatoes

Prep time: 7 minutes | Cook time: 18 to 23 minutes | Serves 4

- 2 large sweet potatoes, peeled and sliced
- 1 teaspoon olive oil
- 1 tablespoon white
- balsamic vinegar
- 1 teaspoon dried thyme
- ¼ cup grated Parmesan cheese

1. In a large bowl, drizzle the sweet potato slices with the olive oil and toss. 2. Sprinkle with the balsamic vinegar and thyme and toss again. 3. Sprinkle the potatoes with the Parmesan cheese and toss to coat. 4. Roast the slices, in batches, in the air fryer basket at 400ºF (204ºC) for 18 to 23 minutes, tossing the sweet potato slices in the basket once during cooking, until tender. 5. Repeat with the remaining sweet potato slices. Serve immediately.

Pecan Rolls

Prep time: 20 minutes | Cook time: 20 to 24 minutes | Makes 12 rolls

- 2 cups all-purpose flour, plus more for dusting
- 2 tablespoons granulated sugar, plus ¼ cup, divided
- 1 teaspoon salt
- 3 tablespoons butter, at room temperature
- ¾ cup milk, whole or 2%
- ¼ cup packed light brown sugar
- ½ cup chopped pecans, toasted
- 1 to 2 tablespoons oil
- ¼ cup confectioners' sugar (optional)

1. In a large bowl, whisk the flour, 2 tablespoons granulated sugar, and salt until blended. Stir in the butter and milk briefly until a sticky dough forms. 2. In a small bowl, stir together the brown sugar and remaining ¼ cup of granulated sugar. 3. Place a piece of parchment paper on a work surface and dust it with flour. Roll the dough on the prepared surface to ¼ inch thickness. 4. Spread the sugar mixture over the dough. Sprinkle the pecans on top. Roll up the dough jelly roll-style, pinching the ends to seal. Cut the dough into 12 rolls. 5. Preheat the air fryer to 320ºF (160ºC). 6. Line the air fryer basket with parchment paper and spritz the parchment with oil. Place 6 rolls on the prepared parchment. 7. Bake for 5 minutes. Flip the rolls and bake for 5 to 7 minutes more until lightly browned. Repeat with the remaining rolls. 8. Sprinkle with confectioners' sugar (if using).

Beignets

Prep time: 30 minutes | Cook time: 6 minutes | Makes 9 beignets

- Oil, for greasing and spraying
- 3 cups all-purpose flour, plus more for dusting
- 1½ teaspoons salt
- 1 (2¼ teaspoons) envelope active dry yeast
- 1 cup milk
- 2 tablespoons packed light brown sugar
- 1 tablespoon unsalted butter
- 1 large egg
- 1 cup confectioners' sugar

1. Oil a large bowl. 2. In a small bowl, mix together the flour, salt, and yeast. Set aside. 3. Pour the milk into a glass measuring cup and microwave in 1-minute intervals until it boils. 4. In a large bowl, mix together the brown sugar and butter. Pour in the hot milk and whisk until the sugar has dissolved. Let cool to room temperature. 5. Whisk the egg into the cooled milk mixture and fold in the flour mixture until a dough forms. 6. On a lightly floured work surface, knead the dough for 3 to 5 minutes. 7. Place the dough in the oiled bowl and cover with a clean kitchen towel. Let rise in a warm place for about 1 hour, or until doubled in size. 8. Roll the dough out on a lightly floured work surface until it's about ¼ inch thick. Cut the dough into 3-inch squares and place them on a lightly floured baking sheet. Cover loosely with a kitchen towel and let rise again until doubled in size, about 30 minutes. 9. Line the air fryer basket with parchment and spray lightly with oil. 10. Place the dough squares in the prepared basket and spray lightly with oil. You may need to work in batches, depending on the size of your air fryer. 11. Air fry at 390°F (199°C) for 3 minutes, flip, spray with oil, and cook for another 3 minutes, until crispy. 12. Dust with the confectioners' sugar before serving.

Steak and Vegetable Kebabs

Prep time: 15 minutes | Cook time: 5 to 7 minutes | Serves 4

- 2 tablespoons balsamic vinegar
- 2 teaspoons olive oil
- ½ teaspoon dried marjoram
- ⅛ teaspoon freshly ground black pepper
- ¾ pound (340 g) round steak, cut into 1-inch pieces
- 1 red bell pepper, sliced
- 16 button mushrooms
- 1 cup cherry tomatoes

1. In a medium bowl, stir together the balsamic vinegar, olive oil, marjoram, and black pepper. 2. Add the steak and stir to coat. Let stand for 10 minutes at room temperature. 3. Alternating items, thread the beef, red bell pepper, mushrooms, and tomatoes onto 8 bamboo or metal skewers that fit in the air fryer. 4. Air fry at 390°F (199°C) for 5 to 7 minutes, or until the beef is browned and reaches at least 145°F (63°C) on a meat thermometer. Serve immediately.

Meatball Subs

Prep time: 15 minutes | Cook time: 19 minutes | Serves 6

- Oil, for spraying
- 1 pound (454 g) 85% lean ground beef
- ½ cup Italian bread crumbs
- 1 tablespoon dried minced onion
- 1 tablespoon minced garlic
- 1 large egg
- 1 teaspoon salt
- 1 teaspoon freshly ground black pepper
- 6 hoagie rolls
- 1 (18 ounces / 510 g) jar marinara sauce
- 1½ cups shredded Mozzarella cheese

1. Line the air fryer basket with parchment and spray lightly with oil. 2. In a large bowl, mix together the ground beef, bread crumbs, onion, garlic, egg, salt, and black pepper. Roll the mixture into 18 meatballs. 3. Place the meatballs in the prepared basket. 4. Air fry at 390°F (199°C) for 15 minutes. 5. Place 3 meatballs in each hoagie roll. Top with marinara and Mozzarella cheese. 6. Place the loaded rolls in the air fryer and cook for 3 to 4 minutes, or until the cheese is melted. You may need to work in batches, depending on the size of your air fryer. Serve immediately.

Phyllo Vegetable Triangles

Prep time: 15 minutes | Cook time: 6 to 11 minutes | Serves 6

- 3 tablespoons minced onion
- 2 garlic cloves, minced
- 2 tablespoons grated carrot
- 1 teaspoon olive oil
- 3 tablespoons frozen baby peas, thawed
- 2 tablespoons nonfat cream cheese, at room temperature
- 6 sheets frozen phyllo dough, thawed
- Olive oil spray, for coating the dough

1. In a baking pan, combine the onion, garlic, carrot, and olive oil. Air fry at 390°F (199°C) for 2 to 4 minutes, or until the vegetables are crisp-tender. Transfer to a bowl. 2. Stir in the peas and cream cheese to the vegetable mixture. Let cool while you prepare the dough. 3. Lay one sheet of phyllo on a work surface and lightly spray with olive oil spray. Top with another sheet of phyllo. Repeat with the remaining 4 phyllo sheets; you'll have 3 stacks with 2 layers each. Cut each stack lengthwise into 4 strips (12 strips total). 4. Place a scant 2 teaspoons of the filling near the bottom of each strip. Bring one corner up over the filling to make a triangle; continue folding the triangles over, as you would fold a flag. Seal the edge with a bit of water. Repeat with the remaining strips and filling. 5. Air fry the triangles, in 2 batches, for 4 to 7 minutes, or until golden brown. Serve.

Avocado and Egg Burrito

Prep time: 10 minutes | Cook time: 3 to 5 minutes | Serves 4

- 2 hard-boiled egg whites, chopped
- 1 hard-boiled egg, chopped
- 1 avocado, peeled, pitted, and chopped
- 1 red bell pepper, chopped
- 3 tablespoons low-sodium salsa, plus additional for serving (optional)
- 1 (1.2 ounces / 34 g) slice low-sodium, low-fat American cheese, torn into pieces
- 4 low-sodium whole-wheat flour tortillas

1. In a medium bowl, thoroughly mix the egg whites, egg, avocado, red bell pepper, salsa, and cheese. 2. Place the tortillas on a work surface and evenly divide the filling among them. Fold in the edges and roll up. Secure the burritos with toothpicks if necessary. 3. Put the burritos in the air fryer basket. Air fry at 390ºF (199ºC) for 3 to 5 minutes, or until the burritos are light golden brown and crisp. Serve with more salsa (if using).

Chinese-Inspired Spareribs

Prep time: 30 minutes | Cook time: 8 minutes | Serves 4

- Oil, for spraying
- 12 ounces (340 g) boneless pork spareribs, cut into 3-inch-long pieces
- 1 cup soy sauce
- ¾ cup sugar
- ½ cup beef or chicken stock
- ¼ cup honey
- 2 tablespoons minced garlic
- 1 teaspoon ground ginger
- 2 drops red food coloring (optional)

1. Line the air fryer basket with parchment and spray lightly with oil. 2. Combine the ribs, soy sauce, sugar, beef stock, honey, garlic, ginger, and food coloring (if using) in a large zip-top plastic bag, seal, and shake well until completely coated. Refrigerate for at least 30 minutes. 3. Place the ribs in the prepared basket. 4. Air fry at 375ºF (191ºC) for 8 minutes, or until the internal temperature reaches 165ºF (74ºC).

Chapter 3

Fast and Easy Everyday Favorites

Buttery Sweet Potatoes

Prep time: 5 minutes | Cook time: 10 minutes | Serves 4

- 2 tablespoons butter, melted
- 1 tablespoon light brown sugar
- 2 sweet potatoes, peeled and cut into ½-inch cubes
- Cooking spray

1. Preheat the air fryer to 400ºF (204ºC). Line the air fryer basket with parchment paper. 2. In a medium bowl, stir together the melted butter and brown sugar until blended. Toss the sweet potatoes in the butter mixture until coated. 3. Place the sweet potatoes on the parchment and spritz with oil. 4. Air fry for 5 minutes. Shake the basket, spritz the sweet potatoes with oil, and air fry for 5 minutes more until they're soft enough to cut with a fork. 5. Serve immediately.

Easy Cinnamon Toast

Prep time: 5 minutes | Cook time: 20 minutes | Serves 6

- 1½ teaspoons cinnamon
- 1½ teaspoons vanilla extract
- ½ cup sugar
- 2 teaspoons ground black
- pepper
- 2 tablespoons melted coconut oil
- 12 slices whole wheat bread

1. Preheat the air fryer to 400ºF (204ºC). 2. Combine all the ingredients, except for the bread, in a large bowl. Stir to mix well. 3. Dunk the bread in the bowl of mixture gently to coat and infuse well. Shake the excess off. 4. Arrange the bread slices in the preheated air fryer. Air fry for 5 minutes or until golden brown. Flip the bread halfway through. You may need to cook in batches to avoid overcrowding. 5. Remove the bread slices from the air fryer and slice to serve.

Garlicky Baked Cherry Tomatoes

Prep time: 5 minutes | Cook time: 4 to 6 minutes | Serves 2

- 2 cups cherry tomatoes
- 1 clove garlic, thinly sliced
- 1 teaspoon olive oil
- ⅛ teaspoon kosher salt
- 1 tablespoon freshly chopped basil, for topping
- Cooking spray

1. Preheat the air fryer to 360ºF (182ºC). Spritz the air fryer baking pan with cooking spray and set aside. 2. In a large bowl, toss together the cherry tomatoes, sliced garlic, olive oil, and kosher salt. Spread the mixture in an even layer in the prepared pan. 3. Bake in the preheated air fryer for 4 to 6 minutes, or until the tomatoes become soft and wilted. 4. Transfer to a bowl and rest for 5 minutes. Top with the chopped basil and serve warm.

South Carolina Shrimp and Corn Bake

Prep time: 10 minutes | Cook time: 18 minutes | Serves 2

- 1 ear corn, husk and silk removed, cut into 2-inch rounds
- 8 ounces (227 g) red potatoes, unpeeled, cut into 1-inch pieces
- 2 teaspoons Old Bay Seasoning, divided
- 2 teaspoons vegetable oil, divided
- ¼ teaspoon ground black
- pepper
- 8 ounces (227 g) large shrimps (about 12 shrimps), deveined
- 6 ounces (170 g) andouille or chorizo sausage, cut into 1-inch pieces
- 2 garlic cloves, minced
- 1 tablespoon chopped fresh parsley

1. Preheat the air fryer to 400ºF (204ºC). 2. Put the corn rounds and potatoes in a large bowl. Sprinkle with 1 teaspoon of Old Bay seasoning and drizzle with vegetable oil. Toss to coat well. 3. Transfer the corn rounds and potatoes on a baking sheet, then put in the preheated air fryer. 4. Bake for 12 minutes or until soft and browned. Shake the basket halfway through the cooking time. 5. Meanwhile, cut slits into the shrimps but be careful not to cut them through. Combine the shrimps, sausage, remaining Old Bay seasoning, and remaining vegetable oil in the large bowl. Toss to coat well. 6. When the baking of the potatoes and corn rounds is complete, add the shrimps and sausage and bake for 6 more minutes or until the shrimps are opaque. Shake the basket halfway through the cooking time. 7. When the baking is finished, serve them on a plate and spread with parsley before serving.

Traditional Queso Fundido

Prep time: 10 minutes | Cook time: 25 minutes | Serves 4

- 4 ounces (113 g) fresh Mexican chorizo, casings removed
- 1 medium onion, chopped
- 3 cloves garlic, minced
- 1 cup chopped tomato
- 2 jalapeños, deseeded and diced
- 2 teaspoons ground cumin
- 2 cups shredded Oaxaca or Mozzarella cheese
- ½ cup half-and-half
- Celery sticks or tortilla chips, for serving

1. Preheat the air fryer to 400ºF (204ºC). 2. In a baking pan, combine the chorizo, onion, garlic, tomato, jalapeños, and cumin. Stir to combine. 3. Place the pan in the air fryer basket. Air fry for 15 minutes, or until the sausage is cooked, stirring halfway through the cooking time to break up the sausage. 4. Add the cheese and half-and-half; stir to combine. Air fry for 10 minutes, or until the cheese has melted. 5. Serve with celery sticks or tortilla chips.

Southwest Corn and Bell Pepper Roast

Prep time: 10 minutes | Cook time: 10 minutes | Serves 4

- For the Corn:
- 1½ cups thawed frozen corn kernels
- 1 cup mixed diced bell peppers
- 1 jalapeño, diced
- 1 cup diced yellow onion
- ½ teaspoon ancho chile powder
- 1 tablespoon fresh lemon
- juice
- 1 teaspoon ground cumin
- ½ teaspoon kosher salt
- Cooking spray
- For Serving:
- ¼ cup feta cheese
- ¼ cup chopped fresh cilantro
- 1 tablespoon fresh lemon juice

1. Preheat the air fryer to 375ºF (191ºC). Spritz the air fryer with cooking spray. 2. Combine the ingredients for the corn in a large bowl. Stir to mix well. 3. Pout the mixture into the air fryer. Air fry for 10 minutes or until the corn and bell peppers are soft. Shake the basket halfway through the cooking time. 4. Transfer them onto a large plate, then spread with feta cheese and cilantro. Drizzle with lemon juice and serve.

Classic Poutine

Prep time: 15 minutes | Cook time: 25 minutes | Serves 2

- 2 russet potatoes, scrubbed and cut into ½-inch sticks
- 2 teaspoons vegetable oil
- 2 tablespoons butter
- ¼ onion, minced
- ¼ teaspoon dried thyme
- 1 clove garlic, smashed
- 3 tablespoons all-purpose
- flour
- 1 teaspoon tomato paste
- 1½ cups beef stock
- 2 teaspoons Worcestershire sauce
- Salt and freshly ground black pepper, to taste
- ⅔ cup chopped string cheese

1. Bring a pot of water to a boil, then put in the potato sticks and blanch for 4 minutes. 2. Preheat the air fryer to 400ºF (204ºC). 3. Drain the potato sticks and rinse under running cold water, then pat dry with paper towels. 4. Transfer the sticks in a large bowl and drizzle with vegetable oil. Toss to coat well. 5. Place the potato sticks in the preheated air fryer. Air fry for 25 minutes or until the sticks are golden brown. Shake the basket at least three times during the frying. 6. Meanwhile, make the gravy: Heat the butter in a saucepan over medium heat until melted. 7. Add the onion, thyme, and garlic and sauté for 5 minutes or until the onion is translucent. 8. Add the flour and sauté for an additional 2 minutes. Pour in the tomato paste and beef stock and cook for 1 more minute or until lightly thickened. 9. Drizzle the gravy with Worcestershire sauce and sprinkle with salt and ground black pepper. Reduce the heat to low to keep the gravy warm until ready to serve. 10. Transfer the fried potato sticks onto a plate, then sprinkle with salt and ground black pepper. Scatter with string cheese and pour the gravy over. Serve warm.

Easy Devils on Horseback

Prep time: 5 minutes | Cook time: 7 minutes | Serves 12

- 24 petite pitted prunes (4½ ounces / 128 g)
- ¼ cup crumbled blue
- cheese, divided
- 8 slices center-cut bacon, cut crosswise into thirds

1. Preheat the air fryer to 400ºF (204ºC). 2. Halve the prunes lengthwise, but don't cut them all the way through. Place ½ teaspoon of cheese in the center of each prune. Wrap a piece of bacon around each prune and secure the bacon with a toothpick. 3. Working in batches, arrange a single layer of the prunes in the air fryer basket. Air fry for about 7 minutes, flipping halfway, until the bacon is cooked through and crisp. 4. Let cool slightly and serve warm.

Air Fried Shishito Peppers

Prep time: 5 minutes | Cook time: 5 minutes | Serves 4

- ½ pound (227 g) shishito peppers (about 24)
- 1 tablespoon olive oil
- Coarse sea salt, to taste
- Lemon wedges, for serving
- Cooking spray

1. Preheat the air fryer to 400ºF (204ºC). Spritz the air fryer basket with cooking spray. 2. Toss the peppers with olive oil in a large bowl to coat well. 3. Arrange the peppers in the preheated air fryer. 4. Air fryer for 5 minutes or until blistered and lightly charred. Shake the basket and sprinkle the peppers with salt halfway through the cooking time. 5. Transfer the peppers onto a plate and squeeze the lemon wedges on top before serving.

Easy Roasted Asparagus

Prep time: 5 minutes | Cook time: 6 minutes | Serves 4

- 1 pound (454 g) asparagus, trimmed and halved crosswise
- 1 teaspoon extra-virgin
- olive oil
- Salt and pepper, to taste
- Lemon wedges, for serving

1. Preheat the air fryer to 400ºF (204ºC). 2. Toss the asparagus with the oil, ⅛ teaspoon salt, and ⅛ teaspoon pepper in bowl. Transfer to air fryer basket. 3. Place the basket in air fryer and roast for 6 to 8 minutes, or until tender and bright green, tossing halfway through cooking. 4. Season with salt and pepper and serve with lemon wedges.

Simple Baked Green Beans

Prep time: 5 minutes | Cook time: 10 minutes | Makes 2 cups

- ½ teaspoon lemon pepper
- 2 teaspoons granulated garlic
- ½ teaspoon salt
- 1 tablespoon olive oil
- 2 cups fresh green beans, trimmed and snapped in half

1. Preheat the air fryer to 370ºF (188ºC). 2. Combine the lemon pepper, garlic, salt, and olive oil in a bowl. Stir to mix well. 3. Add the green beans to the bowl of mixture and toss to coat well. 4. Arrange the green beans in the preheated air fryer. Bake for 10 minutes or until tender and crispy. Shake the basket halfway through to make sure the green beans are cooked evenly. 5. Serve immediately.

Golden Salmon and Carrot Croquettes

Prep time: 15 minutes | Cook time: 10 minutes | Serves 6

- 2 egg whites
- 1 cup almond flour
- 1 cup panko breadcrumbs
- 1 pound (454 g) chopped salmon fillet
- ⅔ cup grated carrots
- 2 tablespoons minced garlic cloves
- ½ cup chopped onion
- 2 tablespoons chopped chives
- Cooking spray

1. Preheat the air fryer to 350ºF (177ºC). Spritz the air fryer basket with cooking spray. 2. Whisk the egg whites in a bowl. Put the flour in a second bowl. Pour the breadcrumbs in a third bowl. Set aside. 3. Combine the salmon, carrots, garlic, onion, and chives in a large bowl. Stir to mix well. 4. Form the mixture into balls with your hands. Dredge the balls into the flour, then egg, and then breadcrumbs to coat well. 5. Arrange the salmon balls in the preheated air fryer and spritz with cooking spray. 6. Air fry for 10 minutes or until crispy and browned. Shake the basket halfway through. 7. Serve immediately.

Crispy Green Tomatoes Slices

Prep time: 10 minutes | Cook time: 8 minutes | Makes 12 slices

- ½ cup all-purpose flour
- 1 egg
- ½ cup buttermilk
- 1 cup cornmeal
- 1 cup panko
- 2 green tomatoes, cut
- into ¼-inch-thick slices, patted dry
- ½ teaspoon salt
- ½ teaspoon ground black pepper
- Cooking spray

1. Preheat the air fryer to 400ºF (204ºC). Line the air fryer basket with parchment paper. 2. Pour the flour in a bowl. Whisk the egg and buttermilk in a second bowl. Combine the cornmeal and panko in a third bowl. 3. Dredge the tomato slices in the bowl of flour first, then into the egg mixture, and then dunk the slices into the cornmeal mixture. Shake the excess off. 4. Transfer the well-coated tomato slices in the preheated air fryer and sprinkle with salt and ground black pepper. 5. Spritz the tomato slices with cooking spray. Air fry for 8 minutes or until crispy and lightly browned. Flip the slices halfway through the cooking time. 6. Serve immediately.

Classic Latkes

Prep time: 15 minutes | Cook time: 10 minutes | Makes 4 latkes

- 1 egg
- 2 tablespoons all-purpose flour
- 2 medium potatoes, peeled and shredded,
- rinsed and drained
- ¼ teaspoon granulated garlic
- ½ teaspoon salt
- Cooking spray

1. Preheat the air fryer to 380ºF (193ºC). Spritz the air fryer basket with cooking spray. 2. Whisk together the egg, flour, potatoes, garlic, and salt in a large bowl. Stir to mix well. 3. Divide the mixture into four parts, then flatten them into four circles. Arrange the circles into the preheated air fryer. 4. Spritz the circles with cooking spray, then air fry for 10 minutes or until golden brown and crispy. Flip the latkes halfway through. 5. Serve immediately.

Purple Potato Chips with Rosemary

Prep time: 10 minutes | Cook time: 9 to 14 minutes | Serves 6

- 1 cup Greek yogurt
- 2 chipotle chiles, minced
- 2 tablespoons adobo sauce
- 1 teaspoon paprika
- 1 tablespoon lemon juice
- 10 purple fingerling potatoes
- 1 teaspoon olive oil
- 2 teaspoons minced fresh rosemary leaves
- ⅛ teaspoon cayenne pepper
- ¼ teaspoon coarse sea salt

1. Preheat the air fryer to 400ºF (204ºC). 2. In a medium bowl, combine the yogurt, minced chiles, adobo sauce, paprika, and lemon juice. Mix well and refrigerate. 3. Wash the potatoes and dry them with paper towels. Slice the potatoes lengthwise, as thinly as possible. You can use a mandoline, a vegetable peeler, or a very sharp knife. 4. Combine the potato slices in a medium bowl and drizzle with the olive oil; toss to coat. 5. Air fry the chips, in batches, in the air fryer basket, for 9 to 14 minutes. Use tongs to gently rearrange the chips halfway during cooking time. 6. Sprinkle the chips with the rosemary, cayenne pepper, and sea salt. Serve with the chipotle sauce for dipping.

Baked Halloumi with Greek Salsa

Prep time: 15 minutes | Cook time: 6 minutes | Serves 4

- Salsa:
- 1 small shallot, finely diced
- 3 garlic cloves, minced
- 2 tablespoons fresh lemon juice
- 2 tablespoons extra-virgin olive oil
- 1 teaspoon freshly cracked black pepper
- Pinch of kosher salt
- ½ cup finely diced English cucumber
- 1 plum tomato, deseeded
- and finely diced
- 2 teaspoons chopped fresh parsley
- 1 teaspoon snipped fresh dill
- 1 teaspoon snipped fresh oregano
- Cheese:
- 8 ounces (227 g) Halloumi cheese, sliced into ½-inch-thick pieces
- 1 tablespoon extra-virgin olive oil

1. Preheat the air fryer to 375ºF (191ºC). 2. For the salsa: Combine the shallot, garlic, lemon juice, olive oil, pepper, and salt in a medium bowl. Add the cucumber, tomato, parsley, dill, and oregano. Toss gently to combine; set aside. 3. For the cheese: Place the cheese slices in a medium bowl. Drizzle with the olive oil. Toss gently to coat. Arrange the cheese in a single layer in the air fryer basket. Bake for 6 minutes. 4. Divide the cheese among four serving plates. Top with the salsa and serve immediately.

Easy Air Fried Edamame

Prep time: 5 minutes | Cook time: 7 minutes | Serves 6

- 1½ pounds (680 g) unshelled edamame
- 2 tablespoons olive oil
- 1 teaspoon sea salt

1. Preheat the air fryer to 400ºF (204ºC). 2. Place the edamame in a large bowl, then drizzle with olive oil. Toss to coat well. 3. Transfer the edamame to the preheated air fryer. Cook for 7 minutes or until tender and warmed through. Shake the basket at least three times during the cooking. 4. Transfer the cooked edamame onto a plate and sprinkle with salt. Toss to combine well and set aside for 3 minutes to infuse before serving.

Beef Bratwursts

Prep time: 5 minutes | Cook time: 15 minutes | Serves 4

- 4 (3-ounce / 85-g) beef bratwursts

1. Preheat the air fryer to 375ºF (191ºC). 2. Place the beef bratwursts in the air fryer basket and air fry for 15 minutes, turning once halfway through. 3. Serve hot.

Corn Fritters

Prep time: 15 minutes | Cook time: 8 minutes | Serves 6

- 1 cup self-rising flour
- 1 tablespoon sugar
- 1 teaspoon salt
- 1 large egg, lightly beaten
- ¼ cup buttermilk
- ¾ cup corn kernels
- ¼ cup minced onion
- Cooking spray

1. Preheat the air fryer to 350ºF (177ºC). Line the air fryer basket with parchment paper. 2. In a medium bowl, whisk the flour, sugar, and salt until blended. Stir in the egg and buttermilk. Add the corn and minced onion. Mix well. Shape the corn fritter batter into 12 balls. 3. Place the fritters on the parchment and spritz with oil. Bake for 4 minutes. Flip the fritters, spritz them with oil, and bake for 4 minutes more until firm and lightly browned. 4. Serve immediately.

Simple and Easy Croutons

Prep time: 5 minutes | Cook time: 8 minutes | Serves 4

- 2 slices friendly bread
- 1 tablespoon olive oil
- Hot soup, for serving

1. Preheat the air fryer to 390ºF (199ºC). 2. Cut the slices of bread into medium-size chunks. 3. Brush the air fryer basket with the oil. 4. Place the chunks inside and air fry for at least 8 minutes. 5. Serve with hot soup.

Chapter 4

Beef, Pork, and Lamb

Spicy Sirloin Tip Steak

Prep time: 25 minutes | Cook time: 12 to 18 minutes | Serves 4

- 2 tablespoons salsa
- 1 tablespoon minced chipotle pepper
- 1 tablespoon apple cider vinegar
- 1 teaspoon ground cumin
- ⅛ teaspoon freshly ground black pepper
- ⅛ teaspoon red pepper flakes
- 12 ounces (340 g) sirloin tip steak, cut into 4 pieces and gently pounded to about ⅓ inch thick
- Cooking oil spray

1. In a small bowl, thoroughly mix the salsa, chipotle pepper, vinegar, cumin, black pepper, and red pepper flakes. Rub this mixture into both sides of each steak piece. Let stand for 15 minutes at room temperature. 2. Insert the crisper plate into the basket and place the basket into the unit. Preheat the unit by selecting AIR FRY, setting the temperature to 390°F (199°C), and setting the time to 3 minutes. Select START/STOP to begin. 3. Once the unit is preheated, spray the crisper plate with cooking oil. Working in batches, place 2 steaks into the basket. 4. Select AIR FRY, set the temperature to 390°F (199°C), and set the time to 9 minutes. Select START/STOP to begin. 5. After about 6 minutes, check the steaks. If a food thermometer inserted into the meat registers at least 145°F (63°C), they are done. If not, resume cooking. 6. When the cooking is done, transfer the steaks to a clean plate and cover with aluminum foil to keep warm. Repeat steps 3, 4, and 5 with the remaining steaks. 7. Thinly slice the steaks against the grain and serve.

Reuben Beef Rolls with Thousand Island Sauce

Prep time: 15 minutes | Cook time: 10 minutes per batch | Makes 10 rolls

- ½ pound (227 g) cooked corned beef, chopped
- ½ cup drained and chopped sauerkraut
- 1 (8-ounce / 227-g) package cream cheese, softened
- ½ cup shredded Swiss cheese
- 20 slices prosciutto
- Cooking spray
- Thousand Island Sauce:
- ¼ cup chopped dill pickles
- ¼ cup tomato sauce
- ¾ cup mayonnaise
- Fresh thyme leaves, for garnish
- 2 tablespoons sugar
- ⅛ teaspoon fine sea salt
- Ground black pepper, to taste

1. Preheat the air fryer to 400°F (204°C) and spritz with cooking spray. 2. Combine the beef, sauerkraut, cream cheese, and Swiss cheese in a large bowl. Stir to mix well. 3. Unroll a slice of prosciutto on a clean work surface, then top with another slice of prosciutto crosswise. Scoop up 4 tablespoons of the beef mixture in the center. 4. Fold the top slice sides over the filling as the ends of the roll, then roll up the long sides of the bottom prosciutto and make it into a roll shape. Overlap the sides by about 1 inch. Repeat with remaining filling and prosciutto. 5. Arrange the rolls in the preheated air fryer, seam side down, and spritz with cooking spray. 6. Air fry for 10 minutes or until golden and crispy. Flip the rolls halfway through. Work in batches to avoid overcrowding. 7. Meanwhile, combine the ingredients for the sauce in a small bowl. Stir to mix well. 8. Serve the rolls with the dipping sauce.

Beef Whirls

Prep time: 30 minutes | Cook time: 18 minutes | Serves 6

- 3 cube steaks (6 ounces / 170 g each)
- 1 (16-ounce / 454-g) bottle Italian dressing
- 1 cup Italian-style bread crumbs
- ½ cup grated Parmesan cheese
- 1 teaspoon dried basil
- 1 teaspoon dried oregano
- 1 teaspoon dried parsley
- ¼ cup beef broth
- 1 to 2 tablespoons oil

1. In a large resealable bag, combine the steaks and Italian dressing. Seal the bag and refrigerate to marinate for 2 hours. 2. In a medium bowl, whisk the bread crumbs, cheese, basil, oregano, and parsley until blended. Stir in the beef broth. 3. Place the steaks on a cutting board and cut each in half so you have 6 equal pieces. Sprinkle with the bread crumb mixture. Roll up the steaks, jelly roll-style, and secure with toothpicks. 4. Preheat the air fryer to 400°F (204°C). 5. Place 3 roll-ups in the air fryer basket. 6. Cook for 5 minutes. Flip the roll-ups and spritz with oil. Cook for 4 minutes more until the internal temperature reaches 145°F (63°C). Repeat with the remaining roll-ups. Let rest for 5 to 10 minutes before serving.

Rosemary Ribeye Steaks

Prep time: 10 minutes | Cook time: 15 minutes | Serves 2

- ¼ cup butter
- 1 clove garlic, minced
- Salt and ground black pepper, to taste
- 1½ tablespoons balsamic vinegar
- ¼ cup rosemary, chopped
- 2 ribeye steaks

1. Melt the butter in a skillet over medium heat. Add the garlic and fry until fragrant. 2. Remove the skillet from the heat and add the salt, pepper, and vinegar. Allow it to cool. 3. Add the rosemary, then pour the mixture into a Ziploc bag. 4. Put the ribeye steaks in the bag and shake well, coating the meat well. Refrigerate for an hour, then allow to sit for a further twenty minutes. 5. Preheat the air fryer to 400°F (204°C). 6. Air fry the ribeye steaks for 15 minutes. 7. Take care when removing the steaks from the air fryer and plate up. 8. Serve immediately.

Bone-in Pork Chops

Prep time: 5 minutes | Cook time: 10 to 12 minutes | Serves 2

- 1 pound (454 g) bone-in pork chops
- 1 tablespoon avocado oil
- 1 teaspoon smoked paprika
- ½ teaspoon onion powder
- ¼ teaspoon cayenne pepper
- Sea salt and freshly ground black pepper, to taste

1. Brush the pork chops with the avocado oil. In a small dish, mix together the smoked paprika, onion powder, cayenne pepper, and salt and black pepper to taste. Sprinkle the seasonings over both sides of the pork chops. 2. Set the air fryer to 400ºF (204ºC). Place the chops in the air fryer basket in a single layer, working in batches if necessary. Air fry for 10 to 12 minutes, until an instant-read thermometer reads 145ºF (63ºC) at the chops' thickest point. 3. Remove the chops from the air fryer and allow them to rest for 5 minutes before serving.

Red Curry Flank Steak

Prep time: 30 minutes | Cook time: 12 to 18 minutes | Serves 4

- 3 tablespoons red curry paste
- ¼ cup olive oil
- 2 teaspoons grated fresh ginger
- 2 tablespoons soy sauce
- 2 tablespoons rice wine vinegar
- 3 scallions, minced
- 1½ pounds (680 g) flank steak
- Fresh cilantro (or parsley) leaves

1. Mix the red curry paste, olive oil, ginger, soy sauce, rice vinegar and scallions together in a bowl. Place the flank steak in a shallow glass dish and pour half the marinade over the steak. Pierce the steak several times with a fork or meat tenderizer to let the marinade penetrate the meat. Turn the steak over, pour the remaining marinade over the top and pierce the steak several times again. Cover and marinate the steak in the refrigerator for 6 to 8 hours. 2. When you are ready to cook, remove the steak from the refrigerator and let it sit at room temperature for 30 minutes. 3. Preheat the air fryer to 400ºF (204ºC). 4. Cut the flank steak in half so that it fits more easily into the air fryer and transfer both pieces to the air fryer basket. Pour the marinade over the steak. Air fry for 12 to 18 minutes, depending on your preferred degree of doneness of the steak (12 minutes = medium rare). Flip the steak over halfway through the cooking time. 5. When your desired degree of doneness has been reached, remove the steak to a cutting board and let it rest for 5 minutes before slicing. Thinly slice the flank steak against the grain of the meat. Transfer the slices to a serving platter, pour any juice from the bottom of the air fryer over the sliced flank steak and sprinkle the fresh cilantro on top.

Hamburger Steak with Mushroom Gravy

Prep time: 20 minutes | Cook time: 29 to 34 minutes | Serves 4

- Mushroom Gravy:
- 1 (1 ounce / 28 g) envelope dry onion soup mix
- ⅓ cup cornstarch
- 1 cup diced mushrooms
- Hamburger Steak:
- 1 pound (454 g) ground beef (85% lean)
- ¾ cup minced onion
- ½ cup Italian-style bread crumbs
- 2 teaspoons Worcestershire sauce
- 1 teaspoon salt
- 1 teaspoon freshly ground black pepper
- 1 to 2 tablespoons oil

Make the Mushroom Gravy 1. In a metal bowl, whisk the soup mix, cornstarch, mushrooms, and 2 cups water until blended. 2. Preheat the air fryer to 350ºF (177ºC). 3. Place the bowl in the air fryer basket. 4. Cook for 10 minutes. Stir and cook for 5 to 10 minutes more to your desired thickness. Make the Hamburger Steak 5. In a large bowl, mix the ground beef, onion, bread crumbs, Worcestershire sauce, salt, and pepper until blended. Shape the beef mixture into 4 patties. 6. Decrease the air fryer's temperature to 320ºF (160ºC). 7. Place the patties in the air fryer basket. 8. Cook for 7 minutes. Flip the patties, spritz them with oil, and cook for 7 minutes more, until the internal temperature reaches 145ºF (63ºC).

Kheema Meatloaf

Prep time: 10 minutes | Cook time: 15 minutes | Serves 4

- 1 pound (454 g) 85% lean ground beef
- 2 large eggs, lightly beaten
- 1 cup diced yellow onion
- ¼ cup chopped fresh cilantro
- 1 tablespoon minced fresh ginger
- 1 tablespoon minced garlic
- 2 teaspoons garam masala
- 1 teaspoon kosher salt
- 1 teaspoon ground turmeric
- 1 teaspoon cayenne pepper
- ½ teaspoon ground cinnamon
- ⅛ teaspoon ground cardamom

1. In a large bowl, gently mix the ground beef, eggs, onion, cilantro, ginger, garlic, garam masala, salt, turmeric, cayenne, cinnamon, and cardamom until thoroughly combined. 2. Place the seasoned meat in a baking pan. Place the pan in the air fryer basket. Set the air fryer to 350ºF (177ºC) for 15 minutes. Use a meat thermometer to ensure the meat loaf has reached an internal temperature of 160ºF / 71ºC (medium). 3. Drain the fat and liquid from the pan and let stand for 5 minutes before slicing. 4. Slice and serve hot.

Pork Loin Roast

Prep time: 30 minutes | Cook time: 55 minutes | Serves 6

- 1½ pounds (680 g) boneless pork loin roast, washed
- 1 teaspoon mustard seeds
- 1 teaspoon garlic powder
- 1 teaspoon porcini powder
- 1 teaspoon shallot
- powder
- ¾ teaspoon sea salt flakes
- 1 teaspoon red pepper flakes, crushed
- 2 dried sprigs thyme, crushed
- 2 tablespoons lime juice

1. Firstly, score the meat using a small knife; make sure to not cut too deep. 2. In a small-sized mixing dish, combine all seasonings in the order listed above; mix to combine well. 3. Massage the spice mix into the pork meat to evenly distribute. Drizzle with lemon juice. 4. Set the air fryer to 360°F (182°C). Place the pork in the air fryer basket; roast for 25 to 30 minutes. Pause the machine, check for doneness and cook for 25 minutes more.

German Rouladen-Style Steak

Prep time: 20 minutes | Cook time: 15 minutes | Serves 4

- Onion Sauce:
- 2 medium onions, cut into ½-inch-thick slices
- Kosher salt and black pepper, to taste
- ½ cup sour cream
- 1 tablespoon tomato paste
- 2 teaspoons chopped fresh parsley
- Rouladen:
- ¼ cup Dijon mustard
- 1 pound (454 g) flank or skirt steak, ¼ to ½ inch thick
- 1 teaspoon black pepper
- 4 slices bacon
- ¼ cup chopped fresh parsley

1. For the sauce: In a small bowl, mix together the onions with salt and pepper to taste. Place the onions in the air fryer basket. Set the air fryer to 400°F (204°C) for 6 minutes, or until the onions are softened and golden brown. 2. Set aside half of the onions to use in the rouladen. Place the rest in a small bowl and add the sour cream, tomato paste, parsley, ½ teaspoon salt, and ½ teaspoon pepper. Stir until well combined, adding 1 to 2 tablespoons of water, if necessary, to thin the sauce slightly. Set the sauce aside. 3. For the rouladen: Evenly spread the mustard over the meat. Sprinkle with the pepper. Top with the bacon slices, reserved onions, and parsley. Starting at the long end, roll up the steak as tightly as possible, ending seam side down. Use 2 or 3 wooden toothpicks to hold the roll together. Using a sharp knife, cut the roll in half so that it better fits in the air fryer basket. 4. Place the steak, seam side down, in the air fryer basket. Set the air fryer to 400°F (204°C) for 9 minutes. Use a meat thermometer to ensure the steak has reached an internal temperature of 145°F (63°C). (It is critical to not overcook flank steak, so as to not toughen the

meat.) 5. Let the steak rest for 10 minutes before cutting into slices. Serve with the sauce.

Smothered Chops

Prep time: 20 minutes | Cook time: 30 minutes | Serves 4

- 4 bone-in pork chops (8 ounces / 227 g each)
- 2 teaspoons salt, divided
- 1½ teaspoons freshly ground black pepper, divided
- 1 teaspoon garlic powder
- 1 cup tomato purée
- 1½ teaspoons Italian seasoning
- 1 tablespoon sugar
- 1 tablespoon cornstarch
- ½ cup chopped onion
- ½ cup chopped green bell pepper
- 1 to 2 tablespoons oil

1. Evenly season the pork chops with 1 teaspoon salt, 1 teaspoon pepper, and the garlic powder. 2. In a medium bowl, stir together the tomato purée, Italian seasoning, sugar, remaining 1 teaspoon of salt, and remaining ½ teaspoon of pepper. 3. In a small bowl, whisk ¾ cup water and the cornstarch until blended. Stir this slurry into the tomato purée, with the onion and green bell pepper. Transfer to a baking pan. 4. Preheat the air fryer to 350°F (177°C). 5. Place the sauce in the fryer and cook for 10 minutes. Stir and cook for 10 minutes more. Remove the pan and keep warm. 6. Increase the air fryer temperature to 400°F (204°C). Line the air fryer basket with parchment paper. 7. Place the pork chops on the parchment and spritz with oil. 8. Cook for 5 minutes. Flip and spritz the chops with oil and cook for 5 minutes more, until the internal temperature reaches 145°F (63°C). Serve with the tomato mixture spooned on top.

Lemony Pork Loin Chop Schnitzel

Prep time: 15 minutes | Cook time: 15 minutes | Serves 4

- 4 thin boneless pork loin chops
- 2 tablespoons lemon juice
- ½ cup flour
- ¼ teaspoon marjoram
- 1 teaspoon salt
- 1 cup panko breadcrumbs
- 2 eggs
- Lemon wedges, for serving
- Cooking spray

1. Preheat the air fryer to 390°F (199°C) and spritz with cooking spray. 2. On a clean work surface, drizzle the pork chops with lemon juice on both sides. 3. Combine the flour with marjoram and salt on a shallow plate. Pour the breadcrumbs on a separate shallow dish. Beat the eggs in a large bowl. 4. Dredge the pork chops in the flour, then dunk in the beaten eggs to coat well. Shake the excess off and roll over the breadcrumbs. 5. Arrange the chops in the preheated air fryer and spritz with cooking spray. Air fry for 15 minutes or until the chops are golden and crispy. Flip the chops halfway through. Squeeze the lemon wedges over the fried chops and serve immediately.

Short Ribs with Chimichurri

Prep time: 30 minutes | Cook time: 13 minutes | Serves 4

- 1 pound (454 g) boneless short ribs
- 1½ teaspoons sea salt, divided
- ½ teaspoon freshly ground black pepper, divided
- ½ cup fresh parsley leaves
- ½ cup fresh cilantro
- leaves
- 1 teaspoon minced garlic
- 1 tablespoon freshly squeezed lemon juice
- ½ teaspoon ground cumin
- ¼ teaspoon red pepper flakes
- 2 tablespoons extra-virgin olive oil
- Avocado oil spray

1. Pat the short ribs dry with paper towels. Sprinkle the ribs all over with 1 teaspoon salt and ¼ teaspoon black pepper. Let sit at room temperature for 45 minutes. 2. Meanwhile, place the parsley, cilantro, garlic, lemon juice, cumin, red pepper flakes, the remaining ½ teaspoon salt, and the remaining ¼ teaspoon black pepper in a blender or food processor. With the blender running, slowly drizzle in the olive oil. Blend for about 1 minute, until the mixture is smooth and well combined. 3. Set the air fryer to 400°F (204°C). Spray both sides of the ribs with oil. Place in the basket and air fry for 8 minutes. Flip and cook for another 5 minutes, until an instant-read thermometer reads 125°F (52°C) for medium-rare (or to your desired doneness). 4. Allow the meat to rest for 5 to 10 minutes, then slice. Serve warm with the chimichurri sauce.

Vietnamese "Shaking" Beef

Prep time: 30 minutes | Cook time: 4 minutes per batch | Serves 4

- Meat:
- 4 garlic cloves, minced
- 2 teaspoons soy sauce
- 2 teaspoons sugar
- 1 teaspoon toasted sesame oil
- 1 teaspoon kosher salt
- ¼ teaspoon black pepper
- 1½ pounds (680 g) flat iron or top sirloin steak, cut into 1-inch cubes
- Salad:
- 2 tablespoons rice vinegar or apple cider vinegar
- 2 tablespoons vegetable oil
- 1 garlic clove, minced
- 2 teaspoons sugar
- ¼ teaspoon kosher salt
- ¼ teaspoon black pepper
- ½ red onion, halved and very thinly sliced
- 1 head Bibb lettuce, leaves separated and torn into large pieces
- ½ cup halved grape tomatoes
- ¼ cup fresh mint leaves
- For Serving:
- Lime wedges
- Coarse salt and freshly cracked black pepper, to taste

1. For the meat: In a small bowl, combine the garlic, soy sauce, sugar, sesame oil, salt, and pepper. Place the meat in a gallon-size resealable plastic bag. Pour the marinade over

the meat. Seal and place the bag in a large bowl. Marinate for 30 minutes, or cover and refrigerate for up to 24 hours. 2. Place half the meat in the air fryer basket. Set the air fryer to 450°F (232°C) for 4 minutes, shaking the basket to redistribute the meat halfway through the cooking time. Transfer the meat to a plate (it should be medium-rare, still pink in the middle). Cover lightly with aluminum foil. Repeat to cook the remaining meat. 3. Meanwhile, for the salad: In a large bowl, whisk together the vinegar, vegetable oil, garlic, sugar, salt, and pepper. Add the onion. Stir to combine. Add the lettuce, tomatoes, and mint and toss to combine. Arrange the salad on a serving platter. 4. Arrange the cooked meat over the salad. Drizzle any accumulated juices from the plate over the meat. Serve with lime wedges, coarse salt, and cracked black pepper.

Italian Pork Loin

Prep time: 30 minutes | Cook time: 16 minutes | Serves 3

- 1 teaspoon Celtic sea salt
- ½ teaspoon black pepper, freshly cracked
- ¼ cup red wine
- 2 tablespoons mustard
- 2 garlic cloves, minced
- 1 pound (454 g) pork top loin
- 1 tablespoon Italian herb seasoning blend

1. In a ceramic bowl, mix the salt, black pepper, red wine, mustard, and garlic. Add the pork top loin and let it marinate at least 30 minutes. 2. Spritz the sides and bottom of the air fryer basket with nonstick cooking spray. 3. Place the pork top loin in the basket; sprinkle with the Italian herb seasoning blend. 4. Cook the pork tenderloin at 370°F (188°C) for 10 minutes. Flip halfway through, spraying with cooking oil and cook for 5 to 6 minutes more. Serve immediately.

Cheese Crusted Chops

Prep time: 10 minutes | Cook time: 12 minutes | Serves 4 to 6

- ¼ teaspoon pepper
- ½ teaspoons salt
- 4 to 6 thick boneless pork chops
- 1 cup pork rind crumbs
- ¼ teaspoon chili powder
- ½ teaspoons onion
- powder
- 1 teaspoon smoked paprika
- 2 beaten eggs
- 3 tablespoons grated Parmesan cheese
- Cooking spray

1. Preheat the air fryer to 400°F (205°C). 2. Rub the pepper and salt on both sides of pork chops. 3. In a food processor, pulse pork rinds into crumbs. Mix crumbs with chili powder, onion powder, and paprika in a bowl. 4. Beat eggs in another bowl. 5. Dip pork chops into eggs then into pork rind crumb mixture. 6. Spritz the air fryer basket with cooking spray and add pork chops to the basket. 7. Air fry for 12 minutes. 8. Serve garnished with the Parmesan cheese.

Currywurst

Prep time: 15 minutes | Cook time: 12 minutes | Serves 4

- 1 cup tomato sauce
- 2 tablespoons cider vinegar
- 2 teaspoons curry powder
- 2 teaspoons sweet paprika
- 1 teaspoon sugar
- ¼ teaspoon cayenne pepper
- 1 small onion, diced
- 1 pound (454 g) bratwurst, sliced diagonally into 1-inch pieces

1. In a large bowl, combine the tomato sauce, vinegar, curry powder, paprika, sugar, and cayenne. Whisk until well combined. Stir in the onion and bratwurst. 2. Transfer the mixture to a baking pan. Place the pan in the air fryer basket. Set the air fryer to 400ºF (204ºC) for 12 minutes, or until the sausage is heated through and the sauce is bubbling.

Southern Chili

Prep time: 20 minutes | Cook time: 25 minutes | Serves 4

- 1 pound (454 g) ground beef (85% lean)
- 1 cup minced onion
- 1 (28-ounce / 794-g) can tomato purée
- 1 (15-ounce / 425-g)
- can diced tomatoes with green chilies
- 1 (15-ounce / 425-g) can light red kidney beans, rinsed and drained
- ¼ cup Chili seasoning

1. Preheat the air fryer to 400ºF (204ºC). 2. In a baking pan, mix the ground beef and onion. Place the pan in the air fryer. 3. Cook for 4 minutes. Stir and cook for 4 minutes more until browned. Remove the pan from the fryer. Drain the meat and transfer to a large bowl. 4. Reduce the air fryer temperature to 350ºF (177ºC). 5. To the bowl with the meat, add in the tomato purée, diced tomatoes and green chilies, kidney beans, and Chili seasoning. Mix well. Pour the mixture into the baking pan. 6. Cook for 25 minutes, stirring every 10 minutes, until thickened.

Pepper Steak

Prep time: 30 minutes | Cook time: 16 to 20 minutes | Serves 4

- 1 pound (454 g) cube steak, cut into 1-inch pieces
- 1 cup Italian dressing
- 1½ cups beef broth
- 1 tablespoon soy sauce
- ½ teaspoon salt
- ¼ teaspoon freshly
- ground black pepper
- ¼ cup cornstarch
- 1 cup thinly sliced bell pepper, any color
- 1 cup chopped celery
- 1 tablespoon minced garlic
- 1 to 2 tablespoons oil

1. In a large resealable bag, combine the beef and Italian dressing. Seal the bag and refrigerate to marinate for 8 hours.

2. In a small bowl, whisk the beef broth, soy sauce, salt, and pepper until blended. 3. In another small bowl, whisk ¼ cup water and the cornstarch until dissolved. Stir the cornstarch mixture into the beef broth mixture until blended. 4. Preheat the air fryer to 375ºF (191ºC). 5. Pour the broth mixture into a baking pan. Cook for 4 minutes. Stir and cook for 4 to 5 minutes more. Remove and set aside. 6. Increase the air fryer temperature to 400ºF (204ºC). Line the air fryer basket with parchment paper. 7. Remove the steak from the marinade and place it in a medium bowl. Discard the marinade. Stir in the bell pepper, celery, and garlic. 8. Place the steak and pepper mixture on the parchment. Spritz with oil. 9. Cook for 4 minutes. Shake the basket and cook for 4 to 7 minutes more, until the vegetables are tender and the meat reaches an internal temperature of 145ºF (63ºC). Serve with the gravy.

Cheddar Bacon Burst with Spinach

Prep time: 5 minutes | Cook time: 60 minutes | Serves 8

- 30 slices bacon
- 1 tablespoon Chipotle seasoning
- 2 teaspoons Italian
- seasoning
- 2½ cups Cheddar cheese
- 4 cups raw spinach

1. Preheat the air fryer to 375ºF (191ºC). 2. Weave the bacon into 15 vertical pieces and 12 horizontal pieces. Cut the extra 3 in half to fill in the rest, horizontally. 3. Season the bacon with Chipotle seasoning and Italian seasoning. 4. Add the cheese to the bacon. 5. Add the spinach and press down to compress. 6. Tightly roll up the woven bacon. 7. Line a baking sheet with kitchen foil and add plenty of salt to it. 8. Put the bacon on top of a cooling rack and put that on top of the baking sheet. 9. Bake for 60 minutes. 10. Let cool for 15 minutes before slicing and serving.

Kielbasa and Cabbage

Prep time: 10 minutes | Cook time: 20 to 25 minutes | Serves 4

- 1 pound (454 g) smoked kielbasa sausage, sliced into ½-inch pieces
- 1 head cabbage, very coarsely chopped
- ½ yellow onion, chopped
- 2 cloves garlic, chopped
- 2 tablespoons olive oil
- ½ teaspoon salt
- ½ teaspoon freshly ground black pepper
- ¼ cup water

1. Preheat the air fryer to 400ºF (204ºC). 2. In a large bowl, combine the sausage, cabbage, onion, garlic, olive oil, salt, and black pepper. Toss until thoroughly combined. 3. Transfer the mixture to the basket of the air fryer and pour the water over the top. Pausing two or three times during the cooking time to shake the basket, air fry for 20 to 25 minutes, until the sausage is browned and the vegetables are tender.

Cantonese BBQ Pork

Prep time: 30 minutes | Cook time: 15 minutes | Serves 4

- ¼ cup honey
- 2 tablespoons dark soy sauce
- 1 tablespoon sugar
- 1 tablespoon Shaoxing wine (rice cooking wine)
- 1 tablespoon hoisin sauce
- 2 teaspoons minced garlic
- 2 teaspoons minced fresh ginger
- 1 teaspoon Chinese five-spice powder
- 1 pound (454 g) fatty pork shoulder, cut into long, 1-inch-thick pieces

1. In a small microwave-safe bowl, combine the honey, soy sauce, sugar, wine, hoisin, garlic, ginger, and five-spice powder. Microwave in 10-second intervals, stirring in between, until the honey has dissolved. 2. Use a fork to pierce the pork slices to allow the marinade to penetrate better. Place the pork in a large bowl or resealable plastic bag and pour in half the marinade; set aside the remaining marinade to use for the sauce. Toss to coat. Marinate the pork at room temperature for 30 minutes, or cover and refrigerate for up 24 hours. 3. Place the pork in a single layer in the air fryer basket. Set the air fryer to 400°F (204°C) for 15 minutes, turning and basting the pork halfway through the cooking time. 4. While the pork is cooking, microwave the reserved marinade on high for 45 to 60 seconds, stirring every 15 seconds, to thicken it slightly to the consistency of a sauce. 5. Transfer the pork to a cutting board and let rest for 10 minutes. Brush with the sauce and serve.

Five-Spice Pork Belly

Prep time: 10 minutes | Cook time: 17 minutes | Serves 4

- 1 pound (454 g) unsalted pork belly
- 2 teaspoons Chinese five-spice powder
- Sauce:
- 1 tablespoon coconut oil
- 1 (1-inch) piece fresh ginger, peeled and grated
- 2 cloves garlic, minced
- ½ cup beef or chicken broth
- ¼ to ½ cup Swerve confectioners'-style sweetener or equivalent amount of liquid or powdered sweetener
- 3 tablespoons wheat-free tamari, or ½ cup coconut aminos
- 1 green onion, sliced, plus more for garnish

1. Spray the air fryer basket with avocado oil. Preheat the air fryer to 400°F (204°C). 2. Cut the pork belly into ½-inch-thick slices and season well on all sides with the five-spice powder. Place the slices in a single layer in the air fryer basket (if you're using a smaller air fryer, work in batches if necessary) and cook for 8 minutes, or until cooked to your liking, flipping halfway through. 3. While the pork belly cooks, make the sauce: Heat the coconut oil in a small saucepan over medium heat. Add the ginger

and garlic and sauté for 1 minute, or until fragrant. Add the broth, sweetener, and tamari and simmer for 10 to 15 minutes, until thickened. Add the green onion and cook for another minute, until the green onion is softened. Taste and adjust the seasoning to your liking. 4. Transfer the pork belly to a large bowl. Pour the sauce over the pork belly and coat well. Place the pork belly slices on a serving platter and garnish with sliced green onions. 5. Best served fresh. Store leftovers in an airtight container in the fridge for up to 4 days. Reheat in a preheated 400°F (204°C) air fryer for 3 minutes, or until heated through.

Crescent Dogs

Prep time: 15 minutes | Cook time: 8 minutes | Makes 24 crescent dogs

- Oil, for spraying
- 1 (8-ounce / 227-g) can refrigerated crescent rolls
- 8 slices Cheddar cheese, cut into thirds
- 24 cocktail sausages or 8
- (6-inch) hot dogs, cut into thirds
- 2 tablespoons unsalted butter, melted
- 1 tablespoon sea salt flakes

1. Line the air fryer basket with parchment and spray lightly with oil. 2. Separate the dough into 8 triangles. Cut each triangle into 3 narrow triangles so you have 24 total triangles. 3. Top each triangle with 1 piece of cheese and 1 cocktail sausage. 4. Roll up each piece of dough, starting at the wide end and rolling toward the point. 5. Place the rolls in the prepared basket in a single layer. You may need to cook in batches, depending on the size of your air fryer. 6. Air fry at 325°F (163°C) for 3 to 4 minutes, flip, and cook for another 3 to 4 minutes, or until golden brown. 7. Brush with the melted butter and sprinkle with the sea salt flakes before serving.

Italian Sausage Links

Prep time: 10 minutes | Cook time: 24 minutes | Serves 4

- 1 bell pepper (any color), sliced
- 1 medium onion, sliced
- 1 tablespoon avocado oil
- 1 teaspoon Italian seasoning
- Sea salt and freshly ground black pepper, to taste
- 1 pound (454 g) Italian sausage links

1. Place the bell pepper and onion in a medium bowl, and toss with the avocado oil, Italian seasoning, and salt and pepper to taste. 2. Set the air fryer to 400°F (204°C). Put the vegetables in the air fryer basket and cook for 12 minutes. 3. Push the vegetables to the side of the basket and arrange the sausage links in the bottom of the basket in a single layer. Spoon the vegetables over the sausages. Cook for 12 minutes, tossing halfway through, until an instant-read thermometer inserted into the sausage reads 160°F (71°C).

Italian Sausages with Peppers and Onions

Prep time: 5 minutes | Cook time: 28 minutes | Serves 3

- 1 medium onion, thinly sliced
- 1 yellow or orange bell pepper, thinly sliced
- 1 red bell pepper, thinly sliced
- ¼ cup avocado oil or melted coconut oil
- 1 teaspoon fine sea salt
- 6 Italian sausages
- Dijon mustard, for serving (optional)

1. Preheat the air fryer to 400°F (204°C). 2. Place the onion and peppers in a large bowl. Drizzle with the oil and toss well to coat the veggies. Season with the salt. 3. Place the onion and peppers in a pie pan and cook in the air fryer for 8 minutes, stirring halfway through. Remove from the air fryer and set aside. 4. Spray the air fryer basket with avocado oil. Place the sausages in the air fryer basket and air fry for 20 minutes, or until crispy and golden brown. During the last minute or two of cooking, add the onion and peppers to the basket with the sausages to warm them through. 5. Place the onion and peppers on a serving platter and arrange the sausages on top. Serve Dijon mustard on the side, if desired. 6. Store leftovers in an airtight container in the fridge for up to 7 days or in the freezer for up to a month. Reheat in a preheated 390°F (199°C) air fryer for 3 minutes, or until heated through.

Beef Empanadas

Prep time: 15 minutes | Cook time: 25 minutes | Serves 5

- 2 garlic cloves, chopped
- ⅓ cup chopped green bell pepper
- ⅓ medium onion, chopped
- 8 ounces (227 g) 93% lean ground beef
- 1 teaspoon hamburger seasoning
- Salt and freshly ground black pepper, to taste
- 15 empanada wrappers
- 1 cup shredded Mozzarella cheese
- 1 cup shredded pepper Jack cheese
- 1 tablespoon butter
- Cooking oil spray

1. Spray a skillet with the cooking oil and place it over medium-high heat. Add the garlic, green bell pepper, and onion. Cook until fragrant, about 2 minutes. 2. Add the ground beef to the skillet. Season it with the hamburger seasoning, salt, and pepper. Using a spatula or spoon, break up the beef into small pieces. Cook the beef for about 5 minutes until browned. Drain any excess fat. 3. Lay the empanada wrappers on a work surface. 4. Dip a basting brush in water. Glaze each wrapper along the edges with the wet brush. This will soften the crust and make it easier to roll. You can also dip your fingers in water to moisten the edges. 5. Scoop 2 to 3 tablespoons of the ground beef mixture onto each empanada wrapper. Sprinkle the Mozzarella and pepper Jack cheeses over the beef. 6. Close the empanadas by folding the empanada wrapper in half over the filling. Using the back of a fork, press along the edges to seal. 7. Insert the crisper plate into the basket and the basket into the unit. Preheat the unit by selecting AIR FRY, setting the temperature to 400°F (204°C), and setting the time to 3 minutes. Select START/STOP to begin. 8. Once the unit is preheated, spray the crisper plate with cooking oil. Working in batches, place 7 or 8 empanadas into the basket. Spray each with cooking oil. 9. Select AIR FRY, set the temperature to 400°F (204°C), and set the time to 12 minutes. Select START/STOP to begin. 10. After 8 minutes, flip the empanadas and spray them with more cooking oil. Resume cooking. 11. When the cooking is complete, transfer the empanadas to a plate. For added flavor, top each hot empanada with a bit of butter and let melt. Repeat steps 8, 9, and 10 for the remaining empanadas. 12. Cool for 5 minutes before serving.

Beef Fried Steak with Cream Gravy

Prep time: 5 minutes | Cook time: 10 minutes | Serves 4

- 4 small thin cube steaks (about 1 pound / 454 g)
- ½ teaspoon salt
- ½ teaspoon freshly ground black pepper
- ¼ teaspoon garlic powder
- 1 egg, lightly beaten
- 1 cup crushed pork rinds (about 3 ounces / 85 g)
- Cream Gravy:
- ½ cup heavy cream
- 2 ounces (57 g) cream cheese
- ¼ cup bacon grease
- 2 to 3 tablespoons water
- 2 to 3 dashes Worcestershire sauce
- Salt and freshly ground black pepper, to taste

1. Preheat the air fryer to 400°F (204°C). 2. Working one at a time, place the steak between two sheets of parchment paper and use a meat mallet to pound to an even thickness. 3. In a small bowl, combine the salt, pepper, and garlic power. Season both sides of each steak with the mixture. 4. Place the egg in a small shallow dish and the pork rinds in another small shallow dish. Dip each steak first in the egg wash, followed by the pork rinds, pressing lightly to form an even coating. Working in batches if necessary, arrange the steaks in a single layer in the air fryer basket. Air fry for 10 minutes until crispy and cooked through. 5. To make the cream gravy: In a heavy-bottomed pot, warm the cream, cream cheese, and bacon grease over medium heat, whisking until smooth. Lower the heat if the mixture begins to boil. Continue whisking as you slowly add the water, 1 tablespoon at a time, until the sauce reaches the desired consistency. Season with the Worcestershire sauce and salt and pepper to taste. Serve over the beef fried steaks.

Italian Steak Rolls

Prep time: 30 minutes | Cook time: 9 minutes | Serves 4

- 1 tablespoon vegetable oil
- 2 cloves garlic, minced
- 2 teaspoons dried Italian seasoning
- 1 teaspoon kosher salt
- 1 teaspoon black pepper
- 1 pound (454 g) flank or skirt steak, ¼ to ½ inch

- thick
- 1 (10-ounce / 283-g) package frozen spinach, thawed and squeezed dry
- ½ cup diced jarred roasted red pepper
- 1 cup shredded Mozzarella cheese

1. In a large bowl, combine the oil, garlic, Italian seasoning, salt, and pepper. Whisk to combine. Add the steak to the bowl, turning to ensure the entire steak is covered with the seasonings. Cover and marinate at room temperature for 30 minutes or in the refrigerator for up to 24 hours. 2. Lay the steak on a flat surface. Spread the spinach evenly over the steak, leaving a ¼-inch border at the edge. Evenly top each steak with the red pepper and cheese. 3. Starting at a long end, roll up the steak as tightly as possible, ending seam side down. Use 2 or 3 wooden toothpicks to hold the roll together. Using a sharp knife, cut the roll in half so that it better fits in the air fryer basket. 4. Place the steak roll, seam side down, in the air fryer basket. Set the air fryer to 400°F (204°C) for 9 minutes. Use a meat thermometer to ensure the steak has reached an internal temperature of 145°F (63°C). (It is critical to not overcook flank steak, so as to not toughen the meat.) 5. Let the steak rest for 10 minutes before cutting into slices to serve.

Bulgogi Burgers

Prep time: 30 minutes | Cook time: 10 minutes | Serves 4

- Burgers:
- 1 pound (454 g) 85% lean ground beef
- ¼ cup chopped scallions
- 2 tablespoons gochujang (Korean red chile paste)
- 1 tablespoon dark soy sauce
- 2 teaspoons minced garlic
- 2 teaspoons minced fresh ginger
- 2 teaspoons sugar

- 1 tablespoon toasted sesame oil
- ½ teaspoon kosher salt
- Gochujang Mayonnaise:
- ¼ cup mayonnaise
- ¼ cup chopped scallions
- 1 tablespoon gochujang (Korean red chile paste)
- 1 tablespoon toasted sesame oil
- 2 teaspoons sesame seeds
- 4 hamburger buns

1. For the burgers: In a large bowl, mix the ground beef, scallions, gochujang, soy sauce, garlic, ginger, sugar, sesame oil, and salt. Marinate at room temperature for 30 minutes, or cover and refrigerate for up to 24 hours. 2. Divide the meat into four portions and form them into round patties. Make a slight depression in the middle of each patty with your thumb to prevent them from puffing up into a dome shape while cooking. 3. Place the patties in a single layer in the air fryer basket. Set the air fryer to 350°F (177°C) for 10 minutes. 4. Meanwhile, for the gochujang mayonnaise: Stir together the mayonnaise, scallions, gochujang, sesame oil, and sesame seeds. 5. At the end of the cooking time, use a meat thermometer to ensure the burgers have reached an internal temperature of 160°F / 71°C (medium). 6. To serve, place the burgers on the buns and top with the mayonnaise.

Beef and Broccoli Stir-Fry

Prep time: 30 minutes | Cook time: 20 minutes | Serves 2

- ½ pound (227 g) sirloin steak, thinly sliced
- 2 tablespoons coconut aminos
- ¼ teaspoon grated ginger
- ¼ teaspoon finely minced garlic

- 1 tablespoon coconut oil
- 2 cups broccoli florets
- ¼ teaspoon crushed red pepper
- ⅛ teaspoon xanthan gum
- ½ teaspoon sesame seeds

1. To marinate beef, place it into a large bowl or storage bag and add coconut aminos, ginger, garlic, and coconut oil. Allow to marinate for 1 hour in refrigerator. 2. Remove beef from marinade, reserving marinade, and place beef into the air fryer basket. 3. Adjust the temperature to 320°F (160°C) and air fry for 20 minutes. 4. After 10 minutes, add broccoli and sprinkle red pepper into the basket and shake. 5. Pour the marinade into a skillet over medium heat and bring to a boil, then reduce to simmer. Stir in xanthan gum and allow to thicken. 6. When done, quickly empty fryer basket into skillet and toss. Sprinkle with sesame seeds. Serve immediately.

Fruited Ham

Prep time: 15 minutes | Cook time: 8 to 10 minutes | Serves 4

- 1 cup orange marmalade
- ¼ cup packed light brown sugar
- ¼ teaspoon ground cloves
- ½ teaspoon dry mustard
- 1 to 2 tablespoons oil

- 1 pound (454 g) cooked ham, cut into 1-inch cubes
- ½ cup canned mandarin oranges, drained and chopped

1. In a small bowl, stir together the orange marmalade, brown sugar, cloves, and dry mustard until blended. Set aside. 2. Preheat the air fryer to 320°F (160°C). Spritz a baking pan with oil. 3. Place the ham cubes in the prepared pan. Pour the marmalade sauce over the ham to glaze it. 4. Cook for 4 minutes. Stir and cook for 2 minutes more. 5. Add the mandarin oranges and cook for 2 to 4 minutes more until the sauce begins to thicken and the ham is tender.

Spicy Tomato Beef Meatballs

Prep time: 10 minutes | Cook time: 15 minutes | Serves 4

- 3 scallions, minced
- 1 garlic clove, minced
- 1 egg yolk
- ¼ cup saltine cracker crumbs
- Pinch salt
- Freshly ground black pepper, to taste
- 1 pound (454 g) 95% lean ground beef
- Olive oil spray
- 1¼ cups any tomato pasta sauce (from a 16-ounce / 454-g jar)
- 2 tablespoons Dijon mustard

1. In a large bowl, combine the scallions, garlic, egg yolk, cracker crumbs, salt, and pepper and mix well. 2. Add the ground beef and gently but thoroughly mix with your hands until combined. Form the meat mixture into 1½-inch round meatballs. 3. Insert the crisper plate into the basket and the basket into the unit. Preheat the unit by selecting BAKE, setting the temperature to 400°F (204°C), and setting the time to 3 minutes. Select START/STOP to begin. 4. Once the unit is preheated, spray the crisper plate with olive oil. Working in batches, spray the meatballs with olive oil and place them into the basket in a single layer, without touching. 5. Select BAKE, set the temperature to 400°F (204°C), and set the time to 11 minutes. Select START/STOP to begin. 6. When the cooking is complete, a food thermometer inserted into the meatballs should register 165°F (74°C). Transfer the meatballs to a 6-inch metal bowl. 7. Repeat steps 4, 5, and 6 with the remaining meatballs. 8. Top the meatballs with the pasta sauce and Dijon mustard, and mix gently. Place the bowl into the basket. 9. Select BAKE, set the temperature to 400°F (204°C), and set the time to 4 minutes. Select START/STOP to begin. 10. When the cooking is complete, serve hot.

Beef and Spinach Rolls

Prep time: 10 minutes | Cook time: 14 minutes | Serves 2

- 3 teaspoons pesto
- 2 pounds (907 g) beef flank steak
- 6 slices provolone cheese
- 3 ounces (85 g) roasted
- red bell peppers
- ¾ cup baby spinach
- 1 teaspoon sea salt
- 1 teaspoon black pepper

1. Preheat the air fryer to 400°F (204°C). 2. Spoon equal amounts of the pesto onto each flank steak and spread it across evenly. 3. Put the cheese, roasted red peppers and spinach on top of the meat, about three-quarters of the way down. 4. Roll the steak up, holding it in place with toothpicks. Sprinkle with the sea salt and pepper. 5. Put inside the air fryer and air fry for 14 minutes, turning halfway through the cooking time. 6. Allow the beef to rest for 10 minutes before slicing up and serving.

Almond and Caraway Crust Steak

Prep time: 16 minutes | Cook time: 10 minutes | Serves 4

- ⅓ cup almond flour
- 2 eggs
- 2 teaspoons caraway seeds
- 4 beef steaks
- 2 teaspoons garlic
- powder
- 1 tablespoon melted butter
- Fine sea salt and cayenne pepper, to taste

1. Generously coat steaks with garlic powder, caraway seeds, salt, and cayenne pepper. 2. In a mixing dish, thoroughly combine melted butter with seasoned crumbs. In another bowl, beat the eggs until they're well whisked. 3. First, coat steaks with the beaten egg; then, coat beef steaks with the buttered crumb mixture. Place the steaks in the air fryer basket; cook for 10 minutes at 355°F (179°C). Bon appétit!

Steak with Bell Pepper

Prep time: 30 minutes | Cook time: 20 to 23 minutes | Serves 6

- ¼ cup avocado oil
- ¼ cup freshly squeezed lime juice
- 2 teaspoons minced garlic
- 1 tablespoon chili powder
- ½ teaspoon ground cumin
- Sea salt and freshly ground black pepper, to taste
- 1 pound (454 g) top
- sirloin steak or flank steak, thinly sliced against the grain
- 1 red bell pepper, cored, seeded, and cut into ½-inch slices
- 1 green bell pepper, cored, seeded, and cut into ½-inch slices
- 1 large onion, sliced

1. In a small bowl or blender, combine the avocado oil, lime juice, garlic, chili powder, cumin, and salt and pepper to taste. 2. Place the sliced steak in a zip-top bag or shallow dish. Place the bell peppers and onion in a separate zip-top bag or dish. Pour half the marinade over the steak and the other half over the vegetables. Seal both bags and let the steak and vegetables marinate in the refrigerator for at least 1 hour or up to 4 hours. 3. Line the air fryer basket with an air fryer liner or aluminum foil. Remove the vegetables from their bag or dish and shake off any excess marinade. Set the air fryer to 400°F (204°C). Place the vegetables in the air fryer basket and cook for 13 minutes. 4. Remove the steak from its bag or dish and shake off any excess marinade. Place the steak on top of the vegetables in the air fryer, and cook for 7 to 10 minutes or until an instant-read thermometer reads 120°F (49°C) for medium-rare (or cook to your desired doneness). 5. Serve with desired fixings, such as keto tortillas, lettuce, sour cream, avocado slices, shredded Cheddar cheese, and cilantro.

Sesame Beef Lettuce Tacos

Prep time: 30 minutes | Cook time: 8 to 10 minutes | Serves 4

- ¼ cup coconut aminos
- ¼ cup avocado oil
- 2 tablespoons cooking sherry
- 1 tablespoon Swerve
- 1 tablespoon ground cumin
- 1 teaspoon minced garlic
- Sea salt and freshly ground black pepper, to taste
- 1 pound (454 g) flank steak
- 8 butter lettuce leaves
- 2 scallions, sliced
- 1 tablespoon toasted sesame seeds
- Hot sauce, for serving
- Lime wedges, for serving
- Flaky sea salt (optional)

1. In a small bowl, whisk together the coconut aminos, avocado oil, cooking sherry, Swerve, cumin, garlic, and salt and pepper to taste. 2. Place the steak in a shallow dish. Pour the marinade over the beef. Cover the dish with plastic wrap and let it marinate in the refrigerator for at least 2 hours or overnight. 3. Remove the flank steak from the dish and discard the marinade. 4. Set the air fryer to 400°F (204°C). Place the steak in the air fryer basket and air fry for 4 to 6 minutes. Flip the steak and cook for 4 minutes more, until an instant-read thermometer reads 120°F (49°C) at the thickest part (or cook it to your desired doneness). Allow the steak to rest for 10 minutes, then slice it thinly against the grain. 5. Stack 2 lettuce leaves on top of each other and add some sliced meat. Top with scallions and sesame seeds. Drizzle with hot sauce and lime juice, and finish with a little flaky salt (if using). Repeat with the remaining lettuce leaves and fillings.

Korean Beef Tacos

Prep time: 30 minutes | Cook time: 12 minutes | Serves 6

- 2 tablespoons gochujang (Korean red chile paste)
- 2 cloves garlic, minced
- 2 teaspoons minced fresh ginger
- 2 tablespoons toasted sesame oil
- 1 tablespoon soy sauce
- 2 tablespoons sesame seeds
- 2 teaspoons sugar
- ½ teaspoon kosher salt
- 1½ pounds (680 g) thinly sliced beef (chuck, rib eye, or sirloin)
- 1 medium red onion, sliced
- 12 (6-inch) flour tortillas, warmed; or lettuce leaves
- ½ cup chopped green onions
- ¼ cup chopped fresh cilantro (optional)
- ½ cup kimchi (optional)

1. In a small bowl, combine the gochujang, garlic, ginger, sesame oil, soy sauce, sesame seeds, sugar, and salt. Whisk until well combined. Place the beef and red onion in a resealable plastic bag and pour the marinade over. Seal the bag and massage to coat all of the meat and onion. Marinate at room temperature for 30 minutes or in the refrigerator for up to 24 hours. 2. Place the meat and onion in the air fryer basket, leaving behind as much of the marinade as possible; discard the marinade. Set the air fryer to 400°F (204°C) for 12 minutes, shaking halfway through the cooking time. 3. To serve, place meat and onion in the tortillas. Top with the green onions and the cilantro and kimchi, if using, and serve.

Tomato and Bacon Zoodles

Prep time: 10 minutes | Cook time: 15 to 22 minutes | Serves 2

- 8 ounces (227 g) sliced bacon
- ½ cup grape tomatoes
- 1 large zucchini, spiralized
- ½ cup ricotta cheese
- ¼ cup heavy (whipping) cream
- ⅓ cup finely grated Parmesan cheese, plus more for serving
- Sea salt and freshly ground black pepper, to taste

1. Set the air fryer to 400°F (204°C). Arrange the bacon strips in a single layer in the air fryer basket—some overlapping is okay because the bacon will shrink, but cook in batches if needed. Air fry for 8 minutes. Flip the bacon strips and air fry for 2 to 5 minutes more, until the bacon is crisp. Remove the bacon from the air fryer. 2. Put the tomatoes in the air fryer basket and air fry for 3 to 5 minutes, until they are just starting to burst. Remove the tomatoes from the air fryer. 3. Put the zucchini noodles in the air fryer and air fry for 2 to 4 minutes, to the desired doneness. 4. Meanwhile, combine the ricotta, heavy cream, and Parmesan in a saucepan over medium-low heat. Cook, stirring often, until warm and combined. 5. Crumble the bacon. Place the zucchini, bacon, and tomatoes in a bowl. Toss with the ricotta sauce. Season with salt and pepper, and sprinkle with additional Parmesan.

Ground Beef Taco Rolls

Prep time: 20 minutes | Cook time: 10 minutes | Serves 4

- ½ pound (227 g) ground beef
- ⅓ cup water
- 1 tablespoon chili powder
- 2 teaspoons cumin
- ½ teaspoon garlic powder
- ¼ teaspoon dried oregano

- ¼ cup canned diced tomatoes and chiles, drained
- 2 tablespoons chopped cilantro
- 1½ cups shredded Mozzarella cheese
- ½ cup blanched finely ground almond flour
- 2 ounces (57 g) full-fat cream cheese
- 1 large egg

1. In a medium skillet over medium heat, brown the ground beef about 7 to 10 minutes. When meat is fully cooked, drain. 2. Add water to skillet and stir in chili powder, cumin, garlic powder, oregano, and tomatoes with chiles. Add cilantro. Bring to a boil, then reduce heat to simmer for 3 minutes. 3. In a large microwave-safe bowl, place Mozzarella, almond flour, cream cheese, and egg. Microwave for 1 minute. Stir the mixture quickly until smooth ball of dough forms. 4. Cut a piece of parchment for your work surface. Press the dough into a large rectangle on the parchment, wetting your hands to prevent the dough from sticking as necessary. Cut the dough into eight rectangles. 5. On each rectangle place a few spoons of the meat mixture. Fold the short ends of each roll toward the center and roll the length as you would a burrito. 6. Cut a piece of parchment to fit your air fryer basket. Place taco rolls onto the parchment and place into the air fryer basket. 7. Adjust the temperature to 360°F (182°C) and air fry for 10 minutes. 8. Flip halfway through the cooking time. 9. Allow to cool 10 minutes before serving.

Chapter 5

Poultry

French Garlic Chicken

Prep time: 30 minutes | Cook time: 27 minutes | Serves 4

- 2 tablespoon extra-virgin olive oil
- 1 tablespoon Dijon mustard
- 1 tablespoon apple cider vinegar
- 3 cloves garlic, minced
- 2 teaspoons herbes de Provence
- ½ teaspoon kosher salt
- 1 teaspoon black pepper
- 1 pound (454 g) boneless, skinless chicken thighs, halved crosswise
- 2 tablespoons butter
- 8 cloves garlic, chopped
- ¼ cup heavy whipping cream

1. In a small bowl, combine the olive oil, mustard, vinegar, minced garlic, herbes de Provence, salt, and pepper. Use a wire whisk to emulsify the mixture. 2. Pierce the chicken all over with a fork to allow the marinade to penetrate better. Place the chicken in a resealable plastic bag, pour the marinade over, and seal. Massage until the chicken is well coated. Marinate at room temperature for 30 minutes or in the refrigerator for up to 24 hours. 3. When you are ready to cook, place the butter and chopped garlic in a baking pan and place it in the air fryer basket. Set the air fryer to 400°F (204°C) for 5 minutes, or until the butter has melted and the garlic is sizzling. 4. Add the chicken and the marinade to the seasoned butter. Set the air fryer to 350°F (177°C) for 15 minutes. Use a meat thermometer to ensure the chicken has reached an internal temperature of 165°F (74°C). Transfer the chicken to a plate and cover lightly with foil to keep warm. 5. Add the cream to the pan, stirring to combine with the garlic, butter, and cooking juices. Place the pan in the air fryer basket. Set the air fryer to 350°F (177°C) for 7 minutes. 6. Pour the thickened sauce over the chicken and serve.

Jerk Chicken Kebabs

Prep time: 10 minutes | Cook time: 14 minutes | Serves 4

- 8 ounces (227 g) boneless, skinless chicken thighs, cut into 1-inch cubes
- 2 tablespoons jerk seasoning
- 2 tablespoons coconut oil
- ½ medium red bell pepper, seeded and cut into 1-inch pieces
- ¼ medium red onion, peeled and cut into 1-inch pieces
- ½ teaspoon salt

1. Place chicken in a medium bowl and sprinkle with jerk seasoning and coconut oil. Toss to coat on all sides. 2. Using eight (6-inch) skewers, build skewers by alternating chicken, pepper, and onion pieces, about three repetitions per skewer. 3. Sprinkle salt over skewers and place into ungreased air fryer basket. Adjust the temperature to 370°F (188°C) and air fry for 14 minutes, turning skewers halfway through cooking. Chicken will be golden and have an internal temperature of at least 165°F (74°C) when done. Serve warm.

Chicken Parmesan

Prep time: 15 minutes | Cook time: 10 minutes | Serves 4

- Oil, for spraying
- 2 (8 ounces / 227 g) boneless, skinless chicken breasts
- 1 cup Italian-style bread crumbs
- ¼ cup grated Parmesan cheese, plus ½ cup shredded
- 4 tablespoons unsalted butter, melted
- ½ cup marinara sauce

1. Preheat the air fryer to 360°F (182°C). Line the air fryer basket with parchment and spray lightly with oil. 2. Cut each chicken breast in half through its thickness to make 4 thin cutlets. Using a meat tenderizer, pound each cutlet until it is about ¾ inch thick. 3. On a plate, mix together the bread crumbs and grated Parmesan cheese. 4. Lightly brush the chicken with the melted butter, then dip into the bread crumb mixture. 5. Place the chicken in the prepared basket and spray lightly with oil. You may need to work in batches, depending on the size of your air fryer. 6. Cook for 6 minutes. Top the chicken with the marinara and shredded Parmesan cheese, dividing evenly. Cook for another 3 to 4 minutes, or until golden brown, crispy, and the internal temperature reaches 165°F (74°C).

Thanksgiving Turkey Breast

Prep time: 5 minutes | Cook time: 30 minutes | Serves 4

- 1½ teaspoons fine sea salt
- 1 teaspoon ground black pepper
- 1 teaspoon chopped fresh rosemary leaves
- 1 teaspoon chopped fresh sage
- 1 teaspoon chopped fresh tarragon
- 1 teaspoon chopped fresh thyme leaves
- 1 (2 pounds / 907 g) turkey breast
- 3 tablespoons ghee or unsalted butter, melted
- 3 tablespoons Dijon mustard

1. Spray the air fryer with avocado oil. Preheat the air fryer to 390°F (199°C). 2. In a small bowl, stir together the salt, pepper, and herbs until well combined. Season the turkey breast generously on all sides with the seasoning. 3. In another small bowl, stir together the ghee and Dijon. Brush the ghee mixture on all sides of the turkey breast. 4. Place the turkey breast in the air fryer basket and air fry for 30 minutes, or until the internal temperature reaches 165°F (74°C). Transfer the breast to a cutting board and allow it to rest for 10 minutes before cutting it into ½-inch-thick slices. 5. Store leftovers in an airtight container in the refrigerator for up to 4 days or in the freezer for up to a month. Reheat in a preheated 350°F (177°C) air fryer for 4 minutes, or until warmed through.

Crunchy Chicken Tenders

Prep time: 5 minutes | Cook time: 12 minutes | Serves 4

- 1 egg
- ¼ cup unsweetened almond milk
- ¼ cup whole wheat flour
- ¼ cup whole wheat bread crumbs
- ½ teaspoon salt
- ½ teaspoon black pepper
- ½ teaspoon dried thyme
- ½ teaspoon dried sage
- ½ teaspoon garlic powder
- 1 pound (454 g) chicken tenderloins
- 1 lemon, quartered

1. Preheat the air fryer to 360°F(182°C). 2. In a shallow bowl, beat together the egg and almond milk until frothy. 3. In a separate shallow bowl, whisk together the flour, bread crumbs, salt, pepper, thyme, sage, and garlic powder. 4. Dip each chicken tenderloin into the egg mixture, then into the bread crumb mixture, coating the outside with the crumbs. Place the breaded chicken tenderloins into the bottom of the air fryer basket in an even layer, making sure that they don't touch each other. 5. Cook for 6 minutes, then turn and cook for an additional 5 to 6 minutes. Serve with lemon slices.

Chicken Nuggets

Prep time: 10 minutes | Cook time: 15 minutes | Serves 4

- 1 pound (454 g) ground chicken thighs
- ½ cup shredded Mozzarella cheese
- 1 large egg, whisked
- ½ teaspoon salt
- ¼ teaspoon dried oregano
- ¼ teaspoon garlic powder

1. In a large bowl, combine all ingredients. Form mixture into twenty nugget shapes, about 2 tablespoons each. 2. Place nuggets into ungreased air fryer basket, working in batches if needed. Adjust the temperature to 375°F (191°C) and air fry for 15 minutes, turning nuggets halfway through cooking. Let cool 5 minutes before serving.

Ginger Turmeric Chicken Thighs

Prep time: 5 minutes | Cook time: 25 minutes | Serves 4

- 4 (4 ounces / 113 g) boneless, skin-on chicken thighs
- 2 tablespoons coconut oil, melted
- ½ teaspoon ground
- turmeric
- ½ teaspoon salt
- ½ teaspoon garlic powder
- ½ teaspoon ground ginger
- ¼ teaspoon ground black pepper

1. Place chicken thighs in a large bowl and drizzle with coconut oil. Sprinkle with remaining ingredients and toss to coat both sides of thighs. 2. Place thighs skin side up into ungreased air fryer basket. Adjust the temperature to 400°F (204°C) and air fry for 25 minutes. After 10 minutes, turn thighs. When 5 minutes remain, flip thighs once more.

Chicken will be done when skin is golden brown and the internal temperature is at least 165ºF (74ºC). Serve warm.

Brazilian Tempero Baiano Chicken Drumsticks

Prep time: 30 minutes | Cook time: 20 minutes | Serves 4

- 1 teaspoon cumin seeds
- 1 teaspoon dried oregano
- 1 teaspoon dried parsley
- 1 teaspoon ground turmeric
- ½ teaspoon coriander seeds
- 1 teaspoon kosher salt
- ½ teaspoon black peppercorns
- ½ teaspoon cayenne pepper
- ¼ cup fresh lime juice
- 2 tablespoons olive oil
- 1½ pounds (680 g) chicken drumsticks

1. In a clean coffee grinder or spice mill, combine the cumin, oregano, parsley, turmeric, coriander seeds, salt, peppercorns, and cayenne. Process until finely ground. 2. In a small bowl, combine the ground spices with the lime juice and oil. Place the chicken in a resealable plastic bag. Add the marinade, seal, and massage until the chicken is well coated. Marinate at room temperature for 30 minutes or in the refrigerator for up to 24 hours. 3. When you are ready to cook, place the drumsticks skin side up in the air fryer basket. Set the air fryer to 400°F (204°C) for 20 to 25 minutes, turning the legs halfway through the cooking time. Use a meat thermometer to ensure that the chicken has reached an internal temperature of 165ºF (74ºC). 4. Serve with plenty of napkins.

Cheese-Encrusted Chicken Tenderloins with Peanuts

Prep time: 10 minutes | Cook time: 25 minutes | Serves 4

- ½ cup grated Parmesan cheese
- ½ teaspoon garlic powder
- 1 teaspoon red pepper flakes
- Sea salt and ground black pepper, to taste
- 2 tablespoons peanut oil
- 1½ pounds (680 g) chicken tenderloins
- 2 tablespoons peanuts, roasted and roughly chopped
- Cooking spray

1. Preheat the air fryer to 360°F (182°C). Spritz the air fryer basket with cooking spray. 2. Combine the Parmesan cheese, garlic powder, red pepper flakes, salt, black pepper, and peanut oil in a large bow. Stir to mix well. 3. Dip the chicken tenderloins in the cheese mixture, then press to coat well. Shake the excess off. 4. Transfer the chicken tenderloins in the air fryer basket. Air fry for 12 minutes or until well browned. Flip the tenderloin halfway through. You may need to work in batches to avoid overcrowding. 5. Transfer the chicken tenderloins on a large plate and top with roasted peanuts before serving.

Chicken with Lettuce

Prep time: 15 minutes | Cook time: 14 minutes | Serves 4

- 1 pound (454 g) chicken breast tenders, chopped into bite-size pieces
- ½ onion, thinly sliced
- ½ red bell pepper, seeded and thinly sliced
- ½ green bell pepper, seeded and thinly sliced
- 1 tablespoon olive oil
- 1 tablespoon fajita seasoning
- 1 teaspoon kosher salt
- Juice of ½ lime
- 8 large lettuce leaves
- 1 cup prepared guacamole

1. Preheat the air fryer to 400°F (204°C). 2. In a large bowl, combine the chicken, onion, and peppers. Drizzle with the olive oil and toss until thoroughly coated. Add the fajita seasoning and salt and toss again. 3. Working in batches if necessary, arrange the chicken and vegetables in a single layer in the air fryer basket. Pausing halfway through the cooking time to shake the basket, air fry for 14 minutes, or until the vegetables are tender and a thermometer inserted into the thickest piece of chicken registers 165°F (74°C). 4. Transfer the mixture to a serving platter and drizzle with the fresh lime juice. Serve with the lettuce leaves and top with the guacamole.

Herb-Buttermilk Chicken Breast

Prep time: 5 minutes | Cook time: 40 minutes | Serves 2

- 1 large bone-in, skin-on chicken breast
- 1 cup buttermilk
- 1½ teaspoons dried parsley
- 1½ teaspoons dried chives
- ¾ teaspoon kosher salt
- ½ teaspoon dried dill
- ½ teaspoon onion powder
- ¼ teaspoon garlic powder
- ¼ teaspoon dried tarragon
- Cooking spray

1. Place the chicken breast in a bowl and pour over the buttermilk, turning the chicken in it to make sure it's completely covered. Let the chicken stand at room temperature for at least 20 minutes or in the refrigerator for up to 4 hours. 2. Meanwhile, in a bowl, stir together the parsley, chives, salt, dill, onion powder, garlic powder, and tarragon. 3. Preheat the air fryer to 300°F (149°C). 4. Remove the chicken from the buttermilk, letting the excess drip off, then place the chicken skin-side up directly in the air fryer. Sprinkle the seasoning mix all over the top of the chicken breast, then let stand until the herb mix soaks into the buttermilk, at least 5 minutes. 5. Spray the top of the chicken with cooking spray. Bake for 10 minutes, then increase the temperature to 350°F (177°C) and bake until an instant-read thermometer inserted into the thickest part of the breast reads 160°F (71°C) and the chicken is deep golden brown, 30 to 35 minutes. 6. Transfer the chicken breast to a cutting board, let rest for 10 minutes, then cut

the meat off the bone and cut into thick slices for serving.

Korean Flavor Glazed Chicken Wings

Prep time: 10 minutes | Cook time: 25 minutes | Serves 4

- Wings:
- 2 pounds (907 g) chicken wings
- 1 teaspoon salt
- 1 teaspoon ground black pepper
- Sauce:
- 2 tablespoons gochujang
- 1 tablespoon mayonnaise
- 1 tablespoon minced
- ginger
- 1 tablespoon minced garlic
- 1 teaspoon agave nectar
- 2 packets Splenda
- 1 tablespoon sesame oil
- For Garnish:
- 2 teaspoons sesame seeds
- ¼ cup chopped green onions

1. Preheat the air fryer to 400°F (204°C). Line a baking pan with aluminum foil, then arrange the rack on the pan. 2. On a clean work surface, rub the chicken wings with salt and ground black pepper, then arrange the seasoned wings on the rack. 3. Air fry for 20 minutes or until the wings are well browned. Flip the wings halfway through. You may need to work in batches to avoid overcrowding. 4. Meanwhile, combine the ingredients for the sauce in a small bowl. Stir to mix well. Reserve half of the sauce in a separate bowl until ready to serve. 5. Remove the air fried chicken wings from the air fryer and toss with remaining half of the sauce to coat well. 6. Place the wings back to the air fryer and air fry for 5 more minutes or until the internal temperature of the wings reaches at least 165°F (74°C). 7. Remove the wings from the air fryer and place on a large plate. Sprinkle with sesame seeds and green onions. Serve with reserved sauce.

Honey-Glazed Chicken Thighs

Prep time: 5 minutes | Cook time: 14 minutes | Serves 4

- Oil, for spraying
- 4 boneless, skinless chicken thighs, fat trimmed
- 3 tablespoons soy sauce
- 1 tablespoon balsamic vinegar
- 2 teaspoons honey
- 2 teaspoons minced garlic
- 1 teaspoon ground ginger

1. Preheat the air fryer to 400°F (204°C). Line the air fryer basket with parchment and spray lightly with oil. 2. Place the chicken in the prepared basket. 3. Cook for 7 minutes, flip, and cook for another 7 minutes, or until the internal temperature reaches 165°F (74°C) and the juices run clear. 4. In a small saucepan, combine the soy sauce, balsamic vinegar, honey, garlic, and ginger and cook over low heat for 1 to 2 minutes, until warmed through. 5. Transfer the chicken to a serving plate and drizzle with the sauce just before serving.

Mediterranean Stuffed Chicken Breasts

Prep time: 5 minutes | Cook time: 20 to 25 minutes | Serves 4

- 4 small boneless, skinless chicken breast halves (about 1½ pounds / 680 g)
- Salt and freshly ground black pepper, to taste
- 4 ounces (113 g) goat cheese
- 6 pitted Kalamata olives, coarsely chopped
- Zest of ½ lemon
- 1 teaspoon minced fresh rosemary or ½ teaspoon ground dried rosemary
- ½ cup almond meal
- ¼ cup balsamic vinegar
- 6 tablespoons unsalted butter

1. Preheat the air fryer to 360ºF (182ºC). 2. With a boning knife, cut a wide pocket into the thickest part of each chicken breast half, taking care not to cut all the way through. Season the chicken evenly on both sides with salt and freshly ground black pepper. 3. In a small bowl, mix the cheese, olives, lemon zest, and rosemary. Stuff the pockets with the cheese mixture and secure with toothpicks. 4. Place the almond meal in a shallow bowl and dredge the chicken, shaking off the excess. Coat lightly with olive oil spray. 5. Working in batches if necessary, arrange the chicken breasts in a single layer in the air fryer basket. Pausing halfway through the cooking time to flip the chicken, air fry for 20 to 25 minutes, until a thermometer inserted into the thickest part registers 165ºF (74ºC). 6. While the chicken is baking, prepare the sauce. In a small pan over medium heat, simmer the balsamic vinegar until thick and syrupy, about 5 minutes. Set aside until the chicken is done. When ready to serve, warm the sauce over medium heat and whisk in the butter, 1 tablespoon at a time, until melted and smooth. Season to taste with salt and pepper. 7. Serve the chicken breasts with the sauce drizzled on top.

Chicken Kiev

Prep time: 15 minutes | Cook time: 25 minutes | Serves 4

- 1 cup (2 sticks) unsalted butter, softened (or butter-flavored coconut oil for dairy-free)
- 2 tablespoons lemon juice
- 2 tablespoons plus 1 teaspoon chopped fresh parsley leaves, divided, plus more for garnish
- 2 tablespoons chopped fresh tarragon leaves
- 3 cloves garlic, minced
- 1 teaspoon fine sea salt, divided
- 4 (4-ounce / 113-g) boneless, skinless chicken breasts
- 2 large eggs
- 2 cups pork dust
- 1 teaspoon ground black pepper
- Sprig of fresh parsley, for garnish
- Lemon slices, for serving

1. Spray the air fryer basket with avocado oil. Preheat the air fryer to 350ºF (177ºC). 2. In a medium-sized bowl, combine the butter, lemon juice, 2 tablespoons of the parsley, the tarragon, garlic, and ¼ teaspoon of the salt. Cover and place in the fridge to harden for 7 minutes. 3. While the butter mixture chills, place one of the chicken breasts on a cutting board. With a sharp knife held parallel to the cutting board, make a 1-inch-wide incision at the top of the breast. Carefully cut into the breast to form a large pocket, leaving a ½-inch border along the sides and bottom. Repeat with the other 3 breasts. 4. Stuff one-quarter of the butter mixture into each chicken breast and secure the openings with toothpicks. 5. Beat the eggs in a small shallow dish. In another shallow dish, combine the pork dust, the remaining 1 teaspoon of parsley, the remaining ¾ teaspoon of salt, and the pepper. 6. One at a time, dip the chicken breasts in the egg, shake off the excess egg, and dredge the breasts in the pork dust mixture. Use your hands to press the pork dust onto each breast to form a nice crust. If you desire a thicker coating, dip it again in the egg and pork dust. As you finish, spray each coated chicken breast with avocado oil and place it in the air fryer basket. 7. Roast the chicken in the air fryer for 15 minutes, flip the breasts, and cook for another 10 minutes, or until the internal temperature of the chicken is 165ºF (74ºC) and the crust is golden brown. 8. Serve garnished with chopped fresh parsley and a parsley sprig, with lemon slices on the side. 9. Store leftovers in an airtight container in the refrigerator for up to 4 days or in the freezer for up to a month. Reheat in a preheated 350ºF (177ºC) air fryer for 5 minutes, or until heated through.

Buffalo Chicken Wings

Prep time: 10 minutes | Cook time: 20 to 25 minutes | Serves 4

- 2 tablespoons baking powder
- 1 teaspoon smoked paprika
- Sea salt and freshly ground black pepper, to taste
- 2 pounds (907 g) chicken wings or chicken drumettes
- Avocado oil spray
- ⅓ cup avocado oil
- ½ cup Buffalo hot sauce, such as Frank's RedHot
- ¼ cup (4 tablespoons) unsalted butter
- 2 tablespoons apple cider vinegar
- 1 teaspoon minced garlic

1. In a large bowl, stir together the baking powder, smoked paprika, and salt and pepper to taste. Add the chicken wings and toss to coat. 2. Set the air fryer to 400ºF (204ºC). Spray the wings with oil. 3. Place the wings in the basket in a single layer, working in batches, and air fry for 20 to 25 minutes. Check with an instant-read thermometer and remove when they reach 155ºF (68ºC). Let rest until they reach 165ºF (74ºC). 4. While the wings are cooking, whisk together the avocado oil, hot sauce, butter, vinegar, and garlic in a small saucepan over medium-low heat until warm. 5. When the wings are done cooking, toss them with the Buffalo sauce. Serve warm.

Thai-Style Cornish Game Hens

Prep time: 30 minutes | Cook time: 20 minutes | Serves 4

- 1 cup chopped fresh cilantro leaves and stems
- ¼ cup fish sauce
- 1 tablespoon soy sauce
- 1 serrano chile, seeded and chopped
- 8 garlic cloves, smashed
- 2 tablespoons sugar
- 2 tablespoons lemongrass paste
- 2 teaspoons black pepper
- 2 teaspoons ground coriander
- 1 teaspoon kosher salt
- 1 teaspoon ground turmeric
- 2 Cornish game hens, giblets removed, split in half lengthwise

1. In a blender, combine the cilantro, fish sauce, soy sauce, serrano, garlic, sugar, lemongrass, black pepper, coriander, salt, and turmeric. Blend until smooth. 2. Place the game hen halves in a large bowl. Pour the cilantro mixture over the hen halves and toss to coat. Marinate at room temperature for 30 minutes, or cover and refrigerate for up to 24 hours. 3. Arrange the hen halves in a single layer in the air fryer basket. Set the air fryer to 400°F (204°C) for 20 minutes. Use a meat thermometer to ensure the game hens have reached an internal temperature of 165°F (74°C).

Chicken and Broccoli Casserole

Prep time: 5 minutes | Cook time: 20 to 25 minutes | Serves 4

- ½ pound (227 g) broccoli, chopped into florets
- 2 cups shredded cooked chicken
- 4 ounces (113 g) cream cheese
- ⅓ cup heavy cream
- 1½ teaspoons Dijon
- mustard
- ½ teaspoon garlic powder
- Salt and freshly ground black pepper, to taste
- 2 tablespoons chopped fresh basil
- 1 cup shredded Cheddar cheese

1. Preheat the air fryer to 390°F (199°C). Lightly coat a casserole dish that will fit in air fryer, with olive oil and set aside. 2. Place the broccoli in a large glass bowl with 1 tablespoon of water and cover with a microwavable plate. Microwave on high for 2 to 3 minutes until the broccoli is bright green but not mushy. Drain if necessary and add to another large bowl along with the shredded chicken. 3. In the same glass bowl used to microwave the broccoli, combine the cream cheese and cream. Microwave for 30 seconds to 1 minute on high and stir until smooth. Add the mustard and garlic powder and season to taste with salt and freshly ground black pepper. Whisk until the sauce is smooth. 4. Pour the warm sauce over the broccoli and chicken mixture and then add the basil. Using a silicone spatula, gently fold the mixture until thoroughly combined. 5. Transfer the chicken mixture to the prepared casserole dish and top with the cheese. Air fry for 20 to 25 minutes

until warmed through and the cheese has browned.

Chicken Wellington

Prep time: 30 minutes | Cook time: 31 minutes | Serves 2

- 2 (5 ounces / 142 g) boneless, skinless chicken breasts
- ½ cup White Worcestershire sauce
- 3 tablespoons butter
- ½ cup finely diced onion (about ½ onion)
- 8 ounces (227 g) button mushrooms, finely chopped
- ¼ cup chicken stock
- 2 tablespoons White Worcestershire sauce (or white wine)
- Salt and freshly ground black pepper, to taste
- 1 tablespoon chopped fresh tarragon
- 2 sheets puff pastry, thawed
- 1 egg, beaten
- Vegetable oil

1. Place the chicken breasts in a shallow dish. Pour the White Worcestershire sauce over the chicken coating both sides and marinate for 30 minutes. 2. While the chicken is marinating, melt the butter in a large skillet over medium-high heat on the stovetop. Add the onion and sauté for a few minutes, until it starts to soften. Add the mushrooms and sauté for 3 to 5 minutes until the vegetables are brown and soft. Deglaze the skillet with the chicken stock, scraping up any bits from the bottom of the pan. Add the White Worcestershire sauce and simmer for 2 to 3 minutes until the mixture reduces and starts to thicken. Season with salt and freshly ground black pepper. Remove the mushroom mixture from the heat and stir in the fresh tarragon. Let the mushroom mixture cool. 3. Preheat the air fryer to 360°F (182°C). 4. Remove the chicken from the marinade and transfer it to the air fryer basket. Tuck the small end of the chicken breast under the thicker part to shape it into a circle rather than an oval. Pour the marinade over the chicken and air fry for 10 minutes. 5. Roll out the puff pastry and cut out two 6-inch squares. Brush the perimeter of each square with the egg wash. Place half of the mushroom mixture in the center of each puff pastry square. Place the chicken breasts, top side down on the mushroom mixture. Starting with one corner of puff pastry and working in one direction, pull the pastry up over the chicken to enclose it and press the ends of the pastry together in the middle. Brush the pastry with the egg wash to seal the edges. Turn the Wellingtons over and set aside. 6. Make a decorative design with the remaining puff pastry, cut out four 10-inch strips. For each Wellington, twist two of the strips together, place them over the chicken breast wrapped in puff pastry, and tuck the ends underneath to seal it. Brush the entire top and sides of the Wellingtons with the egg wash. 7. Preheat the air fryer to 350°F (177°C). 8. Spray or brush the air fryer basket with vegetable oil. Air fry the chicken Wellingtons for 13 minutes. Carefully turn the Wellingtons over. Air fry for another 8 minutes. Transfer to serving plates, light a candle and enjoy!

Chicken, Zucchini, and Spinach Salad

Prep time: 10 minutes | Cook time: 20 minutes | Serves 4

- 3 (5-ounce / 142-g) boneless, skinless chicken breasts, cut into 1-inch cubes
- 5 teaspoons extra-virgin olive oil
- ½ teaspoon dried thyme
- 1 medium red onion, sliced
- 1 red bell pepper, sliced
- 1 small zucchini, cut into strips
- 3 tablespoons freshly squeezed lemon juice
- 6 cups fresh baby spinach leaves

1. Insert the crisper plate into the basket and the basket into the unit. Preheat the unit by selecting AIR ROAST, setting the temperature to 375°F (191°C), and setting the time to 3 minutes. Select START/STOP to begin. 2. In a large bowl, combine the chicken, olive oil, and thyme. Toss to coat. Transfer to a medium metal bowl that fits into the basket. 3. Once the unit is preheated, place the bowl into the basket. 4. Select AIR ROAST, set the temperature to 375°F (191°C), and set the time to 20 minutes. Select START/STOP to begin. 5. After 8 minutes, add the red onion, red bell pepper, and zucchini to the bowl. Resume cooking. After about 6 minutes more, stir the chicken and vegetables. Resume cooking. 6. When the cooking is complete, a food thermometer inserted into the chicken should register at least 165°F (74°C). Remove the bowl from the unit and stir in the lemon juice. 7. Put the spinach in a serving bowl and top with the chicken mixture. Toss to combine and serve immediately.

Piri-Piri Chicken Thighs

Prep time: 5 minutes | Cook time: 25 minutes | Serves 4

- ¼ cup piri-piri sauce
- 1 tablespoon freshly squeezed lemon juice
- 2 tablespoons brown sugar, divided
- 2 cloves garlic, minced
- 1 tablespoon extra-virgin
- olive oil
- 4 bone-in, skin-on chicken thighs, each weighing approximately 7 to 8 ounces (198 to 227 g)
- ½ teaspoon cornstarch

1. To make the marinade, whisk together the piri-piri sauce, lemon juice, 1 tablespoon of brown sugar, and the garlic in a small bowl. While whisking, slowly pour in the oil in a steady stream and continue to whisk until emulsified. Using a skewer, poke holes in the chicken thighs and place them in a small glass dish. Pour the marinade over the chicken and turn the thighs to coat them with the sauce. Cover the dish and refrigerate for at least 15 minutes and up to 1 hour. 2. Preheat the air fryer to 375°F (191°C). Remove the chicken thighs from the dish, reserving the marinade, and place them skin-side down in the air fryer basket. Air fry until the internal temperature reaches 165°F (74°C), 15 to 20 minutes. 3. Meanwhile, whisk the remaining brown sugar and the cornstarch into the marinade and microwave it on high power for 1 minute until it is bubbling and thickened to a glaze. 4. Once the chicken is cooked, turn the thighs over and brush them with the glaze. Air fry for a few additional minutes until the glaze browns and begins to char in spots. 5. Remove the chicken to a platter and serve with additional piri-piri sauce, if desired.

Personal Cauliflower Pizzas

Prep time: 10 minutes | Cook time: 25 minutes | Serves 2

- 1 (12-ounce / 340-g) bag frozen riced cauliflower
- ⅓ cup shredded Mozzarella cheese
- ¼ cup almond flour
- ¼ grated Parmesan cheese
- 1 large egg
- ½ teaspoon salt
- 1 teaspoon garlic powder
- 1 teaspoon dried oregano
- 4 tablespoons no-sugar-added marinara sauce, divided
- 4 ounces (113 g) fresh Mozzarella, chopped, divided
- 1 cup cooked chicken breast, chopped, divided
- ½ cup chopped cherry tomatoes, divided
- ¼ cup fresh baby arugula, divided

1. Preheat the air fryer to 400°F (204°C). Cut 4 sheets of parchment paper to fit the basket of the air fryer. Brush with olive oil and set aside. 2. In a large glass bowl, microwave the cauliflower according to package directions. Place the cauliflower on a clean towel, draw up the sides, and squeeze tightly over a sink to remove the excess moisture. Return the cauliflower to the bowl and add the shredded Mozzarella along with the almond flour, Parmesan, egg, salt, garlic powder, and oregano. Stir until thoroughly combined. 3. Divide the dough into two equal portions. Place one piece of dough on the prepared parchment paper and pat gently into a thin, flat disk 7 to 8 inches in diameter. Air fry for 15 minutes until the crust begins to brown. Let cool for 5 minutes. 4. Transfer the parchment paper with the crust on top to a baking sheet. Place a second sheet of parchment paper over the crust. While holding the edges of both sheets together, carefully lift the crust off the baking sheet, flip it, and place it back in the air fryer basket. The new sheet of parchment paper is now on the bottom. Remove the top piece of paper and air fry the crust for another 15 minutes until the top begins to brown. Remove the basket from the air fryer. 5. Spread 2 tablespoons of the marinara sauce on top of the crust, followed by half the fresh Mozzarella, chicken, cherry tomatoes, and arugula. Air fry for 5 to 10 minutes longer, until the cheese is melted and beginning to brown. Remove the pizza from the oven and let it sit for 10 minutes before serving. Repeat with the remaining ingredients to make a second pizza.

Coconut Chicken Meatballs

Prep time: 10 minutes | Cook time: 14 minutes | Serves 4

- 1 pound (454 g) ground chicken
- 2 scallions, finely chopped
- 1 cup chopped fresh cilantro leaves
- ¼ cup unsweetened shredded coconut
- 1 tablespoon hoisin sauce
- 1 tablespoon soy sauce
- 2 teaspoons Sriracha or other hot sauce
- 1 teaspoon toasted sesame oil
- ½ teaspoon kosher salt
- 1 teaspoon black pepper

1. In a large bowl, gently mix the chicken, scallions, cilantro, coconut, hoisin, soy sauce, Sriracha, sesame oil, salt, and pepper until thoroughly combined (the mixture will be wet and sticky). 2. Place a sheet of parchment paper in the air fryer basket. Using a small scoop or teaspoon, drop rounds of the mixture in a single layer onto the parchment paper. 3. Set the air fryer to 350ºF (177ºC) for 10 minutes, turning the meatballs halfway through the cooking time. Raise the air fryer temperature to 400ºF (204ºC) and cook for 4 minutes more to brown the outsides of the meatballs. Use a meat thermometer to ensure the meatballs have reached an internal temperature of 165ºF (74ºC). 4. Transfer the meatballs to a serving platter. Repeat with any remaining chicken mixture.

Chicken Enchiladas

Prep time: 10 minutes | Cook time: 8 minutes | Serves 4

- Oil, for spraying
- 3 cups shredded cooked chicken
- 1 package taco seasoning
- 8 flour tortillas, at room temperature
- ½ cup canned black beans, rinsed and drained
- 1 (4-ounce / 113-g) can diced green chiles, drained
- 1 (10-ounce / 283-g) can red or green enchilada sauce
- 1 cup shredded Cheddar cheese

1. Line the air fryer basket with parchment and spray lightly with oil. (Do not skip the step of lining the basket; the parchment will keep the sauce and cheese from dripping through the holes.) 2. In a small bowl, mix together the chicken and taco seasoning. 3. Divide the mixture among the tortillas. Top with the black beans and green chiles. Carefully roll up each tortilla. 4. Place the enchiladas, seam-side down, in the prepared basket. You may need to work in batches, depending on the size of your air fryer. 5. Spoon the enchilada sauce over the enchiladas. Use just enough sauce to keep them from drying out. You can add more sauce when serving. Sprinkle the cheese on top. 6. Air fry at 360ºF (182ºC) for 5 to 8 minutes, or until heated through and the cheese is melted. 7. Place 2 enchiladas on each plate and top with more enchilada sauce, if desired.

Chicken and Vegetable Fajitas

Prep time: 15 minutes | Cook time: 23 minutes | Serves 6

- Chicken:
- 1 pound (454 g) boneless, skinless chicken thighs, cut crosswise into thirds
- 1 tablespoon vegetable oil
- 4½ teaspoons taco seasoning
- Vegetables:
- 1 cup sliced onion
- 1 cup sliced bell pepper
- 1 or 2 jalapeños,
- quartered lengthwise
- 1 tablespoon vegetable oil
- ½ teaspoon kosher salt
- ½ teaspoon ground cumin
- For Serving:
- Tortillas
- Sour cream
- Shredded cheese
- Guacamole
- Salsa

1. For the chicken: In a medium bowl, toss together the chicken, vegetable oil, and taco seasoning to coat. 2. For the vegetables: In a separate bowl, toss together the onion, bell pepper, jalapeño(s), vegetable oil, salt, and cumin to coat. 3. Place the chicken in the air fryer basket. Set the air fryer to 375ºF (191ºC) for 10 minutes. Add the vegetables to the basket, toss everything together to blend the seasonings, and set the air fryer for 13 minutes more. Use a meat thermometer to ensure the chicken has reached an internal temperature of 165ºF (74ºC). 4. Transfer the chicken and vegetables to a serving platter. Serve with tortillas and the desired fajita fixings.

Broccoli and Cheese Stuffed Chicken

Prep time: 15 minutes | Cook time: 20 minutes | Serves 4

- 2 ounces (57 g) cream cheese, softened
- 1 cup chopped fresh broccoli, steamed
- ½ cup shredded sharp Cheddar cheese
- 4 (6-ounce / 170-g) boneless, skinless
- chicken breasts
- 2 tablespoons mayonnaise
- ¼ teaspoon salt
- ¼ teaspoon garlic powder
- ⅛ teaspoon ground black pepper

1. In a medium bowl, combine cream cheese, broccoli, and Cheddar. Cut a 4-inch pocket into each chicken breast. Evenly divide mixture between chicken breasts; stuff the pocket of each chicken breast with the mixture. 2. Spread ¼ tablespoon mayonnaise per side of each chicken breast, then sprinkle both sides of breasts with salt, garlic powder, and pepper. 3. Place stuffed chicken breasts into ungreased air fryer basket so that the open seams face up. Adjust the temperature to 350ºF (177ºC) and air fry for 20 minutes, turning chicken halfway through cooking. When done, chicken will be golden and have an internal temperature of

at least 165°F (74°C). Serve warm.

Almond-Crusted Chicken

Prep time: 15 minutes | Cook time: 25 minutes | Serves 4

- ¼ cup slivered almonds
- 2 (6-ounce / 170-g) boneless, skinless chicken breasts
- 2 tablespoons full-fat mayonnaise
- 1 tablespoon Dijon mustard

1. Pulse the almonds in a food processor or chop until finely chopped. Place almonds evenly on a plate and set aside. 2. Completely slice each chicken breast in half lengthwise. 3. Mix the mayonnaise and mustard in a small bowl and then coat chicken with the mixture. 4. Lay each piece of chicken in the chopped almonds to fully coat. Carefully move the pieces into the air fryer basket. 5. Adjust the temperature to 350°F (177°C) and air fry for 25 minutes. 6. Chicken will be done when it has reached an internal temperature of 165°F (74°C) or more. Serve warm.

Thai Game Hens with Cucumber and Chile Salad

Prep time: 25 minutes | Cook time: 25 minutes | Serves 6

- 2 (1¼-pound / 567-g) Cornish game hens, giblets discarded
- 1 tablespoon fish sauce
- 6 tablespoons chopped fresh cilantro
- 2 teaspoons lime zest
- 1 teaspoon ground coriander
- 2 garlic cloves, minced
- 2 tablespoons packed light brown sugar
- 2 teaspoons vegetable oil
- Salt and ground black

- pepper, to taste
- 1 English cucumber, halved lengthwise and sliced thin
- 1 Thai chile, stemmed, deseeded, and minced
- 2 tablespoons chopped dry-roasted peanuts
- 1 small shallot, sliced thinly
- 1 tablespoon lime juice
- Lime wedges, for serving
- Cooking spray

1. Arrange a game hen on a clean work surface, remove the backbone with kitchen shears, then pound the hen breast to flat. Cut the breast in half. Repeat with the remaining game hen. 2. Loose the breast and thigh skin with your fingers, then pat the game hens dry and pierce about 10 holes into the fat deposits of the hens. Tuck the wings under the hens. 3. Combine 2 teaspoons of fish sauce, ¼ cup of cilantro, lime zest, coriander, garlic, 4 teaspoons of sugar, 1 teaspoon of vegetable oil, ½ teaspoon of salt, and ⅛ teaspoon of ground black pepper in a small bowl. Stir to mix well. 4. Rub the fish sauce mixture under the breast and thigh skin of the game hens, then let sit for 10 minutes to marinate. 5. Preheat the air fryer to 400°F (204°C). Spritz the air fryer

basket with cooking spray. 6. Arrange the marinated game hens in the preheated air fryer, skin side down. 7. Air fry for 15 minutes, then gently turn the game hens over and air fry for 10 more minutes or until the skin is golden brown and the internal temperature of the hens reads at least 165°F (74°C). 8. Meanwhile, combine all the remaining ingredients, except for the lime wedges, in a large bowl and sprinkle with salt and black pepper. Toss to mix well. 9. Transfer the fried hens on a large plate, then sit the salad aside and squeeze the lime wedges over before serving.

Greek Chicken Stir-Fry

Prep time: 15 minutes | Cook time: 15 minutes | Serves 2

- 1 (6-ounce / 170-g) chicken breast, cut into 1-inch cubes
- ½ medium zucchini, chopped
- ½ medium red bell pepper, seeded and

- chopped
- ¼ medium red onion, peeled and sliced
- 1 tablespoon coconut oil
- 1 teaspoon dried oregano
- ½ teaspoon garlic powder
- ¼ teaspoon dried thyme

1. Place all ingredients into a large mixing bowl and toss until the coconut oil coats the meat and vegetables. Pour the contents of the bowl into the air fryer basket. 2. Adjust the temperature to 375°F (191°C) and air fry for 15 minutes. 3. Shake the basket halfway through the cooking time to redistribute the food. Serve immediately.

Wild Rice and Kale Stuffed Chicken Thighs

Prep time: 10 minutes | Cook time: 22 minutes | Serves 4

- 4 boneless, skinless chicken thighs
- 1 cup cooked wild rice
- ½ cup chopped kale
- 2 garlic cloves, minced
- 1 teaspoon salt
- Juice of 1 lemon
- ½ cup crumbled feta
- Olive oil cooking spray
- 1 tablespoon olive oil

1. Preheat the air fryer to 380°F (193°C). 2. Place the chicken thighs between two pieces of plastic wrap, and using a meat mallet or a rolling pin, pound them out to about ¼-inch thick. 3. In a medium bowl, combine the rice, kale, garlic, salt, and lemon juice and mix well. 4. Place a quarter of the rice mixture into the middle of each chicken thigh, then sprinkle 2 tablespoons of feta over the filling. 5. Spray the air fryer basket with olive oil cooking spray. 6. Fold the sides of the chicken thigh over the filling, and then gently place each of them seam-side down into the air fryer basket. Brush each stuffed chicken thigh with olive oil. 7. Roast the stuffed chicken thighs for 12 minutes, then turn them over and cook for an additional 10 minutes, or until the internal temperature reaches 165°F (74°C).

Chicken with Pineapple and Peach

Prep time: 10 minutes | Cook time: 14 to 15 minutes | Serves 4

- 1 pound (454 g) low-sodium boneless, skinless chicken breasts, cut into 1-inch pieces
- 1 medium red onion, chopped
- 1 (8-ounce / 227-g) can pineapple chunks, drained, ¼ cup juice reserved
- 1 tablespoon peanut oil or safflower oil
- 1 peach, peeled, pitted, and cubed
- 1 tablespoon cornstarch
- ½ teaspoon ground ginger
- ¼ teaspoon ground allspice
- Brown rice, cooked (optional)

1. Preheat the air fryer to 380ºF (193ºC). 2. In a medium metal bowl, mix the chicken, red onion, pineapple, and peanut oil. Bake in the air fryer for 9 minutes. Remove and stir. 3. Add the peach and return the bowl to the air fryer. Bake for 3 minutes more. Remove and stir again. 4. In a small bowl, whisk the reserved pineapple juice, the cornstarch, ginger, and allspice well. Add to the chicken mixture and stir to combine. 5. Bake for 2 to 3 minutes more, or until the chicken reaches an internal temperature of 165ºF (74ºC) on a meat thermometer and the sauce is slightly thickened. 6. Serve immediately over hot cooked brown rice, if desired.

Bacon-Wrapped Stuffed Chicken Breasts

Prep time: 15 minutes | Cook time: 30 minutes | Serves 4

- ½ cup chopped frozen spinach, thawed and squeezed dry
- ¼ cup cream cheese, softened
- ¼ cup grated Parmesan cheese
- 1 jalapeño, seeded and chopped
- ½ teaspoon kosher salt
- 1 teaspoon black pepper
- 2 large boneless, skinless chicken breasts, butterflied and pounded to ½-inch thickness
- 4 teaspoons salt-free Cajun seasoning
- 6 slices bacon

1. In a small bowl, combine the spinach, cream cheese, Parmesan cheese, jalapeño, salt, and pepper. Stir until well combined. 2. Place the butterflied chicken breasts on a flat surface. Spread the cream cheese mixture evenly across each piece of chicken. Starting with the narrow end, roll up each chicken breast, ensuring the filling stays inside. Season chicken with the Cajun seasoning, patting it in to ensure it sticks to the meat. 3. Wrap each breast in 3 slices of bacon. Place in the air fryer basket. Set the air fryer to 350ºF (177ºC) for 30 minutes. Use a meat thermometer to ensure the chicken has reached an internal temperature of 165ºF (74ºC). 4. Let the chicken stand 5 minutes before slicing each rolled-up breast in half to serve.

Stuffed Chicken Florentine

Prep time: 10 minutes | Cook time: 20 minutes | Serves 4

- 3 tablespoons pine nuts
- ¾ cup frozen spinach, thawed and squeezed dry
- ⅓ cup ricotta cheese
- 2 tablespoons grated Parmesan cheese
- 3 cloves garlic, minced
- Salt and freshly ground black pepper, to taste
- 4 small boneless, skinless chicken breast halves (about 1½ pounds / 680 g)
- 8 slices bacon

1. Place the pine nuts in a small pan and set in the air fryer basket. Set the air fryer to 400ºF (204ºC) and air fry for 2 to 3 minutes until toasted. Remove the pine nuts to a mixing bowl and continue preheating the air fryer. 2. In a large bowl, combine the spinach, ricotta, Parmesan, and garlic. Season to taste with salt and pepper and stir well until thoroughly combined. 3. Using a sharp knife, cut into the chicken breasts, slicing them across and opening them up like a book, but be careful not to cut them all the way through. Sprinkle the chicken with salt and pepper. 4. Spoon equal amounts of the spinach mixture into the chicken, then fold the top of the chicken breast back over the top of the stuffing. Wrap each chicken breast with 2 slices of bacon. 5. Working in batches if necessary, air fry the chicken for 18 to 20 minutes until the bacon is crisp and a thermometer inserted into the thickest part of the chicken registers 165ºF (74ºC).

Sweet and Spicy Turkey Meatballs

Prep time: 15 minutes | Cook time: 15 minutes | Serves 6

- Olive oil
- 1 pound (454 g) lean ground turkey
- ½ cup whole-wheat panko bread crumbs
- 1 egg, beaten
- 1 tablespoon soy sauce
- ¼ cup plus 1 tablespoon hoisin sauce, divided
- 2 teaspoons minced garlic
- ⅛ teaspoon salt
- ⅛ teaspoon freshly ground black pepper
- 1 teaspoon Sriracha

1. Spray the air fryer basket lightly with olive oil. 2. In a large bowl, mix together the turkey, panko bread crumbs, egg, soy sauce, 1 tablespoon of hoisin sauce, garlic, salt, and black pepper. 3. Using a tablespoon, form 24 meatballs. 4. In a small bowl, combine the remaining ¼ cup of hoisin sauce and Sriracha to make a glaze and set aside. 5. Place the meatballs in the air fryer basket in a single layer. You may need to cook them in batches. 6. Air fry at 350ºF (177ºC) for 8 minutes. Brush the meatballs generously with the glaze and cook until cooked through, an additional 4 to 7 minutes.

Tex-Mex Chicken Breasts

Prep time: 10 minutes | Cook time: 17 to 20 minutes | Serves 4

- 1 pound (454 g) low-sodium boneless, skinless chicken breasts, cut into 1-inch cubes
- 1 medium onion, chopped
- 1 red bell pepper, chopped
- 1 jalapeño pepper,
- minced
- 2 teaspoons olive oil
- ⅔ cup canned low-sodium black beans, rinsed and drained
- ½ cup low-sodium salsa
- 2 teaspoons chili powder

1. Preheat the air fryer to 400°F (204°C). 2. In a medium metal bowl, mix the chicken, onion, bell pepper, jalapeño, and olive oil. Roast for 10 minutes, stirring once during cooking. 3. Add the black beans, salsa, and chili powder. Roast for 7 to 10 minutes more, stirring once, until the chicken reaches an internal temperature of 165°F (74°C) on a meat thermometer. Serve immediately.

Cracked-Pepper Chicken Wings

Prep time: 15 minutes | Cook time: 20 minutes | Serves 4

- 1 pound (454 g) chicken wings
- 3 tablespoons vegetable oil
- ½ cup all-purpose flour
- ½ teaspoon smoked
- paprika
- ½ teaspoon garlic powder
- ½ teaspoon kosher salt
- 1½ teaspoons freshly cracked black pepper

1. Place the chicken wings in a large bowl. Drizzle the vegetable oil over wings and toss to coat. 2. In a separate bowl, whisk together the flour, paprika, garlic powder, salt, and pepper until combined. 3. Dredge the wings in the flour mixture one at a time, coating them well, and place in the air fryer basket. Set the air fryer to 400°F (204°C) for 20 minutes, turning the wings halfway through the cooking time, until the breading is browned and crunchy.

Cilantro Lime Chicken Thighs

Prep time: 15 minutes | Cook time: 22 minutes | Serves 4

- 4 bone-in, skin-on chicken thighs
- 1 teaspoon baking powder
- ½ teaspoon garlic powder
- 2 teaspoons chili powder
- 1 teaspoon cumin
- 2 medium limes
- ¼ cup chopped fresh cilantro

1. Pat chicken thighs dry and sprinkle with baking powder. 2. In a small bowl, mix garlic powder, chili powder, and cumin and sprinkle evenly over thighs, gently rubbing on and under chicken skin. 3. Cut one lime in half and squeeze juice over thighs. Place chicken into the air fryer basket. 4.

Adjust the temperature to 380°F (193°C) and roast for 22 minutes. 5. Cut other lime into four wedges for serving and garnish cooked chicken with wedges and cilantro.

Chicken Shawarma

Prep time: 30 minutes | Cook time: 15 minutes | Serves 4

- Shawarma Spice:
- 2 teaspoons dried oregano
- 1 teaspoon ground cinnamon
- 1 teaspoon ground cumin
- 1 teaspoon ground coriander
- 1 teaspoon kosher salt
- ½ teaspoon ground allspice
- ½ teaspoon cayenne
- pepper
- Chicken:
- 1 pound (454 g) boneless, skinless chicken thighs, cut into large bite-size chunks
- 2 tablespoons vegetable oil
- For Serving:
- Tzatziki
- Pita bread

1. For the shawarma spice: In a small bowl, combine the oregano, cayenne, cumin, coriander, salt, cinnamon, and allspice. 2. For the chicken: In a large bowl, toss together the chicken, vegetable oil, and shawarma spice to coat. Marinate at room temperature for 30 minutes or cover and refrigerate for up to 24 hours. 3. Place the chicken in the air fryer basket. Set the air fryer to 350°F (177°C) for 15 minutes, or until the chicken reaches an internal temperature of 165°F (74°C). 4. Transfer the chicken to a serving platter. Serve with tzatziki and pita bread.

Air Fried Chicken Wings with Buffalo Sauce

Prep time: 10 minutes | Cook time: 20 minutes | Serves 6

- 16 chicken drumettes (party wings)
- Chicken seasoning or rub, to taste
- 1 teaspoon garlic powder
- Ground black pepper, to taste
- ¼ cup buffalo wings sauce
- Cooking spray

1. Preheat the air fryer to 400°F (204°C). Spritz the air fryer basket with cooking spray. 2. Rub the chicken wings with chicken seasoning, garlic powder, and ground black pepper on a clean work surface. 3. Arrange the chicken wings in the preheated air fryer. Spritz with cooking spray. Air fry for 10 minutes or until lightly browned. Shake the basket halfway through. 4. Transfer the chicken wings in a large bowl, then pour in the buffalo wings sauce and toss to coat well. 5. Put the wings back to the air fryer and cook for an additional 7 minutes. 6. Serve immediately.

Butter and Bacon Chicken

Prep time: 10 minutes | Cook time: 65 minutes | Serves 6

- 1 (4-pound / 1.8-kg) whole chicken
- 2 tablespoons salted butter, softened
- 1 teaspoon dried thyme
- ½ teaspoon garlic powder
- 1 teaspoon salt
- ½ teaspoon ground black pepper
- 6 slices sugar-free bacon

1. Pat chicken dry with a paper towel, then rub with butter on all sides. Sprinkle thyme, garlic powder, salt, and pepper over chicken. 2. Place chicken into ungreased air fryer basket, breast side up. Lay strips of bacon over chicken and secure with toothpicks. 3. Adjust the temperature to 350°F (177°C) and air fry for 65 minutes. Halfway through cooking, remove and set aside bacon and flip chicken over. Chicken will be done when the skin is golden and crispy and the internal temperature is at least 165°F (74°C). Serve warm with bacon.

Chapter 6

Fish and Seafood

Mackerel with Spinach

Prep time: 15 minutes | Cook time: 20 minutes | Serves 5

- 1 pound (454 g) mackerel, trimmed
- 1 bell pepper, chopped
- ½ cup spinach, chopped
- 1 tablespoon avocado oil
- 1 teaspoon ground black pepper
- 1 teaspoon keto tomato paste

1. In the mixing bowl, mix bell pepper with spinach, ground black pepper, and tomato paste. 2. Fill the mackerel with spinach mixture. 3. Then brush the fish with avocado oil and put it in the air fryer. 4. Cook the fish at 365ºF (185ºC) for 20 minutes.

Crab Cakes

Prep time: 10 minutes | Cook time: 10 minutes | Serves 4

- 2 (6 ounces / 170 g) cans lump crab meat
- ¼ cup blanched finely ground almond flour
- 1 large egg
- 2 tablespoons full-fat mayonnaise
- ½ teaspoon Dijon mustard
- ½ tablespoon lemon juice
- ½ medium green bell pepper, seeded and chopped
- ¼ cup chopped green onion
- ½ teaspoon Old Bay seasoning

1. In a large bowl, combine all ingredients. Form into four balls and flatten into patties. Place patties into the air fryer basket. 2. Adjust the temperature to 350ºF (177ºC) and air fry for 10 minutes. 3. Flip patties halfway through the cooking time. Serve warm.

Thai Shrimp Skewers with Peanut Dipping Sauce

Prep time: 15 minutes | Cook time: 6 minutes | Serves 2

- Salt and pepper, to taste
- 12 ounces (340 g) extra-large shrimp, peeled and deveined
- 1 tablespoon vegetable oil
- 1 teaspoon honey
- ½ teaspoon grated lime zest plus 1 tablespoon juice, plus lime wedges
- for serving
- 6 (6-inch) wooden skewers
- 3 tablespoons creamy peanut butter
- 3 tablespoons hot tap water
- 1 tablespoon chopped fresh cilantro
- 1 teaspoon fish sauce

1. Preheat the air fryer to 400ºF (204ºC). 2. Dissolve 2 tablespoons salt in 1 quart cold water in a large container. Add shrimp, cover, and refrigerate for 15 minutes. 3.

Remove shrimp from brine and pat dry with paper towels. Whisk oil, honey, lime zest, and ¼ teaspoon pepper together in a large bowl. Add shrimp and toss to coat. Thread shrimp onto skewers, leaving about ¼ inch between each shrimp (3 or 4 shrimp per skewer). 4. Arrange 3 skewers in air fryer basket, parallel to each other and spaced evenly apart. Arrange remaining 3 skewers on top, perpendicular to the bottom layer. Air fry until shrimp are opaque throughout, 6 to 8 minutes, flipping and rotating skewers halfway through cooking. 5. Whisk peanut butter, hot tap water, lime juice, cilantro, and fish sauce together in a bowl until smooth. Serve skewers with peanut dipping sauce and lime wedges.

Chili Prawns

Prep time: 10 minutes | Cook time: 8 minutes | Serves 2

- 8 prawns, cleaned
- Salt and black pepper, to taste
- ½ teaspoon ground cayenne pepper
- ½ teaspoon garlic powder
- ½ teaspoon ground cumin
- ½ teaspoon red chili flakes
- Cooking spray

1. Preheat the air fryer to 340ºF (171ºC). Spritz the air fryer basket with cooking spray. 2. Toss the remaining ingredients in a large bowl until the prawns are well coated. 3. Spread the coated prawns evenly in the basket and spray them with cooking spray. 4. Air fry for 8 minutes, flipping the prawns halfway through, or until the prawns are pink. 5. Remove the prawns from the basket to a plate.

Maple Balsamic Glazed Salmon

Prep time: 5 minutes | Cook time: 10 minutes | Serves 4

- 4 (6-ounce / 170-g) fillets of salmon
- Salt and freshly ground black pepper, to taste
- Vegetable oil
- ¼ cup pure maple syrup
- 3 tablespoons balsamic vinegar
- 1 teaspoon Dijon mustard

1. Preheat the air fryer to 400ºF (204ºC). 2. Season the salmon well with salt and freshly ground black pepper. Spray or brush the bottom of the air fryer basket with vegetable oil and place the salmon fillets inside. Air fry the salmon for 5 minutes. 3. While the salmon is air frying, combine the maple syrup, balsamic vinegar and Dijon mustard in a small saucepan over medium heat and stir to blend well. Let the mixture simmer while the fish is cooking. It should start to thicken slightly, but keep your eye on it so it doesn't burn. 4. Brush the glaze on the salmon fillets and air fry for an additional 5 minutes. The salmon should feel firm to the touch when finished and the glaze should be nicely browned on top. Brush a little more glaze on top before removing and serving with rice and vegetables, or a nice green salad.

Trout Amandine with Lemon Butter Sauce

Prep time: 20 minutes | Cook time:8 minutes | Serves 4

- Trout Amandine:
- ⅔ cup toasted almonds
- ⅓ cup grated Parmesan cheese
- 1 teaspoon salt
- ½ teaspoon freshly ground black pepper
- 2 tablespoons butter, melted
- 4 (4-ounce / 113-g) trout fillets, or salmon fillets
- Cooking spray

- Lemon Butter Sauce:
- 8 tablespoons (1 stick) butter, melted
- 2 tablespoons freshly squeezed lemon juice
- ½ teaspoon Worcestershire sauce
- ½ teaspoon salt
- ½ teaspoon freshly ground black pepper
- ¼ teaspoon hot sauce

1. In a blender or food processor, pulse the almonds for 5 to 10 seconds until finely processed. Transfer to a shallow bowl and whisk in the Parmesan cheese, salt, and pepper. Place the melted butter in another shallow bowl. 2. One at a time, dip the fish in the melted butter, then the almond mixture, coating thoroughly. 3. Preheat the air fryer to 300ºF (149ºC). Line the air fryer basket with parchment paper. 4. Place the coated fish on the parchment and spritz with oil. 5. Bake for 4 minutes. Flip the fish, spritz it with oil, and bake for 4 minutes more until the fish flakes easily with a fork. 6. In a small bowl, whisk the butter, lemon juice, Worcestershire sauce, salt, pepper, and hot sauce until blended. 7. Serve with the fish.

Salmon Burgers with Creamy Broccoli Slaw

Prep time: 15 minutes | Cook time: 10 minutes | Serves 4

- For the salmon burgers
- 1 pound (454 g) salmon fillets, bones and skin removed
- 1 egg
- ¼ cup fresh dill, chopped
- 1 cup whole wheat bread crumbs
- ½ teaspoon salt
- ½ teaspoon cayenne pepper
- 2 garlic cloves, minced

- 4 whole wheat buns
- For the broccoli slaw
- 3 cups chopped or shredded broccoli
- ½ cup shredded carrots
- ¼ cup sunflower seeds
- 2 garlic cloves, minced
- ½ teaspoon salt
- 2 tablespoons apple cider vinegar
- 1 cup nonfat plain Greek yogurt

Make the salmon burgers 1. Preheat the air fryer to 360ºF(182ºC). 2. In a food processor, pulse the salmon fillets until they are finely chopped. 3. In a large bowl, combine the chopped salmon, egg, dill, bread crumbs, salt, cayenne, and garlic until it comes together. 4. Form the salmon into 4 patties. Place them into the air fryer basket, making sure that they don't touch each other. 5. Bake for 5 minutes. Flip the salmon patties and bake for 5 minutes more. Make the broccoli slaw 6. In a large bowl, combine all of the ingredients for the broccoli slaw. Mix well. 7. Serve the salmon burgers on toasted whole wheat buns, and top with a generous portion of broccoli slaw.

Panko Crab Sticks with Mayo Sauce

Prep time: 5 minutes | Cook time: 12 minutes | Serves 4

- Crab Sticks:
- 2 eggs
- 1 cup flour
- ⅓ cup panko bread crumbs
- 1 tablespoon old bay seasoning

- 1 pound (454 g) crab sticks
- Cooking spray
- Mayo Sauce:
- ½ cup mayonnaise
- 1 lime, juiced
- 2 garlic cloves, minced

1. Preheat air fryer to 390ºF (199ºC). 2. In a bowl, beat the eggs. In a shallow bowl, place the flour. In another shallow bowl, thoroughly combine the panko bread crumbs and old bay seasoning. 3. Dredge the crab sticks in the flour, shaking off any excess, then in the beaten eggs, finally press them in the bread crumb mixture to coat well. 4. Arrange the crab sticks in the air fryer basket and spray with cooking spray. 5. Air fry for 12 minutes until golden brown. Flip the crab sticks halfway through the cooking time. 6. Meanwhile, make the sauce by whisking together the mayo, lime juice, and garlic in a small bowl. 7. Serve the crab sticks with the mayo sauce on the side.

Cilantro Lime Baked Salmon

Prep time: 10 minutes | Cook time: 12 minutes | Serves 2

- 2 (3-ounce / 85-g) salmon fillets, skin removed
- 1 tablespoon salted butter, melted
- 1 teaspoon chili powder
- ½ teaspoon finely minced

- garlic
- ¼ cup sliced pickled jalapeños
- ½ medium lime, juiced
- 2 tablespoons chopped cilantro

1. Place salmon fillets into a round baking pan. Brush each with butter and sprinkle with chili powder and garlic. 2. Place jalapeño slices on top and around salmon. Pour half of the lime juice over the salmon and cover with foil. Place pan into the air fryer basket. 3. Adjust the temperature to 370ºF (188ºC) and bake for 12 minutes. 4. When fully cooked, salmon should flake easily with a fork and reach an internal temperature of at least 145ºF (63ºC). 5. To serve, spritz with remaining lime juice and garnish with cilantro.

Shrimp Scampi

Prep time: 8 minutes | Cook time: 8 minutes | Serves 4

- 4 tablespoons (½ stick) salted butter or ghee
- 1 tablespoon fresh lemon juice
- 1 tablespoon minced garlic
- 2 teaspoons red pepper flakes
- 1 pound (454 g) shrimp (21 to 25 count), peeled
- and deveined
- 2 tablespoons chicken broth or dry white wine
- 2 tablespoons chopped fresh basil, plus more for sprinkling, or 1 teaspoon dried
- 1 tablespoon chopped fresh chives, or 1 teaspoon dried

1. Place a baking pan in the air fryer basket. Set the air fryer to 325°F (163°C) for 8 minutes (this will preheat the pan so the butter will melt faster). 2. Carefully remove the pan from the fryer and add the butter, lemon juice, garlic, and red pepper flakes. Place the pan back in the fryer. 3. Cook for 2 minutes, stirring once, until the butter has melted. (Do not skip this step; this is what infuses the butter with garlic flavor, which is what makes it all taste so good.) 4. Carefully remove the pan from the fryer and add the shrimp, broth, basil, and chives. Stir gently until the ingredients are well combined. 5. Return the pan to the air fryer and cook for 5 minutes, stirring once. 6. Thoroughly stir the shrimp mixture and let it rest for 1 minute on a wire rack. (This is so the shrimp cooks in the residual heat rather than getting overcooked and rubbery.) 7. Stir once more, sprinkle with additional chopped fresh basil, and serve.

Garlic Shrimp

Prep time: 15 minutes | Cook time: 10 minutes | Serves 3

- Shrimp:
- Oil, for spraying
- 1 pound (454 g) medium raw shrimp, peeled and deveined
- 6 tablespoons unsalted butter, melted
- 1 cup panko bread crumbs
- 2 tablespoons granulated
- garlic
- 1 teaspoon salt
- ½ teaspoon freshly ground black pepper
- Garlic Butter Sauce:
- ½ cup unsalted butter
- 2 teaspoons granulated garlic
- ¾ teaspoon salt (omit if using salted butter)

Make the Shrimp 1. Preheat the air fryer to 400°F (204°C). Line the air fryer basket with parchment and spray lightly with oil. 2. Place the shrimp and melted butter in a zip-top plastic bag, seal, and shake well, until evenly coated. 3. In a medium bowl, mix together the bread crumbs, garlic, salt, and black pepper. 4. Add the shrimp to the panko mixture and toss until evenly coated. Shake off any excess coating. 5. Place the shrimp in the prepared basket and spray lightly with oil. 6. Cook for 8 to 10 minutes, flipping and spraying with oil after 4 to 5 minutes, until golden brown and crispy. Make the Garlic Butter Sauce 7. In a microwave-safe bowl, combine the butter, garlic, and salt and microwave on 50% power for 30 to 60 seconds, stirring every 15 seconds, until completely melted. 8. Serve the shrimp immediately with the garlic butter sauce on the side for dipping.

Roasted Fish with Almond-Lemon Crumbs

Prep time: 10 minutes | Cook time: 7 to 8 minutes | Serves 4

- ½ cup raw whole almonds
- 1 scallion, finely chopped
- Grated zest and juice of 1 lemon
- ½ tablespoon extra-virgin olive oil
- ¾ teaspoon kosher salt,
- divided
- Freshly ground black pepper, to taste
- 4 (6 ounces / 170 g each) skinless fish fillets
- Cooking spray
- 1 teaspoon Dijon mustard

1. In a food processor, pulse the almonds to coarsely chop. Transfer to a small bowl and add the scallion, lemon zest, and olive oil. Season with ¼ teaspoon of the salt and pepper to taste and mix to combine. 2. Spray the top of the fish with oil and squeeze the lemon juice over the fish. Season with the remaining ½ teaspoon salt and pepper to taste. Spread the mustard on top of the fish. Dividing evenly, press the almond mixture onto the top of the fillets to adhere. 3. Preheat the air fryer to 375°F (191°C). 4. Working in batches, place the fillets in the air fryer basket in a single layer. Air fry for 7 to 8 minutes, until the crumbs start to brown and the fish is cooked through. 5. Serve immediately.

Catfish Bites

Prep time: 15 minutes | Cook time: 20 minutes | Serves 4

- Oil, for spraying
- 1 pound (454 g) catfish fillets, cut into 2-inch pieces
- 1 cup buttermilk
- ½ cup cornmeal
- ¼ cup all-purpose flour
- 2 teaspoons Creole seasoning
- ½ cup yellow mustard

1. Line the air fryer basket with parchment and spray lightly with oil. 2. Place the catfish pieces and buttermilk in a zip-top plastic bag, seal, and refrigerate for about 10 minutes. 3. In a shallow bowl, mix together the cornmeal, flour, and Creole seasoning. 4. Remove the catfish from the bag and pat dry with a paper towel. 5. Spread the mustard on all sides of the catfish, then dip them in the cornmeal mixture until evenly coated. 6. Place the catfish in the prepared basket. You may need to work in batches, depending on the size of your air fryer. Spray lightly with oil. 7. Air fry at 400°F (204°C) for 10 minutes, flip carefully, spray with oil, and cook for another 10 minutes. Serve immediately.

Pesto Shrimp with Wild Rice Pilaf

Prep time: 5 minutes | Cook time: 5 minutes | Serves 4

- 1 pound (454 g) medium shrimp, peeled and deveined
- ¼ cup pesto sauce
- 1 lemon, sliced
- 2 cups cooked wild rice pilaf

1. Preheat the air fryer to 360°F(182°C). 2. In a medium bowl, toss the shrimp with the pesto sauce until well coated. 3. Place the shrimp in a single layer in the air fryer basket. Put the lemon slices over the shrimp and roast for 5 minutes. 4. Remove the lemons and discard. Serve a quarter of the shrimp over ½ cup wild rice with some favorite steamed vegetables.

Parmesan-Crusted Hake with Garlic Sauce

Prep time: 5 minutes | Cook time: 10 minutes | Serves 3

- Fish:
- 6 tablespoons mayonnaise
- 1 tablespoon fresh lime juice
- 1 teaspoon Dijon mustard
- 1 cup grated Parmesan cheese
- Salt, to taste
- ¼ teaspoon ground black

- pepper, or more to taste
- 3 hake fillets, patted dry
- Nonstick cooking spray
- Garlic Sauce:
- ¼ cup plain Greek yogurt
- 2 tablespoons olive oil
- 2 cloves garlic, minced
- ½ teaspoon minced tarragon leaves

1. Preheat the air fryer to 395°F (202°C). 2. Mix the mayo, lime juice, and mustard in a shallow bowl and whisk to combine. In another shallow bowl, stir together the grated Parmesan cheese, salt, and pepper. 3. Dredge each fillet in the mayo mixture, then roll them in the cheese mixture until they are evenly coated on both sides. 4. Spray the air fryer basket with nonstick cooking spray. Arrange the fillets in the basket and air fry for 10 minutes, or until the fish flakes easily with a fork. Flip the fillets halfway through the cooking time. 5. Meanwhile, in a small bowl, whisk all the ingredients for the sauce until well incorporated. 6. Serve the fish warm alongside the sauce.

Calamari with Hot Sauce

Prep time: 10 minutes | Cook time: 6 minutes | Serves 2

- 10 ounces (283 g) calamari, trimmed
- 2 tablespoons keto hot

- sauce
- 1 tablespoon avocado oil

1. Slice the calamari and sprinkle with avocado oil. 2. Put the calamari in the air fryer and cook at 400°F (204°C) for 3 minutes per side. 3. Then transfer the calamari in the serving plate and sprinkle with hot sauce.

Fish Cakes

Prep time: 30 minutes | Cook time: 10 to 12 minutes | Serves 4

- ¾ cup mashed potatoes (about 1 large russet potato)
- 12 ounces (340 g) cod or other white fish
- Salt and pepper, to taste
- Oil for misting or cooking spray
- 1 large egg
- ¼ cup potato starch
- ½ cup panko bread crumbs
- 1 tablespoon fresh chopped chives
- 2 tablespoons minced onion

1. Peel potatoes, cut into cubes, and cook on stovetop till soft. 2. Salt and pepper raw fish to taste. Mist with oil or cooking spray, and air fry at 360°F (182°C) for 6 to 8 minutes, until fish flakes easily. If fish is crowded, rearrange halfway through cooking to ensure all pieces cook evenly. 3. Transfer fish to a plate and break apart to cool. 4. Beat egg in a shallow dish. 5. Place potato starch in another shallow dish, and panko crumbs in a third dish. 6. When potatoes are done, drain in colander and rinse with cold water. 7. In a large bowl, mash the potatoes and stir in the chives and onion. Add salt and pepper to taste, then stir in the fish. 8. If needed, stir in a tablespoon of the beaten egg to help bind the mixture. 9. Shape into 8 small, fat patties. Dust lightly with potato starch, dip in egg, and roll in panko crumbs. Spray both sides with oil or cooking spray. 10. Air fry at 360°F (182°C) for 10 to 12 minutes, until golden brown and crispy.

Paprika Crab Burgers

Prep time: 30 minutes | Cook time: 14 minutes | Serves 3

- 2 eggs, beaten
- 1 shallot, chopped
- 2 garlic cloves, crushed
- 1 tablespoon olive oil
- 1 teaspoon yellow mustard
- 1 teaspoon fresh cilantro, chopped
- 10 ounces (283 g) crab meat
- 1 teaspoon smoked paprika
- ½ teaspoon ground black pepper
- Sea salt, to taste
- ¾ cup Parmesan cheese

1. In a mixing bowl, thoroughly combine the eggs, shallot, garlic, olive oil, mustard, cilantro, crab meat, paprika, black pepper, and salt. Mix until well combined. 2. Shape the mixture into 6 patties. Roll the crab patties over grated Parmesan cheese, coating well on all sides. Place in your refrigerator for 2 hours. 3. Spritz the crab patties with cooking oil on both sides. Cook in the preheated air fryer at 360°F (182°C) for 14 minutes. Serve on dinner rolls if desired. Bon appétit!

Golden Shrimp

Prep time: 20 minutes | Cook time: 7 minutes | Serves 4

- 2 egg whites
- ½ cup coconut flour
- 1 cup Parmigiano-Reggiano, grated
- ½ teaspoon celery seeds
- ½ teaspoon porcini powder
- ½ teaspoon onion powder
- 1 teaspoon garlic powder
- ½ teaspoon dried rosemary
- ½ teaspoon sea salt
- ½ teaspoon ground black pepper
- 1½ pounds (680 g) shrimp, deveined

1. Whisk the egg with coconut flour and Parmigiano-Reggiano. Add in seasonings and mix to combine well. 2. Dip your shrimp in the batter. Roll until they are covered on all sides. 3. Cook in the preheated air fryer at 390°F (199°C) for 5 to 7 minutes or until golden brown. Work in batches. Serve with lemon wedges if desired.

Chili Tilapia

Prep time: 5 minutes | Cook time: 20 minutes | Serves 4

- 4 tilapia fillets, boneless
- 1 teaspoon chili flakes
- 1 teaspoon dried oregano
- 1 tablespoon avocado oil
- 1 teaspoon mustard

1. Rub the tilapia fillets with chili flakes, dried oregano, avocado oil, and mustard and put in the air fryer. 2. Cook it for 10 minutes per side at 360°F (182°C).

Tuna Steak

Prep time: 10 minutes | Cook time: 12 minutes | Serves 4

- 1 pound (454 g) tuna steaks, boneless and cubed
- 1 tablespoon mustard
- 1 tablespoon avocado oil
- 1 tablespoon apple cider vinegar

1. Mix avocado oil with mustard and apple cider vinegar. 2. Then brush tuna steaks with mustard mixture and put in the air fryer basket. 3. Cook the fish at 360°F (182°C) for 6 minutes per side.

Roasted Salmon Fillets

Prep time: 5 minutes | Cook time: 10 minutes | Serves 2

- 2 (8-ounce / 227 -g) skin-on salmon fillets, 1½ inches thick
- 1 teaspoon vegetable oil
- Salt and pepper, to taste
- Vegetable oil spray

1. Preheat the air fryer to 400°F (204°C). 2. Make foil sling for air fryer basket by folding 1 long sheet of aluminum foil so it is 4 inches wide. Lay sheet of foil widthwise across basket, pressing foil into and up sides of basket. Fold excess foil as needed so that edges of foil are flush with top of basket. Lightly spray foil and basket with vegetable oil spray. 3. Pat salmon dry with paper towels, rub with oil, and season with salt and pepper. Arrange fillets skin side down on sling in prepared basket, spaced evenly apart. Air fry salmon until center is still translucent when checked with the tip of a paring knife and registers 125°F (52°C) (for medium-rare), 10 to 14 minutes, using sling to rotate fillets halfway through cooking. 4. Using the sling, carefully remove salmon from air fryer. Slide fish spatula along underside of fillets and transfer to individual serving plates, leaving skin behind. Serve.

White Fish with Cauliflower

Prep time: 30 minutes | Cook time: 13 minutes | Serves 4

- ½ pound (227 g) cauliflower florets
- ½ teaspoon English mustard
- 2 tablespoons butter, room temperature
- ½ tablespoon cilantro, minced
- 2 tablespoons sour cream
- 2½ cups cooked white fish
- Salt and freshly cracked black pepper, to taste

1. Boil the cauliflower until tender. Then, purée the cauliflower in your blender. Transfer to a mixing dish. 2. Now, stir in the fish, cilantro, salt, and black pepper. 3. Add the sour cream, English mustard, and butter; mix until everything's well incorporated. Using your hands, shape into patties. 4. Place in the refrigerator for about 2 hours. Cook for 13 minutes at 395°F (202°C). Serve with some extra English mustard.

Crispy Fish Sticks

Prep time: 15 minutes | Cook time: 10 minutes | Serves 4

- 1 ounce (28 g) pork rinds, finely ground
- ¼ cup blanched finely ground almond flour
- ½ teaspoon Old Bay seasoning
- 1 tablespoon coconut oil
- 1 large egg
- 1 pound (454 g) cod fillet, cut into ¾-inch strips

1. Place ground pork rinds, almond flour, Old Bay seasoning, and coconut oil into a large bowl and mix together. In a medium bowl, whisk egg. 2. Dip each fish stick into the egg and then gently press into the flour mixture, coating as fully and evenly as possible. Place fish sticks into the air fryer basket. 3. Adjust the temperature to 400°F (204°C) and air fry for 10 minutes or until golden. 4. Serve immediately.

Shrimp with Smoky Tomato Dressing

Prep time: 5 minutes | Cook time: 8 minutes | Serves 2

- 3 tablespoons mayonnaise
- 1 tablespoon ketchup
- 1 tablespoon minced garlic
- 1 teaspoon Sriracha
- ½ teaspoon smoked paprika
- ½ teaspoon kosher salt
- 1 pound (454 g) large raw shrimp (21 to 25 count), peeled (tails left on) and deveined
- Vegetable oil spray
- ½ cup chopped scallions

1. In a large bowl, combine the mayonnaise, ketchup, garlic, Sriracha, paprika, and salt. Add the shrimp and toss to coat with the sauce. 2. Spray the air fryer basket with vegetable oil spray. Place the shrimp in the basket. Set the air fryer to 350°F (177°C) for 8 minutes, tossing and spraying the shrimp with vegetable oil spray halfway through the cooking time. 3. Sprinkle with the chopped scallions before serving.

Fish Taco Bowl

Prep time: 10 minutes | Cook time: 12 minutes | Serves 4

- ½ teaspoon salt
- ¼ teaspoon garlic powder
- ¼ teaspoon ground cumin
- 4 (4-ounce / 113-g) cod fillets
- 4 cups finely shredded
- green cabbage
- ⅓ cup mayonnaise
- ¼ teaspoon ground black pepper
- ¼ cup chopped pickled jalapeños

1. Sprinkle salt, garlic powder, and cumin over cod and place into ungreased air fryer basket. Adjust the temperature to 350°F (177°C) and air fry for 12 minutes, turning fillets halfway through cooking. Cod will flake easily and have an internal temperature of at least 145°F (63°C) when done. 2. In a large bowl, toss cabbage with mayonnaise, pepper, and jalapeños until fully coated. Serve cod warm over cabbage slaw on four medium plates.

Blackened Salmon

Prep time: 10 minutes | Cook time: 8 minutes | Serves 2

- 10 ounces (283 g) salmon fillet
- ½ teaspoon ground coriander
- 1 teaspoon ground cumin
- 1 teaspoon dried basil
- 1 tablespoon avocado oil

1. In the shallow bowl, mix ground coriander, ground cumin, and dried basil. 2. Then coat the salmon fillet in the spices and sprinkle with avocado oil. 3. Put the fish in the air fryer basket and cook at 395°F (202°C) for 4 minutes per side.

Cheesy Tuna Patties

Prep time: 5 minutes | Cook time: 17 to 18 minutes | Serves 4

- Tuna Patties:
- 1 pound (454 g) canned tuna, drained
- 1 egg, whisked
- 2 tablespoons shallots, minced
- 1 garlic clove, minced
- 1 cup grated Romano cheese
- Sea salt and ground black pepper, to taste
- 1 tablespoon sesame oil
- Cheese Sauce:
- 1 tablespoon butter
- 1 cup beer
- 2 tablespoons grated Colby cheese

1. Mix together the canned tuna, whisked egg, shallots, garlic, cheese, salt, and pepper in a large bowl and stir to incorporate. 2. Divide the tuna mixture into four equal portions and form each portion into a patty with your hands. Refrigerate the patties for 2 hours. 3. When ready, brush both sides of each patty with sesame oil. 4. Preheat the air fryer to 360°F (182°C). 5. Place the patties in the air fryer basket and bake for 14 minutes, flipping the patties halfway through, or until lightly browned and cooked through. 6. Meanwhile, melt the butter in a pan over medium heat. 7. Pour in the beer and whisk constantly, or until it begins to bubble. 8. Add the grated Colby cheese and mix well. Continue cooking for 3 to 4 minutes, or until the cheese melts. Remove the patties from the basket to a plate. Drizzle them with the cheese sauce and serve immediately.

Cajun Catfish Cakes with Cheese

Prep time: 5 minutes | Cook time: 35 minutes | Serves 4

- 2 catfish fillets
- 3 ounces (85 g) butter
- 1 cup shredded Parmesan cheese
- 1 cup shredded Swiss cheese
- ½ cup buttermilk
- 1 teaspoon baking powder
- 1 teaspoon baking soda
- 1 teaspoon Cajun seasoning

1. Bring a pot of salted water to a boil. Add the catfish fillets to the boiling water and let them boil for 5 minutes until they become opaque. 2. Remove the fillets from the pot to a mixing bowl and flake them into small pieces with a fork. 3. Add the remaining ingredients to the bowl of fish and stir until well incorporated. 4. Divide the fish mixture into 12 equal portions and shape each portion into a patty. 5. Preheat the air fryer to 380°F (193°C). 6. Arrange the patties in the air fryer basket and air fry in batches for 15 minutes until golden brown and cooked through. Flip the patties halfway through the cooking time. 7. Let the patties sit for 5 minutes and serve.

Fried Shrimp

Prep time: 15 minutes | Cook time: 5 minutes | Serves 4

- ½ cup self-rising flour
- 1 teaspoon paprika
- 1 teaspoon salt
- ½ teaspoon freshly ground black pepper
- 1 large egg, beaten
- 1 cup finely crushed panko bread crumbs
- 20 frozen large shrimp (about 1-pound / 907-g), peeled and deveined
- Cooking spray

1. In a shallow bowl, whisk the flour, paprika, salt, and pepper until blended. Add the beaten egg to a second shallow bowl and the bread crumbs to a third. 2. One at a time, dip the shrimp into the flour, the egg, and the bread crumbs, coating thoroughly. 3. Preheat the air fryer to 400°F (204°C). Line the air fryer basket with parchment paper. 4. Place the shrimp on the parchment and spritz with oil. 5. Air fry for 2 minutes. Shake the basket, spritz the shrimp with oil, and air fry for 3 minutes more until lightly browned and crispy. Serve hot.

Sweet Tilapia Fillets

Prep time: 5 minutes | Cook time: 14 minutes | Serves 4

- 2 tablespoons erythritol
- 1 tablespoon apple cider vinegar
- 4 tilapia fillets, boneless
- 1 teaspoon olive oil

1. Mix apple cider vinegar with olive oil and erythritol. 2. Then rub the tilapia fillets with the sweet mixture and put in the air fryer basket in one layer. 3. Cook the fish at 360°F (182°C) for 7 minutes per side.

Tuna Nuggets in Hoisin Sauce

Prep time: 15 minutes | Cook time: 5 to 7 minutes | Serves 4

- ½ cup hoisin sauce
- 2 tablespoons rice wine vinegar
- 2 teaspoons sesame oil
- 1 teaspoon garlic powder
- 2 teaspoons dried lemongrass
- ¼ teaspoon red pepper flakes
- ½ small onion, quartered and thinly sliced
- 8 ounces (227 g) fresh tuna, cut into 1-inch cubes
- Cooking spray
- 3 cups cooked jasmine rice

1. Mix the hoisin sauce, vinegar, sesame oil, and seasonings together. 2. Stir in the onions and tuna nuggets. 3. Spray a baking pan with nonstick spray and pour in tuna mixture. 4. Roast at 390°F (199°C) for 3 minutes. Stir gently. 5. Cook 2 minutes and stir again, checking for doneness. Tuna should be barely cooked through, just beginning to flake and still very moist. If necessary, continue cooking and stirring

in 1-minute intervals until done. 6. Serve warm over hot jasmine rice.

Smoky Shrimp and Chorizo Tapas

Prep time: 15 minutes | Cook time: 10 minutes | Serves 2 to 4

- 4 ounces (113 g) Spanish (cured) chorizo, halved horizontally and sliced crosswise
- ½ pound (227 g) raw medium shrimp, peeled and deveined
- 1 tablespoon extra-virgin olive oil
- 1 small shallot, halved and thinly sliced
- 1 garlic clove, minced
- 1 tablespoon finely chopped fresh oregano
- ½ teaspoon smoked Spanish paprika
- ¼ teaspoon kosher salt
- ¼ teaspoon black pepper
- 3 tablespoons fresh orange juice
- 1 tablespoon minced fresh parsley

1. Place the chorizo in a baking pan. Set the pan in the air fryer basket. Set the air fryer to 375°F (191°C) for 5 minutes, or until the chorizo has started to brown and render its fat. 2. Meanwhile, in a large bowl, combine the shrimp, olive oil, shallot, garlic, oregano, paprika, salt, and pepper. Toss until the shrimp is well coated. 3. Transfer the shrimp to the pan with the chorizo. Stir to combine. Place the pan in the air fryer basket. Cook for 10 minutes, stirring halfway through the cooking time. 4. Transfer the shrimp and chorizo to a serving dish. Drizzle with the orange juice and toss to combine. Sprinkle with the parsley.

Garlicky Cod Fillets

Prep time: 10 minutes | Cook time: 10 to 12 minutes | Serves 4

- 1 teaspoon olive oil
- 4 cod fillets
- ¼ teaspoon fine sea salt
- ¼ teaspoon ground black pepper, or more to taste
- 1 teaspoon cayenne pepper
- ½ cup fresh Italian parsley, coarsely chopped
- ½ cup nondairy milk
- 1 Italian pepper, chopped
- 4 garlic cloves, minced
- 1 teaspoon dried basil
- ½ teaspoon dried oregano

1. Lightly coat the sides and bottom of a baking dish with the olive oil. Set aside. 2. In a large bowl, sprinkle the fillets with salt, black pepper, and cayenne pepper. 3. In a food processor, pulse the remaining ingredients until smoothly puréed. 4. Add the purée to the bowl of fillets and toss to coat, then transfer to the prepared baking dish. 5. Preheat the air fryer to 380°F (193°C). 6. Put the baking dish in the air fryer basket and bake for 10 to 12 minutes, or until the fish flakes when pressed lightly with a fork. 7. Remove from the basket and serve warm.

Fish Tacos with Jalapeño-Lime Sauce

Prep time: 25 minutes | Cook time: 7 to 10 minutes | Serves 4

- Fish Tacos:
- 1 pound (454 g) fish fillets
- ¼ teaspoon cumin
- ¼ teaspoon coriander
- ⅛ teaspoon ground red pepper
- 1 tablespoon lime zest
- ¼ teaspoon smoked paprika
- 1 teaspoon oil
- Cooking spray
- 6 to 8 corn or flour tortillas (6-inch size)
- Jalapeño-Lime Sauce:
- ½ cup sour cream
- 1 tablespoon lime juice
- ¼ teaspoon grated lime zest
- ½ teaspoon minced jalapeño (flesh only)
- ¼ teaspoon cumin
- Napa Cabbage Garnish:
- 1 cup shredded Napa cabbage
- ¼ cup slivered red or green bell pepper
- ¼ cup slivered onion

1. Slice the fish fillets into strips approximately ½-inch thick. 2. Put the strips into a sealable plastic bag along with the cumin, coriander, red pepper, lime zest, smoked paprika, and oil. Massage seasonings into the fish until evenly distributed. 3. Spray the air fryer basket with nonstick cooking spray and place seasoned fish inside. 4. Air fry at 390ºF (199ºC) for approximately 5 minutes. Shake basket to distribute fish. Cook an additional 2 to 5 minutes, until fish flakes easily. 5. While the fish is cooking, prepare the Jalapeño-Lime Sauce by mixing the sour cream, lime juice, lime zest, jalapeño, and cumin together to make a smooth sauce. Set aside. 6. Mix the cabbage, bell pepper, and onion together and set aside. 7. To warm refrigerated tortillas, wrap in damp paper towels and microwave for 30 to 60 seconds. 8. To serve, spoon some of fish into a warm tortilla. Add one or two tablespoons Napa Cabbage Garnish and drizzle with Jalapeño-Lime Sauce.

Blackened Fish

Prep time: 15 minutes | Cook time: 8 minutes | Serves 4

- 1 large egg, beaten
- Blackened seasoning, as needed
- 2 tablespoons light brown
- sugar
- 4 (4-ounce / 113- g) tilapia fillets
- Cooking spray

1. In a shallow bowl, place the beaten egg. In a second shallow bowl, stir together the Blackened seasoning and the brown sugar. 2. One at a time, dip the fish fillets in the egg, then the brown sugar mixture, coating thoroughly. 3. Preheat the air fryer to 300ºF (149ºC). Line the air fryer basket with parchment paper. 4. Place the coated fish on the parchment and spritz with oil. 5. Bake for 4 minutes. Flip the fish, spritz it with oil, and bake for 4 to 6 minutes more

until the fish is white inside and flakes easily with a fork. 6. Serve immediately.

Parmesan Mackerel with Coriander

Prep time: 10 minutes | Cook time: 7 minutes | Serves 2

- 12 ounces (340 g) mackerel fillet
- 2 ounces (57 g) Parmesan, grated
- 1 teaspoon ground coriander
- 1 tablespoon olive oil

1. Sprinkle the mackerel fillet with olive oil and put it in the air fryer basket. 2. Top the fish with ground coriander and Parmesan. 3. Cook the fish at 390ºF (199ºC) for 7 minutes.

Mouthwatering Cod over Creamy Leek Noodles

Prep time: 10 minutes | Cook time: 24 minutes | Serves 4

- 1 small leek, sliced into long thin noodles (about 2 cups)
- ½ cup heavy cream
- 2 cloves garlic, minced
- 1 teaspoon fine sea salt, divided
- 4 (4-ounce / 113-g) cod fillets (about 1 inch thick)
- ½ teaspoon ground black pepper
- Coating:
- ¼ cup grated Parmesan cheese
- 2 tablespoons mayonnaise
- 2 tablespoons unsalted butter, softened
- 1 tablespoon chopped fresh thyme, or ½ teaspoon dried thyme leaves, plus more for garnish

1. Preheat the air fryer to 350ºF (177ºC). 2. Place the leek noodles in a casserole dish or a pan that will fit in your air fryer. 3. In a small bowl, stir together the cream, garlic, and ½ teaspoon of the salt. Pour the mixture over the leeks and cook in the air fryer for 10 minutes, or until the leeks are very tender. 4. Pat the fish dry and season with the remaining ½ teaspoon of salt and the pepper. When the leeks are ready, open the air fryer and place the fish fillets on top of the leeks. Air fry for 8 to 10 minutes, until the fish flakes easily with a fork (the thicker the fillets, the longer this will take). 5. While the fish cooks, make the coating: In a small bowl, combine the Parmesan, mayo, butter, and thyme. 6. When the fish is ready, remove it from the air fryer and increase the heat to 425ºF (218ºC) (or as high as your air fryer can go). Spread the fillets with a ½-inch-thick to ¾-inch-thick layer of the coating. 7. Place the fish back in the air fryer and air fry for 3 to 4 minutes, until the coating browns. 8. Garnish with fresh or dried thyme, if desired. Store leftovers in an airtight container in the refrigerator for up to 3 days. Reheat in a casserole dish in a preheated 350ºF (177ºC) air fryer for 6 minutes, or until heated through.

Country Shrimp

Prep time: 10 minutes | Cook time: 15 to 20 minutes | Serves 4

- 1 pound (454 g) large shrimp, deveined, with tails on
- 1 pound (454 g) smoked turkey sausage, cut into thick slices
- 2 corn cobs, quartered
- 1 zucchini, cut into bite-sized pieces
- 1 red bell pepper, cut into chunks
- 1 tablespoon Old Bay seasoning
- 2 tablespoons olive oil
- Cooking spray

1. Preheat the air fryer to 400ºF (204ºC). Spray the air fryer basket lightly with cooking spray. 2. In a large bowl, mix the shrimp, turkey sausage, corn, zucchini, bell pepper, and Old Bay seasoning, and toss to coat with the spices. Add the olive oil and toss again until evenly coated. 3. Spread the mixture in the air fryer basket in a single layer. You will need to cook in batches. 4. Air fry for 15 to 20 minutes, or until cooked through, shaking the basket every 5 minutes for even cooking. 5. Serve immediately.

Miso Salmon

Prep time: 10 minutes | Cook time: 12 minutes | Serves 2

- 2 tablespoons brown sugar
- 2 tablespoons soy sauce
- 2 tablespoons white miso paste
- 1 teaspoon minced garlic
- 1 teaspoon minced fresh ginger
- ½ teaspoon freshly cracked black pepper
- 2 (5-ounce / 142-g) salmon fillets
- Vegetable oil spray
- 1 teaspoon sesame seeds
- 2 scallions, thinly sliced, for garnish

1. In a small bowl, whisk together the brown sugar, soy sauce, miso, garlic, ginger, and pepper to combine. 2. Place the salmon fillets on a plate. Pour half the sauce over the fillets; turn the fillets to coat the other sides with sauce. 3. Spray the air fryer basket with vegetable oil spray. Place the sauce-covered salmon in the basket. Set the air fryer to 400ºF (204ºC) for 12 minutes. Halfway through the cooking time, brush additional miso sauce on the salmon. 4. Sprinkle the salmon with the sesame seeds and scallions and serve.

Chapter 7

Snacks and Appetizers

Corn Dog Muffins

Prep time: 10 minutes | Cook time: 8 to 10 minutes per batch | Makes 8 muffins

- 1¼ cups sliced kosher hotdogs (3 or 4, depending on size)
- ½ cup flour
- ½ cup yellow cornmeal
- 2 teaspoons baking powder
- ½ cup skim milk
- 1 egg
- 2 tablespoons canola oil
- 8 foil muffin cups, paper liners removed
- Cooking spray
- Mustard or your favorite dipping sauce

1. Slice each hotdog in half lengthwise, then cut in ¼-inch half-moon slices. Set aside. 2. Preheat the air fryer to 390°F (199°C). 3. In a large bowl, stir together flour, cornmeal, and baking powder. 4. In a small bowl, beat together the milk, egg, and oil until just blended. 5. Pour egg mixture into dry ingredients and stir with a spoon to mix well. 6. Stir in sliced hot dogs. 7. Spray the foil cups lightly with cooking spray. 8. Divide mixture evenly into muffin cups. 9. Place 4 muffin cups in the air fryer basket and cook for 5 minutes. 10. Reduce temperature to 360°F (182°C) and cook 3 to 5 minutes or until toothpick inserted in center of muffin comes out clean. 11. Repeat steps 9 and 10 to bake remaining corn dog muffins. 12. Serve with mustard or other sauces for dipping.

Vegetable Pot Stickers

Prep time: 12 minutes | Cook time: 11 to 18 minutes | Makes 12 pot stickers

- 1 cup shredded red cabbage
- ¼ cup chopped button mushrooms
- ¼ cup grated carrot
- 2 tablespoons minced onion
- 2 garlic cloves, minced
- 2 teaspoons grated fresh ginger
- 12 gyoza/pot sticker wrappers
- 2½ teaspoons olive oil, divided

1. In a baking pan, combine the red cabbage, mushrooms, carrot, onion, garlic, and ginger. Add 1 tablespoon of water. Place in the air fryer and air fry at 370°F (188°C) for 3 to 6 minutes, until the vegetables are crisp-tender. Drain and set aside. 2. Working one at a time, place the pot sticker wrappers on a work surface. Top each wrapper with a scant 1 tablespoon of the filling. Fold half of the wrapper over the other half to form a half circle. Dab one edge with water and press both edges together. 3. To another pan, add 1¼ teaspoons of olive oil. Put half of the pot stickers, seam-side up, in the pan. Air fry for 5 minutes, or until the bottoms are light golden brown. Add 1 tablespoon of water and return the pan to the air fryer. 4. Air fry for 4 to 6 minutes more, or until hot. Repeat with the remaining pot stickers, remaining 1¼ teaspoons of oil, and another tablespoon of water. Serve immediately.

Hush Puppies

Prep time: 45 minutes | Cook time: 10 minutes | Serves 12

- 1 cup self-rising yellow cornmeal
- ½ cup all-purpose flour
- 1 teaspoon sugar
- 1 teaspoon salt
- 1 teaspoon freshly ground black pepper
- 1 large egg
- ⅓ cup canned creamed corn
- 1 cup minced onion
- 2 teaspoons minced jalapeño pepper
- 2 tablespoons olive oil, divided

1. Thoroughly combine the cornmeal, flour, sugar, salt, and pepper in a large bowl. 2. Whisk together the egg and corn in a small bowl. Pour the egg mixture into the bowl of cornmeal mixture and stir to combine. Stir in the minced onion and jalapeño. Cover the bowl with plastic wrap and place in the refrigerator for 30 minutes. 3. Preheat the air fryer to 375°F (191°C). Line the air fryer basket with parchment paper and lightly brush it with 1 tablespoon of olive oil. 4. Scoop out the cornmeal mixture and form into 24 balls, about 1 inch. 5. Arrange the balls in the parchment paper-lined basket, leaving space between each ball. 6. Air fry in batches for 5 minutes. Shake the basket and brush the balls with the remaining 1 tablespoon of olive oil. Continue cooking for 5 minutes until golden brown. 7. Remove the balls (hush puppies) from the basket and serve on a plate.

Onion Pakoras

Prep time: 30 minutes | Cook time: 10 minutes per batch | Serves 2

- 2 medium yellow or white onions, sliced (2 cups)
- ½ cup chopped fresh cilantro
- 2 tablespoons vegetable oil
- 1 tablespoon chickpea flour
- 1 tablespoon rice flour, or
- 2 tablespoons chickpea flour
- 1 teaspoon ground turmeric
- 1 teaspoon cumin seeds
- 1 teaspoon kosher salt
- ½ teaspoon cayenne pepper
- Vegetable oil spray

1. In a large bowl, combine the onions, cilantro, oil, chickpea flour, rice flour, turmeric, cumin seeds, salt, and cayenne. Stir to combine. Cover and let stand for 30 minutes or up to overnight. (This allows the onions to release moisture, creating a batter.) Mix well before using. 2. Spray the air fryer basket generously with vegetable oil spray. Drop half of the batter in 6 heaping tablespoons into the basket. Set the air fryer to 350°F (177°C) for 8 minutes. Carefully turn the pakoras over and spray with oil spray. Set the air fryer for 2 minutes, or until the batter is cooked through and crisp. 3. Repeat with remaining batter to make 6 more pakoras, checking at 6 minutes for doneness. Serve hot.

Taco-Spiced Chickpeas

Prep time: 5 minutes | Cook time: 17 minutes | Serves 3

- Oil, for spraying
- 1 (15½-ounce / 439-g) can chickpeas, drained
- 1 teaspoon chili powder
- ½ teaspoon ground cumin
- ½ teaspoon salt
- ½ teaspoon granulated garlic
- 2 teaspoons lime juice

1. Line the air fryer basket with parchment and spray lightly with oil. Place the chickpeas in the prepared basket. 2. Air fry at 390°F (199°C) for 17 minutes, shaking or stirring the chickpeas and spraying lightly with oil every 5 to 7 minutes. 3. In a small bowl, mix together the chili powder, cumin, salt, and garlic. 4. When 2 to 3 minutes of cooking time remain, sprinkle half of the seasoning mix over the chickpeas. Finish cooking. 5. Transfer the chickpeas to a medium bowl and toss with the remaining seasoning mix and the lime juice. Serve immediately.

Mushroom Tarts

Prep time: 15 minutes | Cook time: 38 minutes | Makes 15 tarts

- 2 tablespoons extra-virgin olive oil, divided
- 1 small white onion, sliced
- 8 ounces (227 g) shiitake mushrooms, sliced
- ¼ teaspoon sea salt
- ¼ teaspoon freshly ground black pepper
- ¼ cup dry white wine
- 1 sheet frozen puff pastry, thawed
- 1 cup shredded Gruyère cheese
- Cooking oil spray
- 1 tablespoon thinly sliced fresh chives

1. Insert the crisper plate into the basket and the basket into the unit. Preheat the unit by selecting BAKE, setting the temperature to 300°F (149°C), and setting the time to 3 minutes. Select START/STOP to begin. 2. In a heatproof bowl that fits into the basket, stir together 1 tablespoon of olive oil, the onion, and the mushrooms. 3. Once the unit is preheated, place the bowl into the basket. 4. Select BAKE, set the temperature to 300°F (149°C), and set the time to 7 minutes. Select START/STOP to begin. 5. After about 2½ minutes, stir the vegetables. Resume cooking. After another 2½ minutes, the vegetables should be browned and tender. Season with the salt and pepper and add the wine. Resume cooking until the liquid evaporates, about 2 minutes. 6. When the cooking is complete, place the bowl on a heatproof surface. 7. Increase the air fryer temperature to 390°F (199°C) and set the time to 3 minutes. Select START/STOP to begin. 8. Unfold the puff pastry and cut it into 15 (3-by-3-inch) squares. Using a fork, pierce the dough and brush both sides with the remaining 1 tablespoon of olive oil. 9. Evenly distribute half the cheese among the puff pastry squares, leaving a ½-inch border around the edges. Divide the mushroom-onion mixture among the pastry squares and top with the remaining cheese. 10. Once the unit is preheated, spray the crisper plate with cooking oil. Working in batches, place 5 tarts into the basket; do not stack or overlap. 11. Select BAKE, set the temperature to 390°F (199°C), and set the time to 8 minutes. Select START/STOP to begin. 12. After 6 minutes, check the tarts; if not yet golden brown, resume cooking for about 2 minutes more. 13. When the cooking is complete, remove the tarts and transfer to a wire rack to cool. Repeat steps 10, 11, and 12 with the remaining tarts. 14. Serve garnished with the chives.

Garlic-Roasted Tomatoes and Olives

Prep time: 5 minutes | Cook time: 20 minutes | Serves 6

- 2 cups cherry tomatoes
- 4 garlic cloves, roughly chopped
- ½ red onion, roughly chopped
- 1 cup black olives
- 1 cup green olives
- 1 tablespoon fresh basil, minced
- 1 tablespoon fresh oregano, minced
- 2 tablespoons olive oil
- ¼ to ½ teaspoon salt

1. Preheat the air fryer to 380°F(193°C). 2. In a large bowl, combine all of the ingredients and toss together so that the tomatoes and olives are coated well with the olive oil and herbs. 3. Pour the mixture into the air fryer basket, and roast for 10 minutes. Stir the mixture well, then continue roasting for an additional 10 minutes. 4. Remove from the air fryer, transfer to a serving bowl, and enjoy.

Peppery Chicken Meatballs

Prep time: 5 minutes | Cook time: 13 to 20 minutes | Makes 16 meatballs

- 2 teaspoons olive oil
- ¼ cup minced onion
- ¼ cup minced red bell pepper
- 2 vanilla wafers, crushed
- 1 egg white
- ½ teaspoon dried thyme
- ½ pound (227 g) ground chicken breast

1. Preheat the air fryer to 370°F (188°C). 2. In a baking pan, mix the olive oil, onion, and red bell pepper. Put the pan in the air fryer. Air fry for 3 to 5 minutes, or until the vegetables are tender. 3. In a medium bowl, mix the cooked vegetables, crushed wafers, egg white, and thyme until well combined 4. Mix in the chicken, gently but thoroughly, until everything is combined. 5. Form the mixture into 16 meatballs and place them in the air fryer basket. Air fry for 10 to 15 minutes, or until the meatballs reach an internal temperature of 165°F (74°C) on a meat thermometer. 6. Serve immediately.

Baked Spanakopita Dip

Prep time: 10 minutes | Cook time: 15 minutes | Serves 2

- Olive oil cooking spray
- 3 tablespoons olive oil, divided
- 2 tablespoons minced white onion
- 2 garlic cloves, minced
- 4 cups fresh spinach
- 4 ounces (113 g) cream cheese, softened
- 4 ounces (113 g) feta
- cheese, divided
- Zest of 1 lemon
- ¼ teaspoon ground nutmeg
- 1 teaspoon dried dill
- ½ teaspoon salt
- Pita chips, carrot sticks, or sliced bread for serving (optional)

1. Preheat the air fryer to 360°F(182°C). Coat the inside of a 6-inch ramekin or baking dish with olive oil cooking spray. 2. In a large skillet over medium heat, heat 1 tablespoon of the olive oil. Add the onion, then cook for 1 minute. 3. Add in the garlic and cook, stirring for 1 minute more. 4. Reduce the heat to low and mix in the spinach and water. Let this cook for 2 to 3 minutes, or until the spinach has wilted. Remove the skillet from the heat. 5. In a medium bowl, combine the cream cheese, 2 ounces (57 g) of the feta, and the remaining 2 tablespoons of olive oil, along with the lemon zest, nutmeg, dill, and salt. Mix until just combined. 6. Add the vegetables to the cheese base and stir until combined. 7. Pour the dip mixture into the prepared ramekin and top with the remaining 2 ounces (57 g) of feta cheese. 8. Place the dip into the air fryer basket and cook for 10 minutes, or until heated through and bubbling. 9. Serve with pita chips, carrot sticks, or sliced bread.

Beef and Mango Skewers

Prep time: 10 minutes | Cook time: 4 to 7 minutes | Serves 4

- ¾ pound (340 g) beef sirloin tip, cut into 1-inch cubes
- 2 tablespoons balsamic vinegar
- 1 tablespoon olive oil
- 1 tablespoon honey
- ½ teaspoon dried marjoram
- Pinch of salt
- Freshly ground black pepper, to taste
- 1 mango

1. Preheat the air fryer to 390°F (199°C). 2. Put the beef cubes in a medium bowl and add the balsamic vinegar, olive oil, honey, marjoram, salt, and pepper. Mix well, then massage the marinade into the beef with your hands. Set aside. 3. To prepare the mango, stand it on end and cut the skin off, using a sharp knife. Then carefully cut around the oval pit to remove the flesh. Cut the mango into 1-inch cubes. 4. Thread metal skewers alternating with three beef cubes and two mango cubes. 5. Roast the skewers in the air fryer basket for 4 to 7 minutes, or until the beef is browned and at least 145°F (63°C). 6. Serve hot.

Air Fried Pot Stickers

Prep time: 10 minutes | Cook time: 18 to 20 minutes | Makes 30 pot stickers

- ½ cup finely chopped cabbage
- ¼ cup finely chopped red bell pepper
- 2 green onions, finely chopped
- 1 egg, beaten
- 2 tablespoons cocktail sauce
- 2 teaspoons low-sodium soy sauce
- 30 wonton wrappers
- 1 tablespoon water, for brushing the wrappers

1. Preheat the air fryer to 360°F (182°C). 2. In a small bowl, combine the cabbage, pepper, green onions, egg, cocktail sauce, and soy sauce, and mix well. 3. Put about 1 teaspoon of the mixture in the center of each wonton wrapper. Fold the wrapper in half, covering the filling; dampen the edges with water, and seal. You can crimp the edges of the wrapper with your fingers so they look like the pot stickers you get in restaurants. Brush them with water. 4. Place the pot stickers in the air fryer basket and air fry in 2 batches for 9 to 10 minutes, or until the pot stickers are hot and the bottoms are lightly browned. 5. Serve hot.

Cheese-Stuffed Blooming Onion

Prep time: 10 minutes | Cook time: 15 minutes | Serves 2

- 1 large yellow onion (14 ounces / 397 g)
- 1 tablespoon olive oil
- Kosher salt and freshly ground black pepper, to taste
- ¼ cup plus 2 tablespoons panko bread crumbs
- ¼ cup grated Parmesan cheese
- 3 tablespoons mayonnaise
- 1 tablespoon fresh lemon juice
- 1 tablespoon chopped fresh flat-leaf parsley
- 2 teaspoons whole-grain Dijon mustard
- 1 garlic clove, minced

1. Place the onion on a cutting board and trim the top off and peel off the outer skin. Turn the onion upside down and use a paring knife, cut vertical slits halfway through the onion at ½-inch intervals around the onion, keeping the root intact. When you turn the onion right side up, it should open up like the petals of a flower. Drizzle the cut sides of the onion with the olive oil and season with salt and pepper. Place petal-side up in the air fryer and air fry at 350°F (177°C) for 10 minutes. 2. Meanwhile, in a bowl, stir together the panko, Parmesan, mayonnaise, lemon juice, parsley, mustard, and garlic until incorporated into a smooth paste. 3. Remove the onion from the fryer and stuff the paste all over and in between the onion "petals." Return the onion to the air fryer and air fry at 375°F (191°C) until the onion is tender in the center and the bread crumb mixture is golden brown, about 5 minutes. Remove the onion from the air fryer, transfer to a plate, and serve hot.

Crunchy Chickpeas

Prep time: 5 minutes | Cook time: 15 to 20 minutes | Serves 4

- ½ teaspoon chili powder
- ½ teaspoon ground cumin
- ¼ teaspoon cayenne pepper
- ¼ teaspoon salt
- 1 (19 ounces / 539 g) can chickpeas, drained and rinsed
- Cooking spray

1. Preheat the air fryer to 390ºF (199ºC). Lightly spritz the air fryer basket with cooking spray. 2. Mix the chili powder, cumin, cayenne pepper, and salt in a small bowl. 3. Place the chickpeas in a medium bowl and lightly mist with cooking spray. 4. Add the spice mixture to the chickpeas and toss until evenly coated. 5. Place the chickpeas in the air fryer basket and air fry for 15 to 20 minutes, or until the chickpeas are cooked to your preferred crunchiness. Shake the basket three or four times during cooking. 6. Let the chickpeas cool for 5 minutes before serving.

Spiced Nuts

Prep time: 5 minutes | Cook time: 25 minutes | Makes 3 cups

- 1 egg white, lightly beaten
- ¼ cup sugar
- 1 teaspoon salt
- ½ teaspoon ground cinnamon
- ¼ teaspoon ground cloves
- ¼ teaspoon ground allspice
- Pinch ground cayenne pepper
- 1 cup pecan halves
- 1 cup cashews
- 1 cup almonds

1. Combine the egg white with the sugar and spices in a bowl. 2. Preheat the air fryer to 300ºF (149ºC). 3. Spray or brush the air fryer basket with vegetable oil. Toss the nuts together in the spiced egg white and transfer the nuts to the air fryer basket. 4. Air fry for 25 minutes, stirring the nuts in the basket a few times during the cooking process. Taste the nuts (carefully because they will be very hot) to see if they are crunchy and nicely toasted. Air fry for a few more minutes if necessary. 5. Serve warm or cool to room temperature and store in an airtight container for up to two weeks.

Greek Street Tacos

Prep time: 10 minutes | Cook time: 3 minutes | Makes 8 small tacos

- 8 small flour tortillas (4-inch diameter)
- 8 tablespoons hummus
- 4 tablespoons crumbled feta cheese
- 4 tablespoons chopped kalamata or other olives (optional)
- Olive oil for misting

1. Place 1 tablespoon of hummus or tapenade in the center of each tortilla. Top with 1 teaspoon of feta crumbles and 1 teaspoon of chopped olives, if using. 2. Using your finger or a small spoon, moisten the edges of the tortilla all around with water. 3. Fold tortilla over to make a half-moon shape. Press center gently. Then press the edges firmly to seal in the filling. 4. Mist both sides with olive oil. 5. Place in air fryer basket very close but try not to overlap. 6. Air fry at 390ºF (199ºC) for 3 minutes, just until lightly browned and crispy.

Dark Chocolate and Cranberry Granola Bars

Prep time: 5 minutes | Cook time: 15 minutes | Serves 6

- 2 cups certified gluten-free quick oats
- 2 tablespoons sugar-free dark chocolate chunks
- 2 tablespoons unsweetened dried cranberries
- 3 tablespoons
- unsweetened shredded coconut
- ½ cup raw honey
- 1 teaspoon ground cinnamon
- ⅛ teaspoon salt
- 2 tablespoons olive oil

1. Preheat the air fryer to 360ºF(182ºC). Line an 8-by-8-inch baking dish with parchment paper that comes up the side so you can lift it out after cooking. 2. In a large bowl, mix together all of the ingredients until well combined. 3. Press the oat mixture into the pan in an even layer. 4. Place the pan into the air fryer basket and bake for 15 minutes. 5. Remove the pan from the air fryer, and lift the granola cake out of the pan using the edges of the parchment paper. 6. Allow to cool for 5 minutes before slicing into 6 equal bars. 7. Serve immediately, or wrap in plastic wrap and store at room temperature for up to 1 week.

Greek Yogurt Deviled Eggs

Prep time: 15 minutes | Cook time: 15 minutes | Serves 4

- 4 eggs
- ¼ cup nonfat plain Greek yogurt
- 1 teaspoon chopped fresh dill
- ⅛ teaspoon salt
- ⅛ teaspoon paprika
- ⅛ teaspoon garlic powder
- Chopped fresh parsley, for garnish

1. Preheat the air fryer to 260ºF(127ºC). 2. Place the eggs in a single layer in the air fryer basket and cook for 15 minutes. 3. Quickly remove the eggs from the air fryer and place them into a cold water bath. Let the eggs cool in the water for 10 minutes before removing and peeling them. 4. After peeling the eggs, cut them in half. 5. Spoon the yolk into a small bowl. Add the yogurt, dill, salt, paprika, and garlic powder and mix until smooth. 6. Spoon or pipe the yolk mixture into the halved egg whites. Serve with a sprinkle of fresh parsley on top.

Bruschetta with Basil Pesto

Prep time: 10 minutes | Cook time: 5 to 11 minutes | Serves 4

- 8 slices French bread, ½ inch thick
- 2 tablespoons softened butter
- 1 cup shredded Mozzarella cheese
- ½ cup basil pesto
- 1 cup chopped grape tomatoes
- 2 green onions, thinly sliced

1. Preheat the air fryer to 350°F (177°C). 2. Spread the bread with the butter and place butter-side up in the air fryer basket. Bake for 3 to 5 minutes, or until the bread is light golden brown. 3. Remove the bread from the basket and top each piece with some of the cheese. Return to the basket in 2 batches and bake for 1 to 3 minutes, or until the cheese melts. 4. Meanwhile, combine the pesto, tomatoes, and green onions in a small bowl. 5. When the cheese has melted, remove the bread from the air fryer and place on a serving plate. Top each slice with some of the pesto mixture and serve.

Stuffed Figs with Goat Cheese and Honey

Prep time: 5 minutes | Cook time: 10 minutes | Serves 4

- 8 fresh figs
- 2 ounces (57 g) goat cheese
- ¼ teaspoon ground
- cinnamon
- 1 tablespoon honey, plus more for serving
- 1 tablespoon olive oil

1. Preheat the air fryer to 360°F(182°C). 2. Cut the stem off of each fig. 3. Cut an X into the top of each fig, cutting halfway down the fig. Leave the base intact. 4. In a small bowl, mix together the goat cheese, cinnamon, and honey. 5. Spoon the goat cheese mixture into the cavity of each fig. 6. Place the figs in a single layer in the air fryer basket. Drizzle the olive oil over top of the figs and roast for 10 minutes. 7. Serve with an additional drizzle of honey.

Cheesy Hash Brown Bruschetta

Prep time: 5 minutes | Cook time: 6 to 8 minutes | Serves 4

- 4 frozen hash brown patties
- 1 tablespoon olive oil
- ⅓ cup chopped cherry tomatoes
- 3 tablespoons diced fresh Mozzarella
- 2 tablespoons grated Parmesan cheese
- 1 tablespoon balsamic vinegar
- 1 tablespoon minced fresh basil

1. Preheat the air fryer to 400°F (204°C). 2. Place the hash brown patties in the air fryer in a single layer. Air fry for 6 to 8 minutes, or until the potatoes are crisp, hot, and golden brown. 3. Meanwhile, combine the olive oil, tomatoes, Mozzarella, Parmesan, vinegar, and basil in a small bowl. 4. When the potatoes are done, carefully remove from the basket and arrange on a serving plate. Top with the tomato mixture and serve.

Eggplant Fries

Prep time: 10 minutes | Cook time: 7 to 8 minutes per batch | Serves 4

- 1 medium eggplant
- 1 teaspoon ground coriander
- 1 teaspoon cumin
- 1 teaspoon garlic powder
- ½ teaspoon salt
- 1 cup crushed panko bread crumbs
- 1 large egg
- 2 tablespoons water
- Oil for misting or cooking spray

1. Peel and cut the eggplant into fat fries, ⅜- to ½-inch thick. 2. Preheat the air fryer to 390°F (199°C). 3. In a small cup, mix together the coriander, cumin, garlic, and salt. 4. Combine 1 teaspoon of the seasoning mix and panko crumbs in a shallow dish. 5. Place eggplant fries in a large bowl, sprinkle with remaining seasoning, and stir well to combine. 6. Beat eggs and water together and pour over eggplant fries. Stir to coat. 7. Remove eggplant from egg wash, shaking off excess, and roll in panko crumbs. 8. Spray with oil. 9. Place half of the fries in air fryer basket. You should have only a single layer, but it's fine if they overlap a little. 10. Cook for 5 minutes. Shake basket, mist lightly with oil, and cook 2 to 3 minutes longer, until browned and crispy. 11. Repeat step 10 to cook remaining eggplant.

Lemony Pear Chips

Prep time: 15 minutes | Cook time: 9 to 13 minutes | Serves 4

- 2 firm Bosc pears, cut crosswise into ⅛-inch-thick slices
- 1 tablespoon freshly squeezed lemon juice
- ½ teaspoon ground cinnamon
- ⅛ teaspoon ground cardamom

1. Preheat the air fryer to 380°F (193°C). 2. Separate the smaller stem-end pear rounds from the larger rounds with seeds. Remove the core and seeds from the larger slices. Sprinkle all slices with lemon juice, cinnamon, and cardamom. 3. Put the smaller chips into the air fryer basket. Air fry for 3 to 5 minutes, or until light golden brown, shaking the basket once during cooking. Remove from the air fryer. 4. Repeat with the larger slices, air frying for 6 to 8 minutes, or until light golden brown, shaking the basket once during cooking. 5. Remove the chips from the air fryer. Cool and serve or store in an airtight container at room temperature up for to 2 days.

Caramelized Onion Dip

Prep time: 5 minutes | Cook time: 30 minutes | Serves 8 to 10

- 1 tablespoon butter
- 1 medium yellow onion, halved and thinly sliced
- ¼ teaspoon kosher salt, plus additional for seasoning
- 4 ounces (113 g) cream cheese, softened
- ½ cup sour cream
- ¼ teaspoon onion powder
- 1 tablespoon chopped fresh chives
- Black pepper, to taste
- Thick-cut potato chips or vegetable chips

1. Place the butter in a baking pan. Place the pan in the air fryer basket. Set the air fryer to 200°F (93°C) for 1 minute, or until the butter is melted. Add the onions and salt to the pan. 2. Set the air fryer to 200°F (93°C) for 15 minutes, or until onions are softened. Set the air fryer to 375°F (191°C) for 15 minutes, until onions are a deep golden brown, stirring two or three times during the cooking time. Let cool completely. 3. In a medium bowl, stir together the cooked onions, cream cheese, sour cream, onion powder, and chives. Season with salt and pepper. Cover and refrigerate for 2 hours to allow the flavors to blend. 4. Serve the dip with potato chips or vegetable chips.

Black Bean Corn Dip

Prep time: 10 minutes | Cook time: 10 minutes | Serves 4

- ½ (15 ounces / 425 g) can black beans, drained and rinsed
- ½ (15 ounces / 425 g) can corn, drained and rinsed
- ¼ cup chunky salsa
- 2 ounces (57 g) reduced-fat cream cheese,
- softened
- ¼ cup shredded reduced-fat Cheddar cheese
- ½ teaspoon ground cumin
- ½ teaspoon paprika
- Salt and freshly ground black pepper, to taste

1. Preheat the air fryer to 325°F (163°C). 2. In a medium bowl, mix together the black beans, corn, salsa, cream cheese, Cheddar cheese, cumin, and paprika. Season with salt and pepper and stir until well combined. 3. Spoon the mixture into a baking dish. 4. Place baking dish in the air fryer basket and bake until heated through, about 10 minutes. 5. Serve hot.

Homemade Sweet Potato Chips

Prep time: 5 minutes | Cook time: 15 minutes | Serves 2

- 1 large sweet potato, sliced thin
- ⅛ teaspoon salt
- 2 tablespoons olive oil

1. Preheat the air fryer to 380°F(193°C). 2. In a small bowl, toss the sweet potatoes, salt, and olive oil together until the potatoes are well coated. 3. Put the sweet potato slices into the air fryer and spread them out in a single layer. 4. Fry for 10 minutes. Stir, then air fry for 3 to 5 minutes more, or until the chips reach the preferred level of crispiness.

Buffalo Bites

Prep time: 15 minutes | Cook time: 11 to 12 minutes per batch | Makes 16 meatballs

- 1½ cups cooked jasmine or sushi rice
- ¼ teaspoon salt
- 1 pound (454 g) ground chicken
- 8 tablespoons buffalo wing sauce
- 2 ounces (57 g) Gruyère cheese, cut into 16 cubes
- 1 tablespoon maple syrup

1. Mix 4 tablespoons buffalo wing sauce into all the ground chicken. 2. Shape chicken into a log and divide into 16 equal portions. 3. With slightly damp hands, mold each chicken portion around a cube of cheese and shape into a firm ball. When you have shaped 8 meatballs, place them in air fryer basket. 4. Air fry at 390°F (199°C) for approximately 5 minutes. Shake basket, reduce temperature to 360°F (182°C), and cook for 5 to 6 minutes longer. 5. While the first batch is cooking, shape remaining chicken and cheese into 8 more meatballs. 6. Repeat step 4 to cook second batch of meatballs. 7. In a medium bowl, mix the remaining 4 tablespoons of buffalo wing sauce with the maple syrup. Add all the cooked meatballs and toss to coat. 8. Place meatballs back into air fryer basket and air fry at 390°F (199°C) for 2 to 3 minutes to set the glaze. Skewer each with a toothpick and serve.

Rosemary-Garlic Shoestring Fries

Prep time: 5 minutes | Cook time: 18 minutes | Serves 2

- 1 large russet potato (about 12 ounces / 340 g), scrubbed clean, and julienned
- 1 tablespoon vegetable oil
- Leaves from 1 sprig fresh
- rosemary
- Kosher salt and freshly ground black pepper, to taste
- 1 garlic clove, thinly sliced
- Flaky sea salt, for serving

1. Preheat the air fryer to 400°F (204°C). 2. Place the julienned potatoes in a large colander and rinse under cold running water until the water runs clear. Spread the potatoes out on a double-thick layer of paper towels and pat dry. 3. In a large bowl, combine the potatoes, oil, and rosemary. Season with kosher salt and pepper and toss to coat evenly. Place the potatoes in the air fryer and air fry for 18 minutes, shaking the basket every 5 minutes and adding the garlic in the last 5 minutes of cooking, or until the fries are golden brown and crisp. 4. Transfer the fries to a plate and sprinkle with flaky sea salt while they're hot. Serve immediately.

Tangy Fried Pickle Spears

Prep time: 5 minutes | Cook time: 15 minutes | Serves 6

- 2 jars sweet and sour pickle spears, patted dry
- 2 medium-sized eggs
- ⅓ cup milk
- 1 teaspoon garlic powder
- 1 teaspoon sea salt
- ½ teaspoon shallot powder
- ⅓ teaspoon chili powder
- ⅓ cup all-purpose flour
- Cooking spray

1. Preheat the air fryer to 385°F (196°C). Spritz the air fryer basket with cooking spray. 2. In a bowl, beat together the eggs with milk. In another bowl, combine garlic powder, sea salt, shallot powder, chili powder and all-purpose flour until well blended. 3. One by one, roll the pickle spears in the powder mixture, then dredge them in the egg mixture. Dip them in the powder mixture a second time for additional coating. 4. Arrange the coated pickles in the prepared basket. Air fry for 15 minutes until golden and crispy, shaking the basket halfway through to ensure even cooking. 5. Transfer to a plate and let cool for 5 minutes before serving.

Shrimp Egg Rolls

Prep time: 15 minutes | Cook time: 10 minutes per batch | Serves 4

- 1 tablespoon vegetable oil
- ½ head green or savoy cabbage, finely shredded
- 1 cup shredded carrots
- 1 cup canned bean sprouts, drained
- 1 tablespoon soy sauce
- ½ teaspoon sugar
- 1 teaspoon sesame oil
- ¼ cup hoisin sauce
- Freshly ground black pepper, to taste
- 1 pound (454 g) cooked shrimp, diced
- ¼ cup scallions
- 8 egg roll wrappers
- Vegetable oil
- Duck sauce

1. Preheat a large sauté pan over medium-high heat. Add the oil and cook the cabbage, carrots and bean sprouts until they start to wilt, about 3 minutes. Add the soy sauce, sugar, sesame oil, hoisin sauce and black pepper. Sauté for a few more minutes. Stir in the shrimp and scallions and cook until the vegetables are just tender. Transfer the mixture to a colander in a bowl to cool. Press or squeeze out any excess water from the filling so that you don't end up with soggy egg rolls. 2. Make the egg rolls: Place the egg roll wrappers on a flat surface with one of the points facing towards you so they look like diamonds. Dividing the filling evenly between the eight wrappers, spoon the mixture onto the center of the egg roll wrappers. Spread the filling across the center of the wrappers from the left corner to the right corner, but leave 2 inches from each corner empty. Brush the empty sides of the wrapper with a little water. Fold the bottom corner of the wrapper tightly up over the filling, trying to avoid making any air pockets. Fold the left corner in toward the center and then the right corner toward the center. It should now look like an envelope. Tightly roll the egg roll from the bottom to the top open corner. Press to seal the egg roll together, brushing with a little extra water if need be. Repeat this technique with all 8 egg rolls. 3. Preheat the air fryer to 370°F (188°C). 4. Spray or brush all sides of the egg rolls with vegetable oil. Air fry four egg rolls at a time for 10 minutes, turning them over halfway through the cooking time. 5. Serve hot with duck sauce or your favorite dipping sauce.

Zucchini Feta Roulades

Prep time: 10 minutes | Cook time: 10 minutes | Serves 6

- ½ cup feta
- 1 garlic clove, minced
- 2 tablespoons fresh basil, minced
- 1 tablespoon capers, minced
- ⅛ teaspoon salt
- ⅛ teaspoon red pepper flakes
- 1 tablespoon lemon juice
- 2 medium zucchini
- 12 toothpicks

1. Preheat the air fryer to 360°F (182°C).(If using a grill attachment, make sure it is inside the air fryer during preheating.) 2. In a small bowl, combine the feta, garlic, basil, capers, salt, red pepper flakes, and lemon juice. 3. Slice the zucchini into ⅛-inch strips lengthwise. (Each zucchini should yield around 6 strips.) 4. Spread 1 tablespoon of the cheese filling onto each slice of zucchini, then roll it up and secure it with a toothpick through the middle. 5. Place the zucchini roulades into the air fryer basket in a single layer, making sure that they don't touch each other. 6. Bake or grill in the air fryer for 10 minutes. 7. Remove the zucchini roulades from the air fryer and gently remove the toothpicks before serving.

Kale Chips with Tex-Mex Dip

Prep time: 10 minutes | Cook time: 5 to 6 minutes | Serves 8

- 1 cup Greek yogurt
- 1 tablespoon chili powder
- ⅓ cup low-sodium salsa, well drained
- 1 bunch curly kale
- 1 teaspoon olive oil
- ¼ teaspoon coarse sea salt

1. In a small bowl, combine the yogurt, chili powder, and drained salsa; refrigerate. 2. Rinse the kale thoroughly, and pat dry. Remove the stems and ribs from the kale, using a sharp knife. Cut or tear the leaves into 3-inch pieces. 3. Toss the kale with the olive oil in a large bowl. 4. Air fry the kale in small batches at 390°F (199°C) until the leaves are crisp. This should take 5 to 6 minutes. Shake the basket once during cooking time. 5. As you remove the kale chips, sprinkle them with a bit of the sea salt. 6. When all of the kale chips are done, serve with the dip.

Spinach and Crab Meat Cups

Prep time: 10 minutes | Cook time: 10 minutes | Makes 30 cups

- 1 (6 ounces / 170 g) can crab meat, drained to yield ⅓ cup meat
- ¼ cup frozen spinach, thawed, drained, and chopped
- 1 clove garlic, minced
- ½ cup grated Parmesan cheese
- 3 tablespoons plain yogurt
- ¼ teaspoon lemon juice
- ½ teaspoon Worcestershire sauce
- 30 mini frozen phyllo shells, thawed
- Cooking spray

1. Preheat the air fryer to 390ºF (199ºC). 2. Remove any bits of shell that might remain in the crab meat. 3. Mix the crab meat, spinach, garlic, and cheese together. 4. Stir in the yogurt, lemon juice, and Worcestershire sauce and mix well. 5. Spoon a teaspoon of filling into each phyllo shell. 6. Spray the air fryer basket with cooking spray and arrange half the shells in the basket. Air fry for 5 minutes. Repeat with the remaining shells. 7. Serve immediately.

Carrot Chips

Prep time: 15 minutes | Cook time: 8 to 10 minutes | Serves 4

- 1 tablespoon olive oil, plus more for greasing the basket
- 4 to 5 medium carrots, trimmed and thinly sliced
- 1 teaspoon seasoned salt

1. Preheat the air fryer to 390ºF (199ºC). Grease the air fryer basket with the olive oil. 2. Toss the carrot slices with 1 tablespoon of olive oil and salt in a medium bowl until thoroughly coated. 3. Arrange the carrot slices in the greased basket. You may need to work in batches to avoid overcrowding. 4. Air fry for 8 to 10 minutes until the carrot slices are crisp-tender. Shake the basket once during cooking. 5. Transfer the carrot slices to a bowl and repeat with the remaining carrots. 6. Allow to cool for 5 minutes and serve.

Poutine with Waffle Fries

Prep time: 10 minutes | Cook time: 15 to 17 minutes | Serves 4

- 2 cups frozen waffle cut fries
- 2 teaspoons olive oil
- 1 red bell pepper, chopped
- 2 green onions, sliced
- 1 cup shredded Swiss cheese
- ½ cup bottled chicken gravy

1. Preheat the air fryer to 380ºF (193ºC). 2. Toss the waffle fries with the olive oil and place in the air fryer basket. Air fry for 10 to 12 minutes, or until the fries are crisp and light golden brown, shaking the basket halfway through the cooking time. 3. Transfer the fries to a baking pan and top with the pepper, green onions, and cheese. Air fry for 3 minutes, or until the vegetables are crisp and tender. 4. Remove the pan from the air fryer and drizzle the gravy over the fries. Air fry for 2 minutes, or until the gravy is hot. 5. Serve immediately.

Grilled Ham and Cheese on Raisin Bread

Prep time: 5 minutes | Cook time: 10 minutes | Serves 1

- 2 slices raisin bread
- 2 tablespoons butter, softened
- 2 teaspoons honey mustard
- 3 slices thinly sliced
- honey ham (about 3 ounces / 85 g)
- 4 slices Muenster cheese (about 3 ounces / 85 g)
- 2 toothpicks

1. Preheat the air fryer to 370ºF (188ºC). 2. Spread the softened butter on one side of both slices of raisin bread and place the bread, buttered side down on the counter. Spread the honey mustard on the other side of each slice of bread. Layer 2 slices of cheese, the ham and the remaining 2 slices of cheese on one slice of bread and top with the other slice of bread. Remember to leave the buttered side of the bread on the outside. 3. Transfer the sandwich to the air fryer basket and secure the sandwich with toothpicks. 4. Air fry for 5 minutes. Flip the sandwich over, remove the toothpicks and air fry for another 5 minutes. Cut the sandwich in half and enjoy!

Browned Ricotta with Capers and Lemon

Prep time: 10 minutes | Cook time: 8 to 10 minutes | Serves 4 to 6

- 1½ cups whole milk ricotta cheese
- 2 tablespoons extra-virgin olive oil
- 2 tablespoons capers, rinsed
- Zest of 1 lemon, plus more for garnish
- 1 teaspoon finely chopped fresh rosemary
- Pinch crushed red pepper flakes
- Salt and freshly ground black pepper, to taste
- 1 tablespoon grated Parmesan cheese

1. Preheat the air fryer to 380ºF (193ºC). 2. In a mixing bowl, stir together the ricotta cheese, olive oil, capers, lemon zest, rosemary, red pepper flakes, salt, and pepper until well combined. 3. Spread the mixture evenly in a baking dish and place it in the air fryer basket. 4. Air fry for 8 to 10 minutes until the top is nicely browned. 5. Remove from the basket and top with a sprinkle of grated Parmesan cheese. 6. Garnish with the lemon zest and serve warm.

Lebanese Muhammara

Prep time: 15 minutes | Cook time: 15 minutes | Serves 6

- 2 large red bell peppers
- ¼ cup plus 2 tablespoons extra-virgin olive oil
- 1 cup walnut halves
- 1 tablespoon agave nectar or honey
- 1 teaspoon fresh lemon juice
- 1 teaspoon ground cumin
- 1 teaspoon kosher salt
- 1 teaspoon red pepper flakes
- Raw vegetables (such as cucumber, carrots, zucchini slices, or cauliflower) or toasted pita chips, for serving

1. Drizzle the peppers with 2 tablespoons of the olive oil and place in the air fryer basket. Set the air fryer to 400°F (204°C) for 10 minutes. 2. Add the walnuts to the basket, arranging them around the peppers. Set the air fryer to 400°F (204°C) for 5 minutes. 3. Remove the peppers, seal in a resealable plastic bag, and let rest for 5 to 10 minutes. Transfer the walnuts to a plate and set aside to cool. 4. Place the softened peppers, walnuts, agave, lemon juice, cumin, salt, and ½ teaspoon of the pepper flakes in a food processor and purée until smooth. 5. Transfer the dip to a serving bowl and make an indentation in the middle. Pour the remaining ¼ cup olive oil into the indentation. Garnish the dip with the remaining ½ teaspoon pepper flakes. 6. Serve with vegetables or toasted pita chips.

Garlic-Parmesan Croutons

Prep time: 3 minutes | Cook time: 12 minutes | Serves 4

- Oil, for spraying
- 4 cups cubed French bread
- 1 tablespoon grated Parmesan cheese
- 3 tablespoons olive oil
- 1 tablespoon granulated garlic
- ½ teaspoon unsalted salt

1. Line the air fryer basket with parchment and spray lightly with oil. 2. In a large bowl, mix together the bread, Parmesan cheese, olive oil, garlic, and salt, tossing with your hands to evenly distribute the seasonings. Transfer the coated bread cubes to the prepared basket. 3. Air fry at 350°F (177°C) for 10 to 12 minutes, stirring once after 5 minutes, or until crisp and golden brown.

Turkey Burger Sliders

Prep time: 10 minutes | Cook time: 5 to 7 minutes | Makes 8 sliders

- 1 pound (454 g) ground turkey
- ¼ teaspoon curry powder
- 1 teaspoon Hoisin sauce
- ½ teaspoon salt
- 8 slider buns
- ½ cup slivered red onions
- ½ cup slivered green or red bell pepper
- ½ cup fresh chopped pineapple
- Light cream cheese, softened

1. Combine turkey, curry powder, Hoisin sauce, and salt and mix together well. 2. Shape turkey mixture into 8 small patties. 3. Place patties in air fryer basket and air fry at 360°F (182°C) for 5 to 7 minutes, until patties are well done and juices run clear. 4. Place each patty on the bottom half of a slider bun and top with onions, peppers, and pineapple. Spread the remaining bun halves with cream cheese to taste, place on top, and serve.

Feta and Quinoa Stuffed Mushrooms

Prep time: 5 minutes | Cook time: 8 minutes | Serves 6

- 2 tablespoons finely diced red bell pepper
- 1 garlic clove, minced
- ¼ cup cooked quinoa
- ⅛ teaspoon salt
- ¼ teaspoon dried oregano
- 24 button mushrooms, stemmed
- 2 ounces (57 g) crumbled feta
- 3 tablespoons whole wheat bread crumbs
- Olive oil cooking spray

1. Preheat the air fryer to 360°F(182°C). 2. In a small bowl, combine the bell pepper, garlic, quinoa, salt, and oregano. 3. Spoon the quinoa stuffing into the mushroom caps until just filled. 4. Add a small piece of feta to the top of each mushroom. 5. Sprinkle a pinch bread crumbs over the feta on each mushroom. 6. Spray the basket of the air fryer with olive oil cooking spray, then gently place the mushrooms into the basket, making sure that they don't touch each other. (Depending on the size of the air fryer, you may have to cook them in two batches.) 7. Place the basket into the air fryer and bake for 8 minutes. 8. Remove from the air fryer and serve.

Chapter 8

Vegetables and Side

Maple-Roasted Tomatoes

Prep time: 15 minutes | Cook time: 20 minutes | Serves 2

- 10 ounces (283 g) cherry tomatoes, halved
- Kosher salt, to taste
- 2 tablespoons maple syrup
- 1 tablespoon vegetable oil
- 2 sprigs fresh thyme, stems removed
- 1 garlic clove, minced
- Freshly ground black pepper

1. Place the tomatoes in a colander and sprinkle liberally with salt. Let stand for 10 minutes to drain. 2. Transfer the tomatoes cut-side up to a cake pan, then drizzle with the maple syrup, followed by the oil. Sprinkle with the thyme leaves and garlic and season with pepper. Place the pan in the air fryer and roast at 325°F (163°C) until the tomatoes are soft, collapsed, and lightly caramelized on top, about 20 minutes. 3. Serve straight from the pan or transfer the tomatoes to a plate and drizzle with the juices from the pan to serve.

Butternut Squash Croquettes

Prep time: 5 minutes | Cook time: 17 minutes | Serves 4

- ⅓ butternut squash, peeled and grated
- ⅓ cup all-purpose flour
- 2 eggs, whisked
- 4 cloves garlic, minced
- 1½ tablespoons olive oil
- 1 teaspoon fine sea salt
- ⅓ teaspoon freshly ground black pepper, or more to taste
- ⅓ teaspoon dried sage
- A pinch of ground allspice

1. Preheat the air fryer to 345°F (174°C). Line the air fryer basket with parchment paper. 2. In a mixing bowl, stir together all the ingredients until well combined. 3. Make the squash croquettes: Use a small cookie scoop to drop tablespoonfuls of the squash mixture onto a lightly floured surface and shape into balls with your hands. Transfer them to the air fryer basket. 4. Air fry for 17 minutes until the squash croquettes are golden brown. 5. Remove from the basket to a plate and serve warm.

Parmesan-Rosemary Radishes

Prep time: 5 minutes | Cook time: 15 to 20 minutes | Serves 4

- 1 bunch radishes, stemmed, trimmed, and quartered
- 1 tablespoon avocado oil
- 2 tablespoons finely grated fresh Parmesan
- cheese
- 1 tablespoon chopped fresh rosemary
- Sea salt and freshly ground black pepper, to taste

1. Place the radishes in a medium bowl and toss them with the avocado oil, Parmesan cheese, rosemary, salt, and pepper. 2. Set the air fryer to 375°F (191°C). Arrange the radishes in a single layer in the air fryer basket. Roast for 15 to 20 minutes, until golden brown and tender. Let cool for 5 minutes before serving.

Easy Greek Briami (Ratatouille)

Prep time: 15 minutes | Cook time: 40 minutes | Serves 6

- 2 russet potatoes, cubed
- ½ cup Roma tomatoes, cubed
- 1 eggplant, cubed
- 1 zucchini, cubed
- 1 red onion, chopped
- 1 red bell pepper, chopped
- 2 garlic cloves, minced
- 1 teaspoon dried mint
- 1 teaspoon dried parsley
- 1 teaspoon dried oregano
- ½ teaspoon salt
- ½ teaspoon black pepper
- ¼ teaspoon red pepper flakes
- ⅓ cup olive oil
- 1 (8-ounce / 227-g) can tomato paste
- ¼ cup vegetable broth
- ¼ cup water

1. Preheat the air fryer to 320°F (160°C). 2. In a large bowl, combine the potatoes, tomatoes, eggplant, zucchini, onion, bell pepper, garlic, mint, parsley, oregano, salt, black pepper, and red pepper flakes. 3. In a small bowl, mix together the olive oil, tomato paste, broth, and water. 4. Pour the oil-and-tomato-paste mixture over the vegetables and toss until everything is coated. 5. Pour the coated vegetables into the air fryer basket in an even layer and roast for 20 minutes. After 20 minutes, stir well and spread out again. Roast for an additional 10 minutes, then repeat the process and cook for another 10 minutes.

Broccoli with Sesame Dressing

Prep time: 5 minutes | Cook time: 10 minutes | Serves 4

- 6 cups broccoli florets, cut into bite-size pieces
- 1 tablespoon olive oil
- ¼ teaspoon salt
- 2 tablespoons sesame seeds
- 2 tablespoons rice
- vinegar
- 2 tablespoons coconut aminos
- 2 tablespoons sesame oil
- ½ teaspoon Swerve
- ¼ teaspoon red pepper flakes (optional)

1. Preheat the air fryer to 400°F (204°C). 2. In a large bowl, toss the broccoli with the olive oil and salt until thoroughly coated. 3. Transfer the broccoli to the air fryer basket. Pausing halfway through the cooking time to shake the basket, air fry for 10 minutes until the stems are tender and the edges are beginning to crisp. 4. Meanwhile, in the same large bowl, whisk together the sesame seeds, vinegar, coconut aminos, sesame oil, Swerve, and red pepper flakes (if using). 5. Transfer the broccoli to the bowl and toss until thoroughly coated with the seasonings. Serve warm or at room temperature.

Butter and Garlic Fried Cabbage

Prep time: 5 minutes | Cook time: 9 minutes | Serves 2

- Oil, for spraying
- ½ head cabbage, cut into bite-size pieces
- 2 tablespoons unsalted butter, melted
- 1 teaspoon granulated
- garlic
- ½ teaspoon coarse sea salt
- ¼ teaspoon freshly ground black pepper

1. Line the air fryer basket with parchment and spray lightly with oil. 2. In a large bowl, mix together the cabbage, butter, garlic, salt, and black pepper until evenly coated. 3. Transfer the cabbage to the prepared basket and spray lightly with oil. 4. Air fry at 375°F (191°C) for 5 minutes, toss, and cook for another 3 to 4 minutes, or until lightly crispy.

Air-Fried Okra

Prep time: 10 minutes | Cook time: 10 minutes | Serves 4

- 1 egg
- ½ cup almond milk
- ½ cup crushed pork rinds
- ¼ cup grated Parmesan cheese
- ¼ cup almond flour
- 1 teaspoon garlic powder
- ¼ teaspoon freshly ground black pepper
- ½ pound (227 g) fresh okra, stems removed and chopped into 1-inch slices

1. Preheat the air fryer to 400°F (204°C). 2. In a shallow bowl, whisk together the egg and milk. 3. In a second shallow bowl, combine the pork rinds, Parmesan, almond flour, garlic powder, and black pepper. 4. Working with a few slices at a time, dip the okra into the egg mixture followed by the crumb mixture. Press lightly to ensure an even coating. 5. Working in batches if necessary, arrange the okra in a single layer in the air fryer basket and spray lightly with olive oil. Pausing halfway through the cooking time to turn the okra, air fry for 10 minutes until tender and golden brown. Serve warm.

Fried Asparagus

Prep time: 5 minutes | Cook time: 12 minutes | Serves 4

- 1 tablespoon olive oil
- 1 pound (454 g) asparagus spears, ends trimmed
- ¼ teaspoon salt
- ¼ teaspoon ground black pepper
- 1 tablespoon salted butter, melted

1. In a large bowl, drizzle olive oil over asparagus spears and sprinkle with salt and pepper. 2. Place spears into ungreased air fryer basket. Adjust the temperature to 375°F (191°C) and set the timer for 12 minutes, shaking the basket halfway through cooking. Asparagus will be lightly browned and tender when done. 3. Transfer to a large dish and drizzle with butter. Serve warm.

Asian Tofu Salad

Prep time: 25 minutes | Cook time: 15 minutes | Serves 2

- Tofu:
- 1 tablespoon soy sauce
- 1 tablespoon vegetable oil
- 1 teaspoon minced fresh ginger
- 1 teaspoon minced garlic
- 8 ounces (227 g) extra-firm tofu, drained and cubed
- Salad:
- ¼ cup rice vinegar
- 1 tablespoon sugar
- 1 teaspoon salt
- 1 teaspoon black pepper
- ¼ cup sliced scallions
- 1 cup julienned cucumber
- 1 cup julienned red onion
- 1 cup julienned carrots
- 6 butter lettuce leaves

1. For the tofu: In a small bowl, whisk together the soy sauce, vegetable oil, ginger, and garlic. Add the tofu and mix gently. Let stand at room temperature for 10 minutes. 2. Arrange the tofu in a single layer in the air fryer basket. Set the air fryer to 400°F (204°C) for 15 minutes, shaking halfway through the cooking time. 3. Meanwhile, for the salad: In a large bowl, whisk together the vinegar, sugar, salt, pepper, and scallions. Add the cucumber, onion, and carrots and toss to combine. Set aside to marinate while the tofu cooks. 4. To serve, arrange three lettuce leaves on each of two plates. Pile the marinated vegetables (and marinade) on the lettuce. Divide the tofu between the plates and serve.

Sweet-and-Sour Brussels Sprouts

Prep time: 10 minutes | Cook time: 20 minutes | Serves 2

- ¼ cup Thai sweet chili sauce
- 2 tablespoons black vinegar or balsamic vinegar
- ½ teaspoon hot sauce, such as Tabasco
- 8 ounces (227 g) Brussels sprouts, trimmed (large
- sprouts halved)
- 2 small shallots, cut into ¼-inch-thick slices
- Kosher salt and freshly ground black pepper, to taste
- 2 teaspoons lightly packed fresh cilantro leaves

1. In a large bowl, whisk together the chili sauce, vinegar, and hot sauce. Add the Brussels sprouts and shallots, season with salt and pepper, and toss to combine. Scrape the Brussels sprouts and sauce into a cake pan. 2. Place the pan in the air fryer and roast at 375°F (191°C), stirring every 5 minutes, until the Brussels sprouts are tender and the sauce is reduced to a sticky glaze, about 20 minutes. 3. Remove the pan from the air fryer and transfer the Brussels sprouts to plates. Sprinkle with the cilantro and serve warm.

Dill-and-Garlic Beets

Prep time: 10 minutes | Cook time: 30 minutes | Serves 4

- 4 beets, cleaned, peeled, and sliced
- 1 garlic clove, minced
- 2 tablespoons chopped
- fresh dill
- ¼ teaspoon salt
- ¼ teaspoon black pepper
- 3 tablespoons olive oil

1. Preheat the air fryer to 380°F(193°C). 2. In a large bowl, mix together all of the ingredients so the beets are well coated with the oil. 3. Pour the beet mixture into the air fryer basket, and roast for 15 minutes before stirring, then continue roasting for 15 minutes more.

Roasted Garlic

Prep time: 5 minutes | Cook time: 20 minutes | Makes 12 cloves

- 1 medium head garlic
- 2 teaspoons avocado oil

1. Remove any hanging excess peel from the garlic but leave the cloves covered. Cut off ¼ of the head of garlic, exposing the tips of the cloves. 2. Drizzle with avocado oil. Place the garlic head into a small sheet of aluminum foil, completely enclosing it. Place it into the air fryer basket. 3. Adjust the temperature to 400°F (204°C) and air fry for 20 minutes. If your garlic head is a bit smaller, check it after 15 minutes. 4. When done, garlic should be golden brown and very soft. 5. To serve, cloves should pop out and easily be spread or sliced. Store in an airtight container in the refrigerator up to 5 days. You may also freeze individual cloves on a baking sheet, then store together in a freezer-safe storage bag once frozen.

Mole-Braised Cauliflower

Prep time: 10 minutes | Cook time: 15 minutes | Serves 2

- 8 ounces (227 g) medium cauliflower florets
- 1 tablespoon vegetable oil
- Kosher salt and freshly ground black pepper, to taste
- 1½ cups vegetable broth
- 2 tablespoons New Mexico chile powder (or regular chili powder)
- 2 tablespoons salted roasted peanuts
- 1 tablespoon toasted sesame seeds, plus more for garnish
- 1 tablespoon finely chopped golden raisins
- 1 teaspoon kosher salt
- 1 teaspoon dark brown sugar
- ½ teaspoon dried oregano
- ¼ teaspoon cayenne pepper
- ⅛ teaspoon ground cinnamon

1. In a large bowl, toss the cauliflower with the oil and season with salt and black pepper. Transfer to a cake pan. Place the pan in the air fryer and roast at 375°F (191°C) until the cauliflower is tender and lightly browned at the edges, about 10 minutes, stirring halfway through. 2. Meanwhile, in a small blender, combine the broth, chile powder, peanuts, sesame seeds, raisins, salt, brown sugar, oregano, cayenne, and cinnamon and purée until smooth. Pour into a small saucepan or skillet and bring to a simmer over medium heat, then cook until reduced by half, 3 to 5 minutes. 3. Pour the hot mole sauce over the cauliflower in the pan, stir to coat, then cook until the sauce is thickened and lightly charred on the cauliflower, about 5 minutes more. Sprinkle with more sesame seeds and serve warm.

Blistered Shishito Peppers with Lime Juice

Prep time: 5 minutes | Cook time: 9 minutes | Serves 3

- ½ pound (227 g) shishito peppers, rinsed
- Cooking spray
- Sauce:
- 1 tablespoon tamari or
- shoyu
- 2 teaspoons fresh lime juice
- 2 large garlic cloves, minced

1. Preheat the air fryer to 392°F (200°C). Spritz the air fryer basket with cooking spray. 2. Place the shishito peppers in the basket and spritz them with cooking spray. Roast for 3 minutes. 3. Meanwhile, whisk together all the ingredients for the sauce in a large bowl. Set aside. 4. Shake the basket and spritz them with cooking spray again, then roast for an additional 3 minutes. 5. Shake the basket one more time and spray the peppers with cooking spray. Continue roasting for 3 minutes until the peppers are blistered and nicely browned. 6. Remove the peppers from the basket to the bowl of sauce. Toss to coat well and serve immediately.

Cheese-Walnut Stuffed Mushrooms

Prep time: 5 minutes | Cook time: 10 minutes | Serves 4

- 4 large portobello mushrooms
- 1 tablespoon canola oil
- ½ cup shredded Mozzarella cheese
- ⅓ cup minced walnuts
- 2 tablespoons chopped fresh parsley
- Cooking spray

1. Preheat the air fryer to 350°F (177°C). Spritz the air fryer basket with cooking spray. 2. On a clean work surface, remove the mushroom stems. Scoop out the gills with a spoon and discard. Coat the mushrooms with canola oil. Top each mushroom evenly with the shredded Mozzarella cheese, followed by the minced walnuts. 3. Arrange the mushrooms in the air fryer and roast for 10 minutes until golden brown. 4. Transfer the mushrooms to a plate and sprinkle the parsley on top for garnish before serving.

Air Fried Potatoes with Olives

Prep time: 15 minutes | Cook time: 40 minutes | Serves 1

- 1 medium russet potatoes, scrubbed and peeled
- 1 teaspoon olive oil
- ¼ teaspoon onion powder
- ⅛ teaspoon salt
- Dollop of butter
- Dollop of cream cheese
- 1 tablespoon Kalamata olives
- 1 tablespoon chopped chives

1. Preheat the air fryer to 400°F (204°C). 2. In a bowl, coat the potatoes with the onion powder, salt, olive oil, and butter. 3. Transfer to the air fryer and air fry for 40 minutes, turning the potatoes over at the halfway point. 4. Take care when removing the potatoes from the air fryer and serve with the cream cheese, Kalamata olives and chives on top.

Potato with Creamy Cheese

Prep time: 5 minutes | Cook time: 15 minutes | Serves 2

- 2 medium potatoes
- 1 teaspoon butter
- 3 tablespoons sour cream
- 1 teaspoon chives
- 1½ tablespoons grated Parmesan cheese

1. Preheat the air fryer to 350°F (177°C). 2. Pierce the potatoes with a fork and boil them in water until they are cooked. 3. Transfer to the air fryer and air fry for 15 minutes. 4. In the meantime, combine the sour cream, cheese and chives in a bowl. Cut the potatoes halfway to open them up and fill with the butter and sour cream mixture. 5. Serve immediately.

Garlic Cauliflower with Tahini

Prep time: 10 minutes | Cook time: 20 minutes | Serves 4

- Cauliflower:
- 5 cups cauliflower florets (about 1 large head)
- 6 garlic cloves, smashed and cut into thirds
- 3 tablespoons vegetable oil
- ½ teaspoon ground cumin
- ½ teaspoon ground coriander
- ½ teaspoon kosher salt
- Sauce:
- 2 tablespoons tahini (sesame paste)
- 2 tablespoons hot water
- 1 tablespoon fresh lemon juice
- 1 teaspoon minced garlic
- ½ teaspoon kosher salt

1. For the cauliflower: In a large bowl, combine the cauliflower florets and garlic. Drizzle with the vegetable oil. Sprinkle with the cumin, coriander, and salt. Toss until well coated. 2. Place the cauliflower in the air fryer basket. Set the air fryer to 400°F (204°C) for 20 minutes, turning the cauliflower halfway through the cooking time. 3. Meanwhile, for the sauce: In a small bowl, combine the tahini, water, lemon juice, garlic, and salt. (The sauce will appear curdled at first, but keep stirring until you have a thick, creamy, smooth mixture.) 4. Transfer the cauliflower to a large serving bowl. Pour the sauce over and toss gently to coat. Serve immediately.

Roasted Radishes with Sea Salt

Prep time: 5 minutes | Cook time: 18 minutes | Serves 4

- 1 pound (454 g) radishes, ends trimmed if needed
- 2 tablespoons olive oil
- ½ teaspoon sea salt

1. Preheat the air fryer to 360°F (182°C). 2. In a large bowl, combine the radishes with olive oil and sea salt. 3. Pour the radishes into the air fryer and roast for 10 minutes. Stir or turn the radishes over and roast for 8 minutes more, then serve.

Curried Fruit

Prep time: 10 minutes | Cook time: 20 minutes | Serves 6 to 8

- 1 cup cubed fresh pineapple
- 1 cup cubed fresh pear (firm, not overly ripe)
- 8 ounces (227 g) frozen peaches, thawed
- 1 (15-ounce / 425-g) can dark, sweet, pitted cherries with juice
- 2 tablespoons brown sugar
- 1 teaspoon curry powder

1. Combine all ingredients in large bowl. Stir gently to mix in the sugar and curry. 2. Pour into a baking pan and bake at 360°F (182°C) for 10 minutes. 3. Stir fruit and cook 10 more minutes. 4. Serve hot.

Asparagus Fries

Prep time: 15 minutes | Cook time: 5 to 7 minutes per batch | Serves 4

- 12 ounces (340 g) fresh asparagus spears with tough ends trimmed off
- 2 egg whites
- ¼ cup water
- ¾ cup panko bread crumbs
- ¼ cup grated Parmesan cheese, plus 2 tablespoons
- ¼ teaspoon salt
- Oil for misting or cooking spray

1. Preheat the air fryer to 390°F (199°C). 2. In a shallow dish, beat egg whites and water until slightly foamy. 3. In another shallow dish, combine panko, Parmesan, and salt. 4. Dip asparagus spears in egg, then roll in crumbs. Spray with oil or cooking spray. 5. Place a layer of asparagus in air fryer basket, leaving just a little space in between each spear. Stack another layer on top, crosswise. Air fry at 390°F (199°C) for 5 to 7 minutes, until crispy and golden brown. 6. Repeat to cook remaining asparagus.

Roasted Potatoes and Asparagus

Prep time: 5 minutes | Cook time: 23 minutes | Serves 4

- 4 medium potatoes
- 1 bunch asparagus
- ⅓ cup cottage cheese
- ⅓ cup low-fat crème fraiche
- 1 tablespoon wholegrain mustard
- Salt and pepper, to taste
- Cooking spray

1. Preheat the air fryer to 390ºF (199ºC). Spritz the air fryer basket with cooking spray. 2. Place the potatoes in the basket. Air fry the potatoes for 20 minutes. 3. Boil the asparagus in salted water for 3 minutes. 4. Remove the potatoes and mash them with rest of ingredients. Sprinkle with salt and pepper. 5. Serve immediately.

Easy Potato Croquettes

Prep time: 15 minutes | Cook time: 15 minutes | Serves 10

- ¼ cup nutritional yeast
- 2 cups boiled potatoes, mashed
- 1 flax egg
- 1 tablespoon flour
- 2 tablespoons chopped
- chives
- Salt and ground black pepper, to taste
- 2 tablespoons vegetable oil
- ¼ cup bread crumbs

1. Preheat the air fryer to 400ºF (204ºC). 2. In a bowl, combine the nutritional yeast, potatoes, flax egg, flour, and chives. Sprinkle with salt and pepper as desired. 3. In a separate bowl, mix the vegetable oil and bread crumbs to achieve a crumbly consistency. 4. Shape the potato mixture into small balls and dip each one into the bread crumb mixture. 5. Put the croquettes inside the air fryer and air fry for 15 minutes, ensuring the croquettes turn golden brown. 6. Serve immediately.

Saltine Wax Beans

Prep time: 10 minutes | Cook time: 7 minutes | Serves 4

- ½ cup flour
- 1 teaspoon smoky chipotle powder
- ½ teaspoon ground black pepper
- 1 teaspoon sea salt flakes
- 2 eggs, beaten
- ½ cup crushed saltines
- 10 ounces (283 g) wax beans
- Cooking spray

1. Preheat the air fryer to 360ºF (182ºC). 2. Combine the flour, chipotle powder, black pepper, and salt in a bowl. Put the eggs in a second bowl. Put the crushed saltines in a third bowl. 3. Wash the beans with cold water and discard any tough strings. 4. Coat the beans with the flour mixture, before dipping them into the beaten egg. Cover them with the crushed saltines. 5. Spritz the beans with cooking spray.

6. Air fry for 4 minutes. Give the air fryer basket a good shake and continue to air fry for 3 minutes. Serve hot.

Parmesan Herb Focaccia Bread

Prep time: 10 minutes | Cook time: 10 minutes | Serves 6

- 1 cup shredded Mozzarella cheese
- 1 ounce (28 g) full-fat cream cheese
- 1 cup blanched finely ground almond flour
- ¼ cup ground golden flaxseed
- ¼ cup grated Parmesan cheese
- ½ teaspoon baking soda
- 2 large eggs
- ½ teaspoon garlic powder
- ¼ teaspoon dried basil
- ¼ teaspoon dried rosemary
- 2 tablespoons salted butter, melted and divided

1. Place Mozzarella, cream cheese, and almond flour into a large microwave-safe bowl and microwave for 1 minute. Add the flaxseed, Parmesan, and baking soda and stir until smooth ball forms. If the mixture cools too much, it will be hard to mix. Return to microwave for 10 to 15 seconds to rewarm if necessary. 2. Stir in eggs. You may need to use your hands to get them fully incorporated. Just keep stirring and they will absorb into the dough. 3. Sprinkle dough with garlic powder, basil, and rosemary and knead into dough. Grease a baking pan with 1 tablespoon melted butter. Press the dough evenly into the pan. Place pan into the air fryer basket. 4. Adjust the temperature to 400ºF (204ºC) and bake for 10 minutes. 5. At 7 minutes, cover with foil if bread begins to get too dark. 6. Remove and let cool at least 30 minutes. Drizzle with remaining butter and serve.

Tahini-Lemon Kale

Prep time: 5 minutes | Cook time: 15 minutes | Serves 2 to 4

- ¼ cup tahini
- ¼ cup fresh lemon juice
- 2 tablespoons olive oil
- 1 teaspoon sesame seeds
- ½ teaspoon garlic powder
- ¼ teaspoon cayenne pepper
- 4 cups packed torn kale
- leaves (stems and ribs removed and leaves torn into palm-size pieces; about 4 ounces / 113 g)
- Kosher salt and freshly ground black pepper, to taste

1. In a large bowl, whisk together the tahini, lemon juice, olive oil, sesame seeds, garlic powder, and cayenne until smooth. Add the kale leaves, season with salt and black pepper, and toss in the dressing until completely coated. Transfer the kale leaves to a cake pan. 2. Place the pan in the air fryer and roast at 350ºF (177ºC), stirring every 5 minutes, until the kale is wilted and the top is lightly browned, about 15 minutes. Remove the pan from the air fryer and serve warm.

Citrus Sweet Potatoes and Carrots

Prep time: 5 minutes | Cook time: 20 to 25 minutes | Serves 4

- 2 large carrots, cut into 1-inch chunks
- 1 medium sweet potato, peeled and cut into 1-inch cubes
- ½ cup chopped onion
- 2 garlic cloves, minced
- 2 tablespoons honey
- 1 tablespoon freshly squeezed orange juice
- 2 teaspoons butter, melted

1. Insert the crisper plate into the basket and the basket into the unit. Preheat the unit by selecting AIR ROAST, setting the temperature to 400°F (204°C), and setting the time to 3 minutes. Select START/STOP to begin. 2. In a 6-by-2-inch round pan, toss together the carrots, sweet potato, onion, garlic, honey, orange juice, and melted butter to coat. 3. Once the unit is preheated, place the pan into the basket. 4. Select AIR ROAST, set the temperature to 400°F (204°C), and set the time to 25 minutes. Select START/STOP to begin. 5. After 15 minutes, remove the basket and shake the vegetables. Reinsert the basket to resume cooking. After 5 minutes, if the vegetables are tender and glazed, they are done. If not, resume cooking. 6. When the cooking is complete, serve immediately.

Sweet and Crispy Roasted Pearl Onions

Prep time: 5 minutes | Cook time: 18 minutes | Serves 3

- 1 (14½ ounces / 411 g) package frozen pearl onions (do not thaw)
- 2 tablespoons extra-virgin olive oil
- 2 tablespoons balsamic
- vinegar
- 2 teaspoons finely chopped fresh rosemary
- ½ teaspoon kosher salt
- ¼ teaspoon black pepper

1. In a medium bowl, combine the onions, olive oil, vinegar, rosemary, salt, and pepper until well coated. 2. Transfer the onions to the air fryer basket. Set the air fryer to 400°F (204°C) for 18 minutes, or until the onions are tender and lightly charred, stirring once or twice during the cooking time.

Lush Vegetable Salad

Prep time: 15 minutes | Cook time: 10 minutes | Serves 4

- 6 plum tomatoes, halved
- 2 large red onions, sliced
- 4 long red pepper, sliced
- 2 yellow pepper, sliced
- 6 cloves garlic, crushed
- 1 tablespoon extra-virgin
- olive oil
- 1 teaspoon paprika
- ½ lemon, juiced
- Salt and ground black pepper, to taste
- 1 tablespoon baby capers

1. Preheat the air fryer to 420°F (216°C). 2. Put the tomatoes, onions, peppers, and garlic in a large bowl and cover with the extra-virgin olive oil, paprika, and lemon juice. Sprinkle with salt and pepper as desired. 3. Line the inside of the air fryer basket with aluminum foil. Put the vegetables inside and air fry for 10 minutes, ensuring the edges turn brown. 4. Serve in a salad bowl with the baby capers.

Garlic-Parmesan Crispy Baby Potatoes

Prep time: 10 minutes | Cook time: 15 minutes | Serves 4

- Oil, for spraying
- 1 pound (454 g) baby potatoes
- ½ cup grated Parmesan cheese, divided
- 3 tablespoons olive oil
- 2 teaspoons granulated garlic
- ½ teaspoon onion powder
- ½ teaspoon salt
- ¼ teaspoon freshly ground black pepper
- ¼ teaspoon paprika
- 2 tablespoons chopped fresh parsley, for garnish

1. Line the air fryer basket with parchment and spray lightly with oil. 2. Rinse the potatoes, pat dry with paper towels, and place in a large bowl. 3. In a small bowl, mix together ¼ cup of Parmesan cheese, the olive oil, garlic, onion powder, salt, black pepper, and paprika. Pour the mixture over the potatoes and toss to coat. 4. Transfer the potatoes to the prepared basket and spread them out in an even layer, taking care to keep them from touching. You may need to work in batches, depending on the size of your air fryer. 5. Air fry at 400°F (204°C) for 15 minutes, stirring after 7 to 8 minutes, or until easily pierced with a fork. Continue to cook for another 1 to 2 minutes, if needed. 6. Sprinkle with the parsley and the remaining Parmesan cheese and serve.

Dinner Rolls

Prep time: 10 minutes | Cook time: 12 minutes | Serves 6

- 1 cup shredded Mozzarella cheese
- 1 ounce (28 g) full-fat cream cheese
- 1 cup blanched finely
- ground almond flour
- ¼ cup ground flaxseed
- ½ teaspoon baking powder
- 1 large egg

1. Place Mozzarella, cream cheese, and almond flour in a large microwave-safe bowl. Microwave for 1 minute. Mix until smooth. 2. Add flaxseed, baking powder, and egg until fully combined and smooth. Microwave an additional 15 seconds if it becomes too firm. 3. Separate the dough into six pieces and roll into balls. Place the balls into the air fryer basket. 4. Adjust the temperature to 320°F (160°C) and air fry for 12 minutes. 5. Allow rolls to cool completely before serving.

Dijon Roast Cabbage

Prep time: 10 minutes | Cook time: 10 minutes | Serves 4

- 1 small head cabbage, cored and sliced into 1-inch-thick slices
- 2 tablespoons olive oil, divided
- ½ teaspoon salt
- 1 tablespoon Dijon mustard
- 1 teaspoon apple cider vinegar
- 1 teaspoon granular erythritol

1. Drizzle each cabbage slice with 1 tablespoon olive oil, then sprinkle with salt. Place slices into ungreased air fryer basket, working in batches if needed. Adjust the temperature to 350ºF (177ºC) and air fry for 10 minutes. Cabbage will be tender and edges will begin to brown when done. 2. In a small bowl, whisk remaining olive oil with mustard, vinegar, and erythritol. Drizzle over cabbage in a large serving dish. Serve warm.

Balsamic Brussels Sprouts

Prep time: 5 minutes | Cook time: 12 minutes | Serves 4

- 2 cups trimmed and halved fresh Brussels sprouts
- 2 tablespoons olive oil
- ¼ teaspoon salt
- ¼ teaspoon ground black
- pepper
- 2 tablespoons balsamic vinegar
- 2 slices cooked sugar-free bacon, crumbled

1. In a large bowl, toss Brussels sprouts in olive oil, then sprinkle with salt and pepper. Place into ungreased air fryer basket. Adjust the temperature to 375ºF (191ºC) and set the timer for 12 minutes, shaking the basket halfway through cooking. Brussels sprouts will be tender and browned when done. 2. Place sprouts in a large serving dish and drizzle with balsamic vinegar. Sprinkle bacon over top. Serve warm.

Tingly Chili-Roasted Broccoli

Prep time: 5 minutes | Cook time: 10 minutes | Serves 2

- 12 ounces (340 g) broccoli florets
- 2 tablespoons Asian hot chili oil
- 1 teaspoon ground Sichuan peppercorns (or black pepper)
- 2 garlic cloves, finely
- chopped
- 1 (2-inch) piece fresh ginger, peeled and finely chopped
- Kosher salt and freshly ground black pepper, to taste

1. In a bowl, toss together the broccoli, chili oil, Sichuan peppercorns, garlic, ginger, and salt and black pepper to taste. 2. Transfer to the air fryer and roast at 375ºF (191ºC),

shaking the basket halfway through, until lightly charred and tender, about 10 minutes. Remove from the air fryer and serve warm.

Corn Croquettes

Prep time: 10 minutes | Cook time: 12 to 14 minutes | Serves 4

- ½ cup leftover mashed potatoes
- 2 cups corn kernels (if frozen, thawed, and well drained)
- ¼ teaspoon onion powder
- ⅛ teaspoon ground black
- pepper
- ¼ teaspoon salt
- ½ cup panko bread crumbs
- Oil for misting or cooking spray

1. Place the potatoes and half the corn in food processor and pulse until corn is well chopped. 2. Transfer mixture to large bowl and stir in remaining corn, onion powder, pepper and salt. 3. Shape mixture into 16 balls. 4. Roll balls in panko crumbs, mist with oil or cooking spray, and place in air fryer basket. 5. Air fry at 360ºF (182ºC) for 12 to 14 minutes, until golden brown and crispy.

Caesar Whole Cauliflower

Prep time: 20 minutes | Cook time: 30 minutes | Serves 2 to 4

- 3 tablespoons olive oil
- 2 tablespoons red wine vinegar
- 2 tablespoons Worcestershire sauce
- 2 tablespoons grated Parmesan cheese
- 1 tablespoon Dijon mustard
- 4 garlic cloves, minced
- 4 oil-packed anchovy fillets, drained and finely
- minced
- Kosher salt and freshly ground black pepper, to taste
- 1 small head cauliflower (about 1 pound / 454 g), green leaves trimmed and stem trimmed flush with the bottom of the head
- 1 tablespoon roughly chopped fresh flat-leaf parsley (optional)

1. In a liquid measuring cup, whisk together the olive oil, vinegar, Worcestershire, Parmesan, mustard, garlic, anchovies, and salt and pepper to taste. Place the cauliflower head upside down on a cutting board and use a paring knife to make an "x" through the full length of the core. Transfer the cauliflower head to a large bowl and pour half the dressing over it. Turn the cauliflower head to coat it in the dressing, then let it rest, stem-side up, in the dressing for at least 10 minutes and up to 30 minutes to allow the dressing to seep into all its nooks and crannies. 2. Transfer the cauliflower head, stem-side down, to the air fryer and air fry at 340ºF (171ºC) for 25 minutes. Drizzle the remaining dressing over the cauliflower and air fry at 400ºF (204ºC) until the top of the cauliflower is golden brown and the core is tender, about 5 minutes more. 3. Remove the basket from the air fryer and transfer the cauliflower to a large plate. Sprinkle with the parsley, if you like, and serve hot.

Green Bean Casserole

Prep time: 10 minutes | Cook time: 20 minutes | Serves 4

- 1 pound (454 g) fresh green beans, ends trimmed, strings removed, and chopped into 2-inch pieces
- 1 (8-ounce / 227-g) package sliced brown mushrooms
- ½ onion, sliced
- 1 clove garlic, minced
- 1 tablespoon olive oil
- ½ teaspoon salt
- ¼ teaspoon freshly ground black pepper
- 4 ounces (113 g) cream cheese
- ½ cup chicken stock
- ¼ teaspoon ground nutmeg
- ½ cup grated Cheddar cheese

1. Preheat the air fryer to 400ºF (204ºC). Coat a casserole dish with olive oil and set aside. 2. In a large bowl, combine the green beans, mushrooms, onion, garlic, olive oil, salt, and pepper. Toss until the vegetables are thoroughly coated with the oil and seasonings. 3. Transfer the mixture to the air fryer basket. Pausing halfway through the cooking time to shake the basket, air fry for 10 minutes until tender. 4. While the vegetables are cooking, in a 2-cup glass measuring cup, warm the cream cheese and chicken stock in the microwave on high for 1 to 2 minutes until the cream cheese is melted. Add the nutmeg and whisk until smooth. 5. Transfer the vegetables to the prepared casserole dish and pour the cream cheese mixture over the top. Top with the Cheddar cheese. Air fry for another 10 minutes until the cheese is melted and beginning to brown.

Breaded Green Tomatoes

Prep time: 15 minutes | Cook time: 30 minutes | Serves 4

- ½ cup all-purpose flour
- 2 eggs
- ½ cup yellow cornmeal
- ½ cup panko bread crumbs
- 1 teaspoon garlic powder
- Salt and freshly ground black pepper, to taste
- 2 green tomatoes, cut into ½-inch-thick rounds
- Cooking oil spray

1. Place the flour in a small bowl. 2. In another small bowl, beat the eggs. 3. In a third small bowl, stir together the cornmeal, panko, and garlic powder. Season with salt and pepper. 4. Dip each tomato slice into the flour, the egg, and finally the cornmeal mixture to coat. 5. Insert the crisper plate into the basket and the basket into the unit. Preheat the unit by selecting AIR FRY, setting the temperature to 400ºF (204ºC), and setting the time to 3 minutes. Select START/STOP to begin. 6. Once the unit is preheated, spray the crisper plate and the basket with cooking oil. Working in batches, place the tomato slices in the air fryer in a single layer. Do not stack them. Spray the tomato slices with the cooking oil. 7. Select AIR FRY, set the temperature to 400ºF (204ºC), and set the time to 10 minutes. Select START/STOP to begin. 8. After 5 minutes, use tongs to flip the tomatoes. Resume cooking for 4 to 5 minutes, or until crisp. 9. When the cooking is complete, transfer the fried green tomatoes to a plate. Repeat steps 6, 7, and 8 for the remaining tomatoes.

Ratatouille

Prep time: 15 minutes | Cook time: 20 minutes | Serves 2 to 3

- 2 cups ¾-inch cubed peeled eggplant
- 1 small red, yellow, or orange bell pepper, stemmed, seeded, and diced
- 1 cup cherry tomatoes
- 6 to 8 cloves garlic, peeled and halved lengthwise
- 3 tablespoons olive oil
- 1 teaspoon dried oregano
- ½ teaspoon dried thyme
- 1 teaspoon kosher salt
- ½ teaspoon black pepper

1. In a medium bowl, combine the eggplant, bell pepper, tomatoes, garlic, oil, oregano, thyme, salt, and pepper. Toss to combine. 2. Place the vegetables in the air fryer basket. Set the air fryer to 400ºF (204ºC) for 20 minutes, or until the vegetables are crisp-tender.

Cabbage Wedges with Caraway Butter

Prep time: 30 minutes | Cook time: 35 to 40 minutes | Serves 6

- 1 tablespoon caraway seeds
- ½ cup (1 stick) unsalted butter, at room temperature
- ½ teaspoon grated lemon zest
- 1 small head green or red cabbage, cut into 6 wedges
- 1 tablespoon avocado oil
- ½ teaspoon sea salt
- ¼ teaspoon freshly ground black pepper

1. Place the caraway seeds in a small dry skillet over medium-high heat. Toast the seeds for 2 to 3 minutes, then remove them from the heat and let cool. Lightly crush the seeds using a mortar and pestle or with the back of a knife. 2. Place the butter in a small bowl and stir in the crushed caraway seeds and lemon zest. Form the butter into a log and wrap it in parchment paper or plastic wrap. Refrigerate for at least 1 hour or freeze for 20 minutes. 3. Brush or spray the cabbage wedges with the avocado oil, and sprinkle with the salt and pepper. 4. Set the air fryer to 375ºF (191ºC). Place the cabbage in a single layer in the air fryer basket and roast for 20 minutes. Flip and cook for 15 to 20 minutes more, until the cabbage is tender and lightly charred. Plate the cabbage and dot with caraway butter. Tent with foil for 5 minutes to melt the butter, and serve.

Chapter 9

Vegetarian Mains

Basmati Risotto

Prep time: 10 minutes | Cook time: 30 minutes | Serves 2

- 1 onion, diced
- 1 small carrot, diced
- 2 cups vegetable broth, boiling
- ½ cup grated Cheddar cheese
- 1 clove garlic, minced
- ¾ cup long-grain basmati rice
- 1 tablespoon olive oil
- 1 tablespoon unsalted butter

1. Preheat the air fryer to 390ºF (199ºC). 2. Grease a baking tin with oil and stir in the butter, garlic, carrot, and onion. 3. Put the tin in the air fryer and bake for 4 minutes. 4. Pour in the rice and bake for a further 4 minutes, stirring three times throughout the baking time. 5. Turn the temperature down to 320ºF (160ºC). 6. Add the vegetable broth and give the dish a gentle stir. Bake for 22 minutes, leaving the air fryer uncovered. 7. Pour in the cheese, stir once more and serve.

Mediterranean Pan Pizza

Prep time: 5 minutes | Cook time: 8 minutes | Serves 2

- 1 cup shredded Mozzarella cheese
- ¼ medium red bell pepper, seeded and chopped
- ½ cup chopped fresh spinach leaves
- 2 tablespoons chopped black olives
- 2 tablespoons crumbled feta cheese

1. Sprinkle Mozzarella into an ungreased round nonstick baking dish in an even layer. Add remaining ingredients on top. 2. Place dish into air fryer basket. Adjust the temperature to 350ºF (177ºC) and bake for 8 minutes, checking halfway through to avoid burning. Top of pizza will be golden brown and the cheese melted when done. 3. Remove dish from fryer and let cool 5 minutes before slicing and serving.

Lush Summer Rolls

Prep time: 15 minutes | Cook time: 15 minutes | Serves 4

- 1 cup shiitake mushroom, sliced thinly
- 1 celery stalk, chopped
- 1 medium carrot, shredded
- ½ teaspoon finely chopped ginger
- 1 teaspoon sugar
- 1 tablespoon soy sauce
- 1 teaspoon nutritional yeast
- 8 spring roll sheets
- 1 teaspoon corn starch
- 2 tablespoons water

1. In a bowl, combine the ginger, soy sauce, nutritional yeast, carrots, celery, mushroom, and sugar. 2. Mix the cornstarch and water to create an adhesive for the spring rolls. 3. Scoop a tablespoonful of the vegetable mixture into the middle of the spring roll sheets. Brush the edges of the sheets with the cornstarch adhesive and enclose around the filling to make spring rolls. 4. Preheat the air fryer to 400ºF (204ºC). When warm, place the rolls inside and air fry for 15 minutes or until crisp. 5. Serve hot.

Eggplant Parmesan

Prep time: 15 minutes | Cook time: 17 minutes | Serves 4

- 1 medium eggplant, ends trimmed, sliced into ½-inch rounds
- ¼ teaspoon salt
- 2 tablespoons coconut oil
- ½ cup grated Parmesan cheese
- 1 ounce (28 g) 100% cheese crisps, finely crushed
- ½ cup low-carb marinara sauce
- ½ cup shredded Mozzarella cheese

1. Sprinkle eggplant rounds with salt on both sides and wrap in a kitchen towel for 30 minutes. Press to remove excess water, then drizzle rounds with coconut oil on both sides. 2. In a medium bowl, mix Parmesan and cheese crisps. Press each eggplant slice into mixture to coat both sides. 3. Place rounds into ungreased air fryer basket. Adjust the temperature to 350ºF (177ºC) and air fry for 15 minutes, turning rounds halfway through cooking. They will be crispy around the edges when done. 4. Spoon marinara over rounds and sprinkle with Mozzarella. Continue cooking an additional 2 minutes at 350ºF (177ºC) until cheese is melted. Serve warm.

Crispy Eggplant Slices with Parsley

Prep time: 5 minutes | Cook time: 10 to 12 minutes | Serves 4

- 1 cup flour
- 4 eggs
- Salt, to taste
- 2 cups bread crumbs
- 1 teaspoon Italian seasoning
- 2 eggplants, sliced
- 2 garlic cloves, sliced
- 2 tablespoons chopped parsley
- Cooking spray

1. Preheat the air fryer to 390ºF (199ºC). Spritz the air fryer basket with cooking spray. 2. On a plate, place the flour. In a shallow bowl, whisk the eggs with salt. In another shallow bowl, combine the bread crumbs and Italian seasoning. 3. Dredge the eggplant slices, one at a time, in the flour, then in the whisked eggs, finally in the bread crumb mixture to coat well. 4. Arrange the coated eggplant slices in the air fryer basket and air fry for 10 to 12 minutes until golden brown and crispy. Flip the eggplant slices halfway through the cooking time. 5. Transfer the eggplant slices to a plate and sprinkle the garlic and parsley on top before serving.

Crispy Tofu

Prep time: 30 minutes | Cook time: 15 to 20 minutes | Serves 4

- 1 (16-ounce / 454-g) block extra-firm tofu
- 2 tablespoons coconut aminos
- 1 tablespoon toasted sesame oil
- 1 tablespoon olive oil
- 1 tablespoon chili-garlic sauce
- 1½ teaspoons black sesame seeds
- 1 scallion, thinly sliced

1. Press the tofu for at least 15 minutes by wrapping it in paper towels and setting a heavy pan on top so that the moisture drains. 2. Slice the tofu into bite-size cubes and transfer to a bowl. Drizzle with the coconut aminos, sesame oil, olive oil, and chili-garlic sauce. Cover and refrigerate for 1 hour or up to overnight. 3. Preheat the air fryer to 400ºF (204ºC). 4. Arrange the tofu in a single layer in the air fryer basket. Pausing to shake the pan halfway through the cooking time, air fry for 15 to 20 minutes until crisp. Serve with any juices that accumulate in the bottom of the air fryer, sprinkled with the sesame seeds and sliced scallion.

Garlic White Zucchini Rolls

Prep time: 20 minutes | Cook time: 20 minutes | Serves 4

- 2 medium zucchini
- 2 tablespoons unsalted butter
- ¼ white onion, peeled and diced
- ½ teaspoon finely minced roasted garlic
- ¼ cup heavy cream
- 2 tablespoons vegetable broth
- ⅛ teaspoon xanthan gum
- ½ cup full-fat ricotta cheese
- ¼ teaspoon salt
- ½ teaspoon garlic powder
- ¼ teaspoon dried oregano
- 2 cups spinach, chopped
- ½ cup sliced baby portobello mushrooms
- ¾ cup shredded Mozzarella cheese, divided

1. Using a mandoline or sharp knife, slice zucchini into long strips lengthwise. Place strips between paper towels to absorb moisture. Set aside. 2. In a medium saucepan over medium heat, melt butter. Add onion and sauté until fragrant. Add garlic and sauté 30 seconds. 3. Pour in heavy cream, broth, and xanthan gum. Turn off heat and whisk mixture until it begins to thicken, about 3 minutes. 4. In a medium bowl, add ricotta, salt, garlic powder, and oregano and mix well. Fold in spinach, mushrooms, and ½ cup Mozzarella. 5. Pour half of the sauce into a round baking pan. To assemble the rolls, place two strips of zucchini on a work surface. Spoon 2 tablespoons of ricotta mixture onto the slices and roll up. Place seam side down on top of sauce. Repeat with remaining ingredients. 6. Pour remaining sauce over the rolls and sprinkle with remaining Mozzarella. Cover with foil and place into the air fryer basket. 7. Adjust the temperature to 350ºF (177ºC) and bake for 20 minutes.

8. In the last 5 minutes, remove the foil to brown the cheese. Serve immediately.

Buffalo Cauliflower Bites with Blue Cheese

Prep time: 10 minutes | Cook time: 8 to 10 minutes | Serves 4

- 1 large head cauliflower, chopped into florets
- 1 tablespoon olive oil
- Salt and freshly ground black pepper, to taste
- ¼ cup unsalted butter, melted
- ¼ cup hot sauce
- Garlic Blue Cheese Dip:
- ½ cup mayonnaise
- ¼ cup sour cream
- 2 tablespoons heavy cream
- 1 tablespoon fresh lemon juice
- 1 clove garlic, minced
- ¼ cup crumbled blue cheese
- Salt and freshly ground black pepper, to taste

1. Preheat the air fryer to 400ºF (204ºC). 2. In a large bowl, combine the cauliflower and olive oil. Season to taste with salt and black pepper. Toss until the vegetables are thoroughly coated. 3. Working in batches, place half of the cauliflower in the air fryer basket. Pausing halfway through the cooking time to shake the basket, air fry for 8 to 10 minutes until the cauliflower is evenly browned. Transfer to a large bowl and repeat with the remaining cauliflower. 4. In a small bowl, whisk together the melted butter and hot sauce. 5. To make the dip: In a small bowl, combine the mayonnaise, sour cream, heavy cream, lemon juice, garlic, and blue cheese. Season to taste with salt and freshly ground black pepper. 6. Just before serving, pour the butter mixture over the cauliflower and toss gently until thoroughly coated. Serve with the dip on the side.

Spaghetti Squash Alfredo

Prep time: 10 minutes | Cook time: 15 minutes | Serves 2

- ½ large cooked spaghetti squash
- 2 tablespoons salted butter, melted
- ½ cup low-carb Alfredo sauce
- ¼ cup grated vegetarian
- Parmesan cheese
- ½ teaspoon garlic powder
- 1 teaspoon dried parsley
- ¼ teaspoon ground peppercorn
- ½ cup shredded Italian blend cheese

1. Using a fork, remove the strands of spaghetti squash from the shell. Place into a large bowl with butter and Alfredo sauce. Sprinkle with Parmesan, garlic powder, parsley, and peppercorn. 2. Pour into a 4-cup round baking dish and top with shredded cheese. Place dish into the air fryer basket. 3. Adjust the temperature to 320ºF (160ºC) and bake for 15 minutes. When finished, cheese will be golden and bubbling. Serve immediately.

Rice and Eggplant Bowl

Prep time: 15 minutes | Cook time: 10 minutes | Serves 4

- ¼ cup sliced cucumber
- 1 teaspoon salt
- 1 tablespoon sugar
- 7 tablespoons Japanese rice vinegar
- 3 medium eggplants, sliced
- 3 tablespoons sweet
- white miso paste
- 1 tablespoon mirin rice wine
- 4 cups cooked sushi rice
- 4 spring onions
- 1 tablespoon toasted sesame seeds

1. Coat the cucumber slices with the rice wine vinegar, salt, and sugar. 2. Put a dish on top of the bowl to weight it down completely. 3. In a bowl, mix the eggplants, mirin rice wine, and miso paste. Allow to marinate for half an hour. 4. Preheat the air fryer to 400ºF (204ºC). 5. Put the eggplant slices in the air fryer and air fry for 10 minutes. 6. Fill the bottom of a serving bowl with rice and top with the eggplants and pickled cucumbers. 7. Add the spring onions and sesame seeds for garnish. Serve immediately.

Cauliflower, Chickpea, and Avocado Mash

Prep time: 10 minutes | Cook time: 25 minutes | Serves 4

- 1 medium head cauliflower, cut into florets
- 1 can chickpeas, drained and rinsed
- 1 tablespoon extra-virgin
- olive oil
- 2 tablespoons lemon juice
- Salt and ground black pepper, to taste
- 4 flatbreads, toasted
- 2 ripe avocados, mashed

1. Preheat the air fryer to 425ºF (218ºC). 2. In a bowl, mix the chickpeas, cauliflower, lemon juice and olive oil. Sprinkle salt and pepper as desired. 3. Put inside the air fryer basket and air fry for 25 minutes. 4. Spread on top of the flatbread along with the mashed avocado. Sprinkle with more pepper and salt and serve.

Pesto Spinach Flatbread

Prep time: 10 minutes | Cook time: 8 minutes | Serves 4

- 1 cup blanched finely ground almond flour
- 2 ounces (57 g) cream cheese
- 2 cups shredded
- Mozzarella cheese
- 1 cup chopped fresh spinach leaves
- 2 tablespoons basil pesto

1. Place flour, cream cheese, and Mozzarella in a large microwave-safe bowl and microwave on high 45 seconds, then stir. 2. Fold in spinach and microwave an additional 15 seconds. Stir until a soft dough ball forms. 3. Cut two pieces of parchment paper to fit air fryer basket. Separate dough into two sections and press each out on ungreased parchment to create 6-inch rounds. 4. Spread 1 tablespoon pesto over each flatbread and place rounds on parchment into ungreased air fryer basket. Adjust the temperature to 350ºF (177ºC) and air fry for 8 minutes, turning crusts halfway through cooking. Flatbread will be golden when done. 5. Let cool 5 minutes before slicing and serving.

Cayenne Tahini Kale

Prep time: 5 minutes | Cook time: 15 minutes | Serves 2 to 4

- Dressing:
- ¼ cup tahini
- ¼ cup fresh lemon juice
- 2 tablespoons olive oil
- 1 teaspoon sesame seeds
- ½ teaspoon garlic powder
- ¼ teaspoon cayenne pepper
- Kale:
- 4 cups packed torn kale leaves (stems and ribs removed and leaves torn into palm-size pieces)
- Kosher salt and freshly ground black pepper, to taste

1. Preheat the air fryer to 350ºF (177ºC). 2. Make the dressing: Whisk together the tahini, lemon juice, olive oil, sesame seeds, garlic powder, and cayenne pepper in a large bowl until well mixed. 3. Add the kale and massage the dressing thoroughly all over the leaves. Sprinkle the salt and pepper to season. 4. Place the kale in the air fryer basket in a single layer and air fry for about 15 minutes, or until the leaves are slightly wilted and crispy. 5. Remove from the basket and serve on a plate.

Super Vegetable Burger

Prep time: 15 minutes | Cook time: 12 minutes | Serves 8

- ½ pound (227 g) cauliflower, steamed and diced, rinsed and drained
- 2 teaspoons coconut oil, melted
- 2 teaspoons minced garlic
- ¼ cup desiccated coconut
- ½ cup oats
- 3 tablespoons flour
- 1 tablespoon flaxseeds
- plus 3 tablespoons water, divided
- 1 teaspoon mustard powder
- 2 teaspoons thyme
- 2 teaspoons parsley
- 2 teaspoons chives
- Salt and ground black pepper, to taste
- 1 cup bread crumbs

1. Preheat the air fryer to 390ºF (199ºC). 2. Combine the cauliflower with all the ingredients, except for the bread crumbs, incorporating everything well. 3. Using the hands, shape 8 equal-sized amounts of the mixture into burger patties. Coat the patties in bread crumbs before putting them in the air fryer basket in a single layer. 4. Air fry for 12 minutes or until crispy. 5. Serve hot.

Super Veg Rolls

Prep time: 20 minutes | Cook time: 10 minutes | Serves 6

- 2 potatoes, mashed
- ¼ cup peas
- ¼ cup mashed carrots
- 1 small cabbage, sliced
- ¼ cups beans
- 2 tablespoons sweetcorn
- 1 small onion, chopped
- ½ cup bread crumbs
- 1 packet spring roll sheets
- ½ cup cornstarch slurry

1. Preheat the air fryer to 390ºF (199ºC). 2. Boil all the vegetables in water over a low heat. Rinse and allow to dry. 3. Unroll the spring roll sheets and spoon equal amounts of vegetable onto the center of each one. Fold into spring rolls and coat each one with the slurry and bread crumbs. 4. Air fry the rolls in the preheated air fryer for 10 minutes. 5. Serve warm.

Roasted Vegetable Mélange with Herbs

Prep time: 10 minutes | Cook time: 14 to 18 minutes | Serves 4

- 1 (8-ounce / 227-g) package sliced mushrooms
- 1 yellow summer squash, sliced
- 1 red bell pepper, sliced
- 3 cloves garlic, sliced
- 1 tablespoon olive oil
- ½ teaspoon dried basil
- ½ teaspoon dried thyme
- ½ teaspoon dried tarragon

1. Preheat the air fryer to 350ºF (177ºC). 2. Toss the mushrooms, squash, and bell pepper with the garlic and olive oil in a large bowl until well coated. Mix in the basil, thyme, and tarragon and toss again. 3. Spread the vegetables evenly in the air fryer basket and roast for 14 to 18 minutes, or until the vegetables are fork-tender. 4. Cool for 5 minutes before serving.

Tangy Asparagus and Broccoli

Prep time: 25 minutes | Cook time: 22 minutes | Serves 4

- ½ pound (227 g) asparagus, cut into 1½-inch pieces
- ½ pound (227 g) broccoli, cut into 1½-inch pieces
- 2 tablespoons olive oil
- Salt and white pepper, to taste
- ½ cup vegetable broth
- 2 tablespoons apple cider vinegar

1. Place the vegetables in a single layer in the lightly greased air fryer basket. Drizzle the olive oil over the vegetables. 2. Sprinkle with salt and white pepper. 3. Cook at 380ºF (193ºC) for 15 minutes, shaking the basket halfway through the cooking time. 4. Add ½ cup of vegetable broth to a saucepan; bring to a rapid boil and add the vinegar. Cook

for 5 to 7 minutes or until the sauce has reduced by half. 5. Spoon the sauce over the warm vegetables and serve immediately. Bon appétit!

Eggplant and Zucchini Bites

Prep time: 30 minutes | Cook time: 30 minutes | Serves 8

- 2 teaspoons fresh mint leaves, chopped
- 1½ teaspoons red pepper chili flakes
- 2 tablespoons melted butter
- 1 pound (454 g) eggplant, peeled and cubed
- 1 pound (454 g) zucchini, peeled and cubed
- 3 tablespoons olive oil

1. Toss all the above ingredients in a large-sized mixing dish. 2. Roast the eggplant and zucchini bites for 30 minutes at 325ºF (163ºC) in your air fryer, turning once or twice. 3. Serve with a homemade dipping sauce.

Mediterranean Air Fried Veggies

Prep time: 10 minutes | Cook time: 6 minutes | Serves 4

- 1 large zucchini, sliced
- 1 cup cherry tomatoes, halved
- 1 parsnip, sliced
- 1 green pepper, sliced
- 1 carrot, sliced
- 1 teaspoon mixed herbs
- 1 teaspoon mustard
- 1 teaspoon garlic purée
- 6 tablespoons olive oil
- Salt and ground black pepper, to taste

1. Preheat the air fryer to 400ºF (204ºC). 2. Combine all the ingredients in a bowl, making sure to coat the vegetables well. 3. Transfer to the air fryer and air fry for 6 minutes, ensuring the vegetables are tender and browned. 4. Serve immediately.

Stuffed Portobellos

Prep time: 10 minutes | Cook time: 8 minutes | Serves 4

- 3 ounces (85 g) cream cheese, softened
- ½ medium zucchini, trimmed and chopped
- ¼ cup seeded and chopped red bell pepper
- 1½ cups chopped fresh
- spinach leaves
- 4 large portobello mushrooms, stems removed
- 2 tablespoons coconut oil, melted
- ½ teaspoon salt

1. In a medium bowl, mix cream cheese, zucchini, pepper, and spinach. 2. Drizzle mushrooms with coconut oil and sprinkle with salt. Scoop ¼ zucchini mixture into each mushroom. 3. Place mushrooms into ungreased air fryer basket. Adjust the temperature to 400ºF (204ºC) and air fry for 8 minutes. Portobellos will be tender and tops will be browned when done. Serve warm.

Chapter
10

Desserts

Blueberry-Cream Cheese Bread Pudding

Prep time: 15 minutes | Cook time: 1 hour 10 minutes | Serves 6

- 1 cup light cream or half-and-half
- 4 large eggs
- ⅓ cup plus 3 tablespoons granulated sugar
- 1 teaspoon pure lemon extract
- 4 cups cubed croissants (4 to 5 croissants)
- 1 cup blueberries
- 4 ounces (113 g) cream cheese, cut into small cubes

1. In a large bowl, combine the cream, eggs, the ⅓ cup sugar, and the extract. Whisk until well combined. Add the cubed croissants, blueberries, and cream cheese. Toss gently until everything is thoroughly combined; set aside. 2. Place a 3-cup Bundt pan in the air fryer basket. Preheat the air fryer to 400°F (204°C). 3. Sprinkle the remaining 3 tablespoons sugar in the bottom of the hot pan. Set the air fryer to 400°F (204°C) for 10 minutes, or until the sugar caramelizes. Tip the pan to spread the caramel evenly across the bottom of the pan. 4. Remove the pan from the air fryer and pour in the bread mixture, distributing it evenly across the pan. Place the pan in the air fryer basket. Set the air fryer to 350°F (177°C) for 60 minutes, or until the custard is set in the middle. Let stand for 10 minutes before unmolding onto a serving plate.

Apple Hand Pies

Prep time: 15 minutes | Cook time: 25 minutes | Serves 8

- 2 apples, cored and diced
- ¼ cup honey
- 1 teaspoon ground cinnamon
- 1 teaspoon vanilla extract
- ⅛ teaspoon ground
- nutmeg
- 2 teaspoons cornstarch
- 1 teaspoon water
- 4 refrigerated piecrusts
- Cooking oil spray

1. Insert the crisper plate into the basket and the basket into the unit. Preheat the unit by selecting AIR FRY, setting the temperature to 400°F (204°C), and setting the time to 3 minutes. Select START/STOP to begin. 2. In a metal bowl that fits into the basket, stir together the apples, honey, cinnamon, vanilla, and nutmeg. 3. In a small bowl, whisk the cornstarch and water until the cornstarch dissolves. 4. Once the unit is preheated, place the metal bowl with the apples into the basket. 5. Select AIR FRY, set the temperature to 400°F (204°C), and set the time to 5 minutes. Select START/STOP to begin. 6. After 2 minutes, stir the apples. Resume cooking for 2 minutes. 7. Remove the bowl and stir the cornstarch mixture into the apples. Reinsert the metal bowl into the basket and resume cooking for about 30 seconds until the sauce thickens slightly. 8. When the cooking is complete, refrigerate the apples while you prepare the piecrust. 9. Cut each piecrust into 2 (4-inch) circles. You should have 8 circles of crust. 10. Lay the piecrusts on a work surface. Divide the apple filling among the piecrusts, mounding the mixture in the center of each round. 11. Fold each piecrust over so the top layer of crust is about an inch short of the bottom layer. (The edges should not meet.) Use the back of a fork to seal the edges. 12. Insert the crisper plate into the basket and the basket into the unit. Preheat the unit by selecting AIR FRY, setting the temperature to 400°F (204°C), and setting the time to 3 minutes. Select START/STOP to begin. 13. Once the unit is preheated, spray the crisper plate with cooking oil, line the basket with parchment paper, and spray it with cooking oil. Working in batches, place the hand pies into the basket in a single layer. 14. Select AIR FRY, set the temperature to 400°F (204°C), and set the time to 10 minutes. Select START/STOP to begin. 15. When the cooking is complete, let the hand pies cool for 5 minutes before removing from the basket. 16. Repeat steps 13, 14, and 15 with the remaining pies.

Pineapple Wontons

Prep time: 15 minutes | Cook time: 15 to 18 minutes per batch | Serves 5

- 1 (8-ounce / 227-g) package cream cheese
- 1 cup finely chopped
- fresh pineapple
- 20 wonton wrappers
- Cooking oil spray

1. In a small microwave-safe bowl, heat the cream cheese in the microwave on high power for 20 seconds to soften. 2. In a medium bowl, stir together the cream cheese and pineapple until mixed well. 3. Lay out the wonton wrappers on a work surface. A clean table or large cutting board works well. 4. Spoon 1½ teaspoons of the cream cheese mixture onto each wrapper. Be careful not to overfill. 5. Fold each wrapper diagonally across to form a triangle. Bring the 2 bottom corners up toward each other. Do not close the wrapper yet. Bring up the 2 open sides and push out any air. Squeeze the open edges together to seal. 6. Insert the crisper plate into the basket and the basket into the unit. Preheat the unit by selecting AIR FRY, setting the temperature to 390°F (199°C), and setting the time to 3 minutes. Select START/STOP to begin. 7. Once the unit is preheated, spray the crisper plate with cooking oil. Place the wontons into the basket. You can work in batches or stack the wontons. Spray the wontons with the cooking oil. 8. Select AIR FRY, set the temperature to 390°F (199°C), and set the time to 18 minutes. Select START/STOP to begin. 9. After 10 minutes, remove the basket, flip each wonton, and spray them with more oil. Reinsert the basket to resume cooking for 5 to 8 minutes more until the wontons are light golden brown and crisp. 10. If cooking in batches, remove the cooked wontons from the basket and repeat steps 7, 8, and 9 for the remaining wontons. 11. When the cooking is complete, cool for 5 minutes before serving.

Eggless Farina Cake

Prep time: 30 minutes | Cook time: 25 minutes | Serves 6

- Vegetable oil
- 2 cups hot water
- 1 cup chopped dried fruit, such as apricots, golden raisins, figs, and/or dates
- 1 cup farina (or very fine semolina)
- 1 cup milk
- 1 cup sugar
- ¼ cup ghee, butter, or
- coconut oil, melted
- 2 tablespoons plain Greek yogurt or sour cream
- 1 teaspoon ground cardamom
- 1 teaspoon baking powder
- ½ teaspoon baking soda
- Whipped cream, for serving

1. Grease a baking pan with vegetable oil. 2. In a small bowl, combine the hot water and dried fruit; set aside for 20 minutes to plump the fruit. 3. Meanwhile, in a large bowl, whisk together the farina, milk, sugar, ghee, yogurt, and cardamom. Let stand for 20 minutes to allow the farina to soften and absorb some of the liquid. 4. Drain the dried fruit and gently stir it into the batter. Add the baking powder and baking soda and stir until thoroughly combined. 5. Pour the batter into the prepared pan. Set the pan in the air fryer basket. Set the air fryer to 325ºF (163ºC) for 25 minutes, or until a toothpick inserted into the center of the cake comes out clean. 6. Let the cake cool in the pan on a wire rack for 10 minutes. Remove the cake from the pan and let cool on the rack for 20 minutes before slicing. 7. Slice and serve topped with whipped cream.

Rhubarb and Strawberry Crumble

Prep time: 10 minutes | Cook time: 12 to 17 minutes | Serves 6

- 1½ cups sliced fresh strawberries
- ¾ cup sliced rhubarb
- ⅓ cup granulated sugar
- ⅔ cup quick-cooking oatmeal
- ½ cup whole-wheat pastry flour, or all-
- purpose flour
- ¼ cup packed light brown sugar
- ½ teaspoon ground cinnamon
- 3 tablespoons unsalted butter, melted

1. Insert the crisper plate into the basket and the basket into the unit. Preheat the unit by selecting BAKE, setting the temperature to 375ºF (191ºC), and setting the time to 3 minutes. Select START/STOP to begin. 2. In a 6-by-2-inch round metal baking pan, combine the strawberries, rhubarb, and granulated sugar. 3. In a medium bowl, stir together the oatmeal, flour, brown sugar, and cinnamon. Stir the melted butter into this mixture until crumbly. Sprinkle the crumble mixture over the fruit. 4. Once the unit is preheated, place the pan into the basket. 5. Select BAKE, set the temperature to 375ºF (191ºC), and set the time to 17 minutes. Select

START/STOP to begin. 6. After about 12 minutes, check the crumble. If the fruit is bubbling and the topping is golden brown, it is done. If not, resume cooking. 7. When the cooking is complete, serve warm.

5-Ingredient Brownies

Prep time: 10 minutes | Cook time: 25 minutes | Serves 6

- Vegetable oil
- ½ cup (1 stick) unsalted butter
- ½ cup chocolate chips
- 3 large eggs
- ½ cup sugar
- 1 teaspoon pure vanilla extract

1. Generously grease a baking pan with vegetable oil. 2. In a microwave-safe bowl, combine the butter and chocolate chips. Microwave on high for 1 minute. Stir very well. (You want the heat from the butter and chocolate to melt the remaining clumps. If you microwave until everything melts, the chocolate will be overcooked. If necessary, microwave for an additional 10 seconds, but stir well before you try that.) 3. In a medium bowl, combine the eggs, sugar, and vanilla. Whisk until light and frothy. While whisking continuously, slowly pour in the melted chocolate in a thin stream and whisk until everything is incorporated. 4. Pour the batter into the prepared pan. Set the pan in the air fryer basket. Set the air fryer to 350ºF (177ºC) for 25 minutes, or until a toothpick inserted into the center comes out clean. 5. Let cool in the pan on a wire rack for 30 minutes before cutting into squares.

Peach Cobbler

Prep time: 15 minutes | Cook time: 12 to 14 minutes | Serves 4

- 16 ounces (454 g) frozen peaches, thawed, with juice (do not drain)
- 6 tablespoons sugar
- 1 tablespoon cornstarch
- 1 tablespoon water
- Crust:
- ½ cup flour
- ¼ teaspoon salt
- 3 tablespoons butter
- 1½ tablespoons cold water
- ¼ teaspoon sugar

1. Place peaches, including juice, and sugar in a baking pan. Stir to mix well. 2. In a small cup, dissolve cornstarch in the water. Stir into peaches. 3. In a medium bowl, combine the flour and salt. Cut in butter using knives or a pastry blender. Stir in the cold water to make a stiff dough. 4. On a floured board or wax paper, pat dough into a square or circle slightly smaller than your baking pan. Cut diagonally into 4 pieces. 5. Place dough pieces on top of peaches, leaving a tiny bit of space between the edges. Sprinkle very lightly with sugar, no more than about ¼ teaspoon. 6. Bake at 360ºF (182ºC) for 12 to 14 minutes, until fruit bubbles and crust browns.

Coconut-Custard Pie

Prep time: 10 minutes | Cook time: 20 to 23 minutes | Serves 4

- 1 cup milk
- ¼ cup plus 2 tablespoons sugar
- ¼ cup biscuit baking mix
- 1 teaspoon vanilla
- 2 eggs
- 2 tablespoons melted butter
- Cooking spray
- ½ cup shredded, sweetened coconut

1. Place all ingredients except coconut in a medium bowl. 2. Using a hand mixer, beat on high speed for 3 minutes. 3. Let sit for 5 minutes. 4. Preheat the air fryer to 330ºF (166ºC). 5. Spray a baking pan with cooking spray and place pan in air fryer basket. 6. Pour filling into pan and sprinkle coconut over top. 7. Cook pie at 330ºF (166ºC) for 20 to 23 minutes or until center sets.

Chocolate Cake

Prep time: 10 minutes | Cook time: 20 to 23 minutes | Serves 8

- ½ cup sugar
- ¼ cup flour, plus 3 tablespoons
- 3 tablespoons cocoa
- ½ teaspoon baking powder
- ½ teaspoon baking soda
- ¼ teaspoon salt
- 1 egg
- 2 tablespoons oil
- ½ cup milk
- ½ teaspoon vanilla extract

1. Preheat the air fryer to 330ºF (166ºC). 2. Grease and flour a baking pan. 3. In a medium bowl, stir together the sugar, flour, cocoa, baking powder, baking soda, and salt. 4. Add all other ingredients and beat with a wire whisk until smooth. 5. Pour batter into prepared pan and bake at 330ºF (166ºC) for 20 to 23 minutes, until toothpick inserted in center comes out clean or with crumbs clinging to it.

Cinnamon and Pecan Pie

Prep time: 10 minutes | Cook time: 25 minutes | Serves 4

- 1 pie dough
- ½ teaspoons cinnamon
- ¾ teaspoon vanilla extract
- 2 eggs
- ¾ cup maple syrup
- ⅛ teaspoon nutmeg
- 3 tablespoons melted butter, divided
- 2 tablespoons sugar
- ½ cup chopped pecans

1. Preheat the air fryer to 370ºF (188ºC). 2. In a small bowl, coat the pecans in 1 tablespoon of melted butter. 3. Transfer the pecans to the air fryer and air fry for about 10 minutes. 4. Put the pie dough in a greased pie pan and add the pecans on top. 5. In a bowl, mix the rest of the ingredients. Pour this over the pecans. 6. Put the pan in the air fryer and bake for 25 minutes. 7. Serve immediately.

Brownies for Two

Prep time: 5 minutes | Cook time: 15 minutes | Serves 2

- ½ cup blanched finely ground almond flour
- 3 tablespoons granular erythritol
- 3 tablespoons unsweetened cocoa powder
- ½ teaspoon baking powder
- 1 teaspoon vanilla extract
- 2 large eggs, whisked
- 2 tablespoons salted butter, melted

1. In a medium bowl, combine flour, erythritol, cocoa powder, and baking powder. 2. Add in vanilla, eggs, and butter, and stir until a thick batter forms. 3. Pour batter into two ramekins greased with cooking spray and place ramekins into air fryer basket. Adjust the temperature to 325ºF (163ºC) and bake for 15 minutes. Centers will be firm when done. Let ramekins cool 5 minutes before serving.

Cinnamon-Sugar Almonds

Prep time: 5 minutes | Cook time: 8 minutes | Serves 4

- 1 cup whole almonds
- 2 tablespoons salted butter, melted
- 1 tablespoon sugar
- ½ teaspoon ground cinnamon

1. In a medium bowl, combine the almonds, butter, sugar, and cinnamon. Mix well to ensure all the almonds are coated with the spiced butter. 2. Transfer the almonds to the air fryer basket and shake so they are in a single layer. Set the air fryer to 300ºF (149ºC) for 8 minutes, stirring the almonds halfway through the cooking time. 3. Let cool completely before serving.

Olive Oil Cake

Prep time: 10 minutes | Cook time: 30 minutes | Serves 8

- 2 cups blanched finely ground almond flour
- 5 large eggs, whisked
- ¾ cup extra-virgin olive oil
- ⅓ cup granular erythritol
- 1 teaspoon vanilla extract
- 1 teaspoon baking powder

1. In a large bowl, mix all ingredients. Pour batter into an ungreased round nonstick baking dish. 2. Place dish into air fryer basket. Adjust the temperature to 300ºF (149ºC) and bake for 30 minutes. The cake will be golden on top and firm in the center when done. 3. Let cake cool in dish 30 minutes before slicing and serving.

Maple-Pecan Tart with Sea Salt

Prep time: 15 minutes | Cook time: 25 minutes | Serves 8

- Tart Crust:
- Vegetable oil spray
- ⅓ cup (⅔ stick) butter, softened
- ¼ cup firmly packed brown sugar
- 1 cup all-purpose flour
- ¼ teaspoon kosher salt
- Filling:
- 4 tablespoons (½ stick) butter, diced
- ½ cup packed brown sugar
- ¼ cup pure maple syrup
- ¼ cup whole milk
- ¼ teaspoon pure vanilla extract
- 1½ cups finely chopped pecans
- ¼ teaspoon flaked sea salt

1. For the crust: Line a baking pan with foil, leaving a couple of inches of overhang. Spray the foil with vegetable oil spray. 2. In a medium bowl, combine the butter and brown sugar. Beat with an electric mixer on medium-low speed until light and fluffy. Add the flour and kosher salt and beat until the ingredients are well blended. Transfer the mixture (it will be crumbly) to the prepared pan. Press it evenly into the bottom of the pan. 3. Place the pan in the air fryer basket. Set the air fryer to 350°F (177°C) for 13 minutes. When the crust has 5 minutes left to cook, start the filling. 4. For the filling: In a medium saucepan, combine the butter, brown sugar, maple syrup, and milk. Bring to a simmer, stirring occasionally. When it begins simmering, cook for 1 minute. Remove from the heat and stir in the vanilla and pecans. 5. Carefully pour the filling evenly over the crust, gently spreading with a rubber spatula so the nuts and liquid are evenly distributed. Set the air fryer to 350°F (177°C) for 12 minutes, or until mixture is bubbling. (The center should still be slightly jiggly, it will thicken as it cools.) 6. Remove the pan from the air fryer and sprinkle the tart with the sea salt. Cool completely on a wire rack until room temperature. 7. Transfer the pan to the refrigerator to chill. When cold (the tart will be easier to cut), use the foil overhang to remove the tart from the pan and cut into 8 wedges. Serve at room temperature.

Fried Golden Bananas

Prep time: 5 minutes | Cook time: 7 minutes | Serves 6

- 1 large egg
- ¼ cup cornstarch
- ¼ cup plain bread crumbs
- 3 bananas, halved
- crosswise
- Cooking oil
- Chocolate sauce, for drizzling

1. Preheat the air fryer to 375°F (191°C) 2. Separate the biscuit dough into 8 biscuits and place them on a flat work surface. Use a small circle cookie cutter or a biscuit cutter to cut a hole in the center of each biscuit. You can also cut the holes using a knife. 3. Spray the air fryer basket with cooking oil. 4. Put 4 donuts in the air fryer. Do not stack. Spray with cooking oil. Air fry for 4 minutes. 5. Open the air fryer and flip the donuts. Air fry for an additional 4 minutes. 6. Remove the cooked donuts from the air fryer, then repeat steps 3 and 4 for the remaining 4 donuts. 7. Drizzle chocolate sauce over the donuts and enjoy while warm.

Bananas Foster

Prep time: 5 minutes | Cook time: 7 minutes | Serves 2

- 1 tablespoon unsalted butter
- 2 teaspoons dark brown sugar
- 1 banana, peeled and halved lengthwise and then crosswise
- 2 tablespoons chopped pecans
- ⅛ teaspoon ground cinnamon
- 2 tablespoons light rum
- Vanilla ice cream, for serving

1. In a baking pan, combine the butter and brown sugar. Place the pan in the air fryer basket. Set the air fryer to 350°F (177°C) for 2 minutes, or until the butter and sugar are melted. Swirl to combine. 2. Add the banana pieces and pecans, turning the bananas to coat. Set the air fryer to 350°F (177°C) for 5 minutes, turning the banana pieces halfway through the cooking time. Sprinkle with the cinnamon. 3. Remove the pan from the air fryer and place on an unlit stovetop for safety. Add the rum to the pan, swirling to combine it with the butter mixture. Carefully light the sauce with a long-reach lighter. Spoon the flaming sauce over the banana pieces until the flames die out. 4. Serve the warm bananas and sauce over vanilla ice cream.

Cream Cheese Shortbread Cookies

Prep time: 30 minutes | Cook time: 20 minutes | Makes 12 cookies

- ¼ cup coconut oil, melted
- 2 ounces (57 g) cream cheese, softened
- ½ cup granular erythritol
- 1 large egg, whisked
- 2 cups blanched finely ground almond flour
- 1 teaspoon almond extract

1. Combine all ingredients in a large bowl to form a firm ball. 2. Place dough on a sheet of plastic wrap and roll into a 12-inch-long log shape. Roll log in plastic wrap and place in refrigerator 30 minutes to chill. 3. Remove log from plastic and slice into twelve equal cookies. Cut two sheets of parchment paper to fit air fryer basket. Place six cookies on each ungreased sheet. Place one sheet with cookies into air fryer basket. Adjust the temperature to 320°F (160°C) and bake for 10 minutes, turning cookies halfway through cooking. They will be lightly golden when done. Repeat with remaining cookies. 4. Let cool 15 minutes before serving to avoid crumbling.

Mixed Berries with Pecan Streusel Topping

Prep time: 5 minutes | Cook time: 17 minutes | Serves 3

- ½ cup mixed berries
- Cooking spray
- Topping:
- 1 egg, beaten
- 3 tablespoons almonds, slivered
- 3 tablespoons chopped pecans
- 2 tablespoons chopped walnuts
- 3 tablespoons granulated Swerve
- 2 tablespoons cold salted butter, cut into pieces
- ½ teaspoon ground cinnamon

1. Preheat the air fryer to 340°F (171°C). Lightly spray a baking dish with cooking spray. 2. Make the topping: In a medium bowl, stir together the beaten egg, nuts, Swerve, butter, and cinnamon until well blended. 3. Put the mixed berries in the bottom of the baking dish and spread the topping over the top. 4. Bake in the preheated air fryer for 17 minutes, or until the fruit is bubbly and topping is golden brown. 5. Allow to cool for 5 to 10 minutes before serving.

Jelly Doughnuts

Prep time: 5 minutes | Cook time: 5 minutes | Serves 8

- 1 (16.3 ounces / 462 g) package large refrigerator biscuits
- Cooking spray
- 1¼ cups good-quality raspberry jam
- Confectioners' sugar, for dusting

1. Preheat the air fryer to 350°F (177°C). 2. Separate biscuits into 8 rounds. Spray both sides of rounds lightly with oil. 3. Spray the basket with oil and place 3 to 4 rounds in the basket. Air fry for 5 minutes, or until golden brown. Transfer to a wire rack; let cool. Repeat with the remaining rounds. 4. Fill a pastry bag, fitted with small plain tip, with raspberry jam; use tip to poke a small hole in the side of each doughnut, then fill the centers with the jam. Dust doughnuts with confectioners' sugar. Serve immediately.

Air Fryer Cooking Chart

Beef

Item	Temp (°F)	Time (mins)	Item	Temp (°F)	Time (mins)
Beef Eye Round Roast (4 lbs.)	400 °F	45 to 55	Meatballs (1-inch)	370 °F	7
Burger Patty (4 oz.)	370 °F	16 to 20	Meatballs (3-inch)	380 °F	10
Filet Mignon (8 oz.)	400 °F	18	Ribeye, bone-in (1-inch, 8 oz)	400 °F	10 to 15
Flank Steak (1.5 lbs.)	400 °F	12	Sirloin steaks (1-inch, 12 oz)	400 °F	9 to 14
Flank Steak (2 lbs.)	400 °F	20 to 28			

Chicken

Item	Temp (°F)	Time (mins)	Item	Temp (°F)	Time (mins)
Breasts, bone in (1 ¼ lb.)	370 °F	25	Legs, bone-in (1 ¾ lb.)	380 °F	30
Breasts, boneless (4 oz)	380 °F	12	Thighs, boneless (1 ½ lb.)	380 °F	18 to 20
Drumsticks (2 ½ lb.)	370 °F	20	Wings (2 lb.)	400 °F	12
Game Hen (halved 2 lb.)	390 °F	20	Whole Chicken	360 °F	75
Thighs, bone-in (2 lb.)	380 °F	22	Tenders	360 °F	8 to 10

Pork & Lamb

Item	Temp (°F)	Time (mins)	Item	Temp (°F)	Time (mins)
Bacon (regular)	400 °F	5 to 7	Pork Tenderloin	370 °F	15
Bacon (thick cut)	400 °F	6 to 10	Sausages	380 °F	15
Pork Loin (2 lb.)	360 °F	55	Lamb Loin Chops (1-inch thick)	400 °F	8 to 12
Pork Chops, bone in (1-inch, 6.5 oz)	400 °F	12	Rack of Lamb (1.5 – 2 lb.)	380 °F	22

Fish & Seafood

Item	Temp (°F)	Time (mins)	Item	Temp (°F)	Time (mins)
Calamari (8 oz)	400 °F	4	Tuna Steak	400 °F	7 to 10
Fish Fillet (1-inch, 8 oz)	400 °F	10	Scallops	400 °F	5 to 7
Salmon, fillet (6 oz)	380 °F	12	Shrimp	400 °F	5
Swordfish steak	400 °F	10			

Vegetables

INGREDIENT	AMOUNT	PREPARATION	OIL	TEMP	COOK TIME
Asparagus	2 bunches	Cut in half, trim stems	2 Tbsp	420°F	12-15 mins
Beets	1½ lbs	Peel, cut in ½-inch cubes	1Tbsp	390°F	28-30 mins
Bell peppers (for roasting)	4 peppers	Cut in quarters, remove seeds	1Tbsp	400°F	15-20 mins
Broccoli	1 large head	Cut in 1-2-inch florets	1Tbsp	400°F	15-20 mins
Brussels sprouts	1lb	Cut in half, remove stems	1Tbsp	425°F	15-20 mins
Carrots	1lb	Peel, cut in ¼-inch rounds	1 Tbsp	425°F	10-15 mins
Cauliflower	1 head	Cut in 1-2-inch florets	2 Tbsp	400°F	20-22 mins
Corn on the cob	7 ears	Whole ears, remove husks	1 Tbps	400°F	14-17 mins
Green beans	1 bag (12 oz)	Trim	1 Tbps	420°F	18-20 mins
Kale (for chips)	4 oz	Tear into pieces,remove stems	None	325°F	5-8 mins
Mushrooms	16 oz	Rinse, slice thinly	1 Tbps	390°F	25-30 mins
Potatoes, russet	1½ lbs	Cut in 1-inch wedges	1 Tbps	390°F	25-30 mins
Potatoes, russet	1lb	Hand-cut fries, soak 30 mins in cold water, then pat dry	½ -3 Tbps	400°F	25-28 mins
Potatoes, sweet	1lb	Hand-cut fries, soak 30 mins in cold water, then pat dry	1 Tbps	400°F	25-28 mins
Zucchini	1lb	Cut in eighths lengthwise, then cut in half	1 Tbps	400°F	15-20 mins

Appendix

2

Index

S

T

V

W

Z

Made in United States
Orlando, FL
05 January 2025

56916309R00057